Elizabeth Speller read Archaeology and Classics at Cambridge as a mature student, followed by a post-graduate degree in Ancient History. She has lived in Berlin and Rome and travelled extensively in Italy, Greece and Turkey. She has written for publications as diverse as the *Observer*, the *Big Issue*, the *Independent on Sunday*, *Woman's Journal* and also for Radio 4 and lectures on many aspects of the ancient world, from astronomy to art and medicine to sexuality.

An award-winning poet, Elizabeth Speller wrote the libretto for the anthem *Farewell* in the bestselling memorial CD for Linda McCartney, *A Garland for Linda*. She lives in Gloucestershire.

Following Hadrian

A Second-Century Journey
through the Roman Empire

Elizabeth Speller

review

First published in 2002
by REVIEW

An imprint of Headline Book Publishing
First published in paperback in 2003

10 9 8 7 6 5 4 3 2 1

Elizabeth Speller would be happy to hear from readers with their
comments on the book at the following e-mail address:
egs@elispell.demon.co.uk

ISBN 0 7472 6662 X

Typeset by Avon DataSet Ltd, Bidford-on-Avon, Warks
Printed and bound in Great Britain by Clays Ltd, St Ives plc

HEADLINE BOOK PUBLISHING
A division of Hodder Headline
338 Euston Road, London NW1 3BH

www.headline.co.uk
www.reviewbooks.co.uk
www.hodderheadline.com

To my father

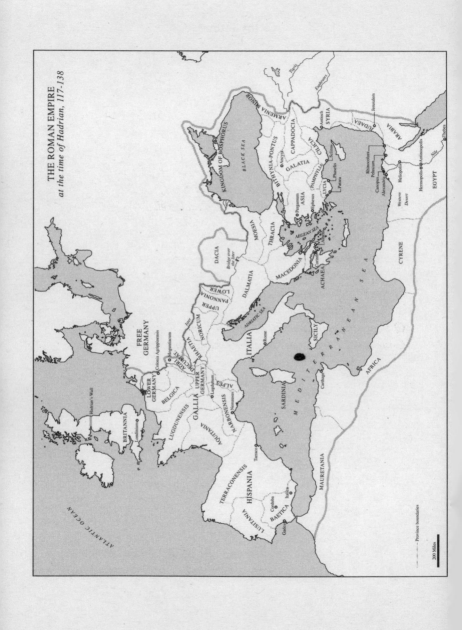

THE ROMAN EMPIRE
at the time of Hadrian, 117-138

FREE GERMANY

Hadrian's Wall
Londinium
BRITANNIA

ATLANTIC OCEAN

LOWER GERMANY
Colonia Agrippinensis
Mogontiacum
UPPER GERMANY

BELGICA
LUGDUNENSIS
Lugdunum
GALLIA
AQUITANIA
NARBONENSIS
Nemausum
ALPES

AGRI DECUMAT

RHAETIA
NORICUM

Iter

TERRACONENSIS
Tarraco
HISPANIA
LUSITANIA
BAETICA
Corduba
Gades
Ilipa

MAURETANIA

ITALIA
Rome
SARDINIA
SICILY
Carthage
AFRICA

MEDITERRANEAN SEA

DACIA
Bridge over the Ister
PANNONIA
UPPER
LOWER
DALMATIA
ADRIATIC SEA

MOESIA
THRACIA
MACEDONIA
ACHAEA
Corinth

KINGDOM OF BOSPHORUS
BLACK SEA

ARMENIA MINOR
BITHYNIA-PONTUS
Nicaea
GALATIA
Pergamum
Ephesus
ASIA
AEGEAN SEA

CAPPADOCIA
Antioch
CILICIA
PAMPHYLIA
LYCIA
Thaustus
Patara

SYRIA
Jerusalem
JUDAEA
ARABIA

Rhinocolura
Pelusium
Canopus
Alexandria
Heliopolis
Hermopolis
Antinoopolis
Western Desert
Nile
Thebes

EGYPT

CYRENE

Tigris
Euphrates

Province boundaries

200 Miles

Phlebas the Phoenician, a fortnight dead,
Forgot the cry of gulls, and the deep sea swell
And the profit and loss.
        A current under sea
Picked his bones in whispers. As he rose and fell
He passed the stages of his age and youth
Entering the whirlpool.
        Gentile or Jew
O you who turn the wheel and look to windward,
Consider Phlebas, who was once handsome and tall as you.

T. S. Eliot, *The Waste Land*

Contents

Acknowledgements

In writing any historical work one inevitably refers to a large amount of secondary literature. These books are listed in the bibliography, but the following are particularly useful or unusual works which I recommend to anyone wanting to discover more about individual aspects of Hadrian's life or to follow his journeys. Anthony Birley's *Hadrian, the Restless Emperor*, is the definitive modern biography. Amanda Claridge's hugely informative and entertaining book on the archaeology of Rome and Michael Haag's *Cadogan Guide to Egypt* are both invaluable sorces. Diana Kleiner's lavishly illustrated *Roman Sculpture* is a wonderful survey of imperial portraiture and William Macdonald and John Pinto's beautiful volume on the substance and legacy of Hadrian's villa considerably amplified my existing knowledge of the site. Mary T. Boatwright's recent *Hadrian and the Cities of the Roman Empire* encompasses the extraordinary breadth of the emperor's foundations and benefactions, and I have returned to it many times. Andrew Dalby's delicious read, *Empire of Pleasures*, was full of tiny and invaluable detail, while Lionel Casson's *Travel in the Ancient World* provided background to the whole subject of Greek and Roman tourism.

The friendship, direction and imagination of my postgraduate supervisors, Christopher Kelly of Corpus Christi College, Cambridge, and Catharine Edwards of Birkbeck College, University of London, as well as explorations enjoyed with

Caroline Vout of Nottingham University, have expanded my view of the Roman world, its complexities and its potential. Caroline's unpublished doctoral thesis illuminated the construction and legacy of Antinous and will, I hope, soon be turned into a book. I am particularly indebted to Corey T. Brennan of Bryn Mawr College, USA, whose scholarly paper on Julia Balbilla inspired me to use her as a central figure in my book, and to Geoffrey Preger of Jerusalem, who helped me find my way among unfamiliar Hebrew sources. Animated lunchtime exchanges with Tom Holland have reinvigorated me when the classical world occasionally became a perplexing and frustrating place to be. Numerous conversations at Cambridge and at the British School at Rome provided fruitful material for new lines of enquiry, and the resources and eccentric pleasures of the libraries of both institutions were invaluable. Keith Hopkins, William Griffin and Michael Hoskins, all of Cambridge University, provided me with crucial pieces of information, and Michael Bywater invested his time and professional expertise in helping me again and again.

Without the patience and investment of my family, particularly my children, Nicholas, Miranda and Abigail, and my ex-husband, Jeremy, I would never have been able to study, to travel or to write. My friends Louise Foxcroft, Caron Freeborn and Catherine Hopkins have in this project, as in all things, offered me their unstinting support, energy and confidence.

My thanks go to Graham Simpson, who first introduced me to the Greek cities of Asia Minor; to my agent Georgina Capel, to Heather Holden-Brown and Celia Kent at Headline books, and to my gifted copy-editor, Gillian Bromley.

Finally, I am enormously grateful to the President and Fellows of Lucy Cavendish College, University of Cambridge, who took a gamble in admitting me as a mature student and so changed my life for ever.

E.S.

Preface

Gaining an impressionistic sense of how it was in ancient Rome is easier, no less valid, and possibly more exciting than attempting to lay out a scrupulous history. It is perhaps why fiction and films have been so successful in conveying a generalised ancient past to a wide audience; in many ways, modern novels and the spectacles of Hollywood capture more of the 'feel' of ancient histories than academic attempts to be scrupulous with the evidence.

Our present insistence on a history well secured in original sources – on the supremacy of *facts* – derives from the growth of scientific disciplines in the nineteenth century and an optimistic illusion that there existed a clear record of the past to be retrieved by diligent scholars. Yet the older history is, the more incomplete the facts become, and ancient history is a mosaic of fragments at best, however confidently historians and biographers fill in the gaps. (Looking at just two areas of source material, one eminent academic calculated that the survival rate of Romano-Egyptian census returns was one in 12,000 and that the survival of praetorian grave inscriptions was of the same order of magnitude.[1])

The Emperor Hadrian has been the subject of several learned monographs, histories, biographies and fictional works. Sturdy biographies by Weber and Henderson emerged in 1907 and 1923 and were the standard works for decades. But then in 1951 Marguérite Yourcenar's beautiful novel *Memoirs of Hadrian* imaginatively filled the enticing gap left by

Hadrian's own long-vanished autobiographical text. In the 1990s Anthony Birley produced a much-needed scholarly biography, *Hadrian, the Restless Emperor*, while Royston Lambert's slightly earlier *Beloved and God* bravely speculated on the relationship between Hadrian and Antinous. I have been very grateful for the labours of all three. Yourcenar's extraordinary work has gained such a hold on the public perception that her re-creation of the emperor is perhaps the most enduring.

Evidence for the reign of Hadrian is sparse in terms of texts, but rich in terms of architecture, statues and inscriptions. Although Hadrian's memoirs have disappeared, it is assumed that some ancient historians used them as source material for their own works. It was said at the time that he attempted to pass them off as written by one of his freedmen so that the favourable picture of his reign and motivation they presented might appear more impartial. The principal literary sources – the *Roman History* of Cassius Dio and the *Scriptores Historiae Augustae* – are both problematic. Dio, like the imperial favourite, Antinous, a Bithynian, lived nearly a century after Hadrian. He was a highly partisan Greek who had reached the highest echelons of public life in the Roman empire and become a senator. He is energetically pro-establishment and his viewpoint is that of his own elite circle. The *SHA* is an enigma, and one much argued over. It is not, as it claims to be, a third-century compilation of individually written biographies but a later, possibly fourth-century, conceit by one man. It is charming, eccentric and unreliable – but not necessarily untrue.

Ancient history was not, in any case, always written with truth as its principal concern; entertainment and persuasion were equally important. My account of Hadrian is based on material accepted as 'true' but, with more than a nod to the style of the early historians, it is at times both circumstantial and anecdotal.

Sabina was Hadrian's wife for nearly forty years. Her relationship with her husband was notoriously poor. She is almost invisible in the literary record, although there are some fine images of her. As such she has always been an irresistible figure on which to project all manner of fantasy, largely negative, in an attempt to illuminate the more central figure of Hadrian. Julia Balbilla was a well-connected, aristocratic friend of the Empress Sabina who travelled to Egypt, and possibly beyond, in Hadrian's entourage. She was a descendant of the deposed royal house of Commagene and sister of Philopappus, a Roman consul and the so-called 'king' of Commagene who lived in exuberant exile in Athens. He was a friend of Hadrian, whom he predeceased by many years, and Julia Balbilla may have been responsible for his grandiose, and surviving, mausoleum on the Hill of the Muses in Athens. Julia Balbilla was evidently a highly educated woman who could write in the formal Greek dialect affected by the literati of the second century. Little else is known of her life. A small number of poems by Balbilla have survived, although her works do not include the diaries extracts from which appear here.

The Roman emperors, 27 BCE–193 CE

Julio-Claudians

Augustus 27 BCE–14 CE	*Rumours of murder*
Tiberius 14–37	*Rumours of murder*
Gaius (Caligula) 37–41	*Assassinated*
Claudius 41–54	*Rumours of murder*
Nero 54–68	*Forced to commit suicide*
Galba 68–9	*Assassinated*
Otho 69	*Committed suicide*
Vitellius 69	*Assassinated*

Flavians

Vespasian 69–79	
Titus 79–81	
Domitian 81–96	*Assassinated*

The adoptive emperors

Nerva 96–8
Trajan 98–117
Hadrian 117–38

Antonines

Antoninus Pius 138–61
Marcus Aurelius 161–80

Lucius Verus 161–9
Commodus 180–92   *Assassinated*

Civil war

Pertinax 193   *Assassinated*
Didius Julianus 193   *Executed*

Hadrian (Publius Aelius Hadrianus): Timeline

76 CE	Hadrian born, Rome, 24 January
96	Domitian murdered; Nerva proclaimed emperor
97	Nerva adopts Trajan; Nerva dies; Trajan proclaimed emperor
100	Hadrian marries Sabina
101	Trajan's first Danube campaign
102	Trajan penetrates Dacia
105–6	Second Dacian War
105	Hadrian made praetor
107	Hadrian made governor of Lower Pannonia
108	Hadrian made consul
111–12	Hadrian's first visit to Athens
114	Trajan advances against Parthia. Hadrian made governor of Syria
114–17	Parthian War: Armenia, Mesopotamia and Assyria become new provinces
114–18	Jews revolt in Cyrenaica, Egypt and Cyprus
117	Trajan dies at Selinus in Cilicia on 7–8 August; Hadrian proclaims himself emperor
117	Hadrian abandons eastward expansion and makes peace with Parthia
118	Hadrian partly withdraws from Dacia
121–5	Hadrian goes to Gaul, Rhine frontiers, Britain, Spain, western Mauritania, the Orient and Danube
128–32	Hadrian goes to Africa, Greece, Asia minor, Syria, Egypt and Cyrene

Introduction

Of the twelve Caesars of the first century CE, six were bloodily assassinated, or were forced to commit suicide, at least two of them in their own palaces in Rome. A further three were the subject of lurid posthumous rumours as to the manner of their deaths, and of the remaining three, only one ruled for more than two years. The writer and philosopher Seneca, who was tutor to the young Nero, summed up the uneasy reality of imperial rule: '*No matter how many you slay, you cannot kill your successor.*'[1] This was the century and the society into which Hadrian was born on 24 January 76 CE.

Yet after Hadrian came to power in 117 CE he ruled for twenty-one years, dying of natural causes at the age of sixty-two. Although the peace achieved by him and his successors proved to be only a hiatus in the bloody politics of the magnificently flawed Roman principate, the great eighteenth-century historian Edward Gibbon made a radiant assessment of the period within which Hadrian ruled: '*If a man were called to fix the period in the history of the world, during which the condition of the race were most happy and most prosperous, he would, without hesitation, name that which elapsed from the death of Domitian to*

the accession of Commodus.[2] Domitian died in 96; Commodus
acceded in 180. Both were assassinated. There were murky
allegations about Hadrian's assumption of power and there
were claims of early plots against his life; yet, having become the
most powerful man in the world, he proceeded to consolidate
the boundaries of an empire which encircled the Mediterranean
and stretched from Britain to Africa, from Spain to Asia minor,
and which contained as many as sixty million people.[3] His
dream of a single, powerful, integrated realm – an ideal first
voiced by Alexander the Great – was a remarkably modern one,
and Hadrian came close to achieving it. Inheriting an empire of
provinces held together by coercion and predatory military
manoeuvring, he tried to implement a policy of mutually
advantageous cooperation.

Until the last years of his life, Hadrian was a passionate
and incessant traveller. More than half his reign was spent
abroad and he used his extensive journeys to augment existing
cities and found new ones, providing public buildings which,
as the products of wealth, technical expertise and soaring
imagination, were beautiful, functional and enduring. Among
the best-known of these are two of the most remarkable
survivals of the Roman world: the 80 mile long Hadrian's
Wall in Britain, which marks the northern limit of the empire,
and the Pantheon, the great temple in Rome which has
remained in use for nearly two thousand years. Hadrian also
completed a palace for his personal use – but for this he
chose a site outside Rome, where he could build as he chose,
unconstrained by the conventions of urban geography and the
pre-existing buildings of his forebears, and far away from
the dark shadows of the past. He moved beyond tradition and
constructed a country house at Tibur, modern Tivoli, 20 miles
from the capital, which outdid any surviving palace in size
and originality and in which he could house his magnificent
collections. It was the wonder of its time, and it is a strange
and enchanting ruin today.

Hadrian's Wall in northern England, the Pantheon in Rome and the villa at Tivoli represent three central themes of imperial rule: military domination, a broad and tolerant religious observance, and a cultured and extravagant private life. All three buildings are emblematic of Hadrian's peaceful and transforming ambitions for the empire which, when he first came to power, was still defined and subdued by military aggression. Hadrian's Wall was a clear declaration of what the empire was and where its limits might be reached; the Pantheon, too, defined known limits in its architectural experimentation; and the villa was an imaginative symbolic representation of the empire in its entirety. The emperor's distinctive structures are highly visible markers of the vast power and resources wielded by all Roman emperors which, when directed by Hadrian's personal interests and drive, went on to instigate the last great flowering of classical art. Hadrian knew how to create his effects, and the impact of his imagination on the landscape of the Mediterranean and beyond is a reflection of the nature and reach of an extraordinary reign. Hadrian built to be remembered, and in that he was entirely successful.

Yet the judgement of posterity has changed over time. Despite his apparent strengths, something went very wrong in the last years of his life, and although modern assessments of Hadrian's reign are usually favourable, at his death in 138 CE he was said to be hated by the people; some even called him a tyrant. The Roman senate delayed a decision as to whether to accord him the posthumous imperial honours which were usually a matter of routine, and they finally did so only when forced to act by Hadrian's adopted son and successor, Antoninus Pius. Why Hadrian, who brought peace to a troubled empire and who endowed its cities so generously, came to be detested is a question concerned as much with the contradictions of his personality as with personal misfortunes and historical events. Hadrian, the cleverest and most cultured of emperors, was little understood by his contemporaries throughout his long reign. A combination of melancholy, quick temper and intellectual competitiveness did not promote friendship or even, at times, respect; and events in the last years of his reign precipitated a sequence of ill-health and misjudgement which for many centuries critically damaged Hadrian's reputation and diminished any appreciation of his contribution to the ancient world.

A long, solitary and uncertain wait for power had perhaps exacerbated his natural lack of warmth, and the graciousness observed in his dealings with ordinary people was not usually extended to his peers. In later life Hadrian's brilliant enthusiasms turned to obsession, his curiosity became dissatisfaction and his lack of trust eventually slipped into something approaching paranoia. Older age and personal crises turned these characteristics into depressive severity and diminished the quick intelligence and statesmanlike qualities which had underpinned the achievements of his earlier reign. The lofty concept of a harmonious empire soon vanished when his ideology and authority were seriously challenged in Judea, and here, in the 130s, Hadrian instituted a campaign of violent suppression equal to the most vicious campaigns of any of his predecessors. His handling of Jewish resistance caused a revolt to escalate into a war which was prosecuted with such brutality that it appeared to have annihilated the Jewish people. The repercussions of this were felt both in Rome at the time and more widely down the centuries.

Perhaps more than with any other emperor, Hadrian's reputation at any given time has depended on current prejudice. Nothing illustrates better the gulf between the values of ancient Rome and those of the twenty-first century than the changing justifications for this opprobrium. Contemporary criticism of the emperor was directed not at his eventual aggression against unequal opponents, nor even at the questions of his sexuality that have so preoccupied modern

4

writers, but at a political scandal right at the start of his reign which became known as the Affair of the Four Consuls and dogged his reputation for twenty years. Many among the more conservative Roman upper classes also considered his ceding of territory a weakness, his abiding passions incomprehensible and the aftermath – not the existence – of his doomed relationship with a Greek youth, Antinous, undignified. In Hadrian's time, a man was judged not by his sexuality in itself but by how his relationships were conducted.

Yet Hadrian *was* a great and brilliant emperor. Behind the inscriptions and the temples, the texts and the coinage, the panegyric and the slander, Hadrian can be clearly distinguished, not only as the figure of a ruler but as an individual – an individual who made such an impact on his times that his immortality was assured. The itinerant emperor attempted with considerable success to integrate the many peoples of his empire. He came close to achieving his aim of peace, and the methods he used to do so created a unique legacy in over 130 cities of the world. Manipulating his presence so that he was simultaneously more accessible to his subjects than his predecessors and yet more elusive in his traditional role, he escaped the untidy fate of so many early emperors, keeping the cult of personality in balance with the welfare of his empire. In satisfying his own desire to collect and commission works of art and by doing so to cement his position, he also became himself an object of desire to cities and powerful individuals throughout his world. He re-invented his life and his times: he played the parts of a Greek or Hellenistic or Egyptian ruler, a philosopher, a magician, a grammarian, an architect and a poet; and one century after the death of Christ he raised a very ordinary, if beautiful, Greek boy to be the last pagan god of ancient Rome. He used the whole Mediterranean world as a stage on which his journeys were the great evolving drama not just of his own life but of the lives of the millions who inhabited his empire.

The ruins of Rome that have drawn travellers since the middle ages, pursued by the Romantics and the Grand Tourists, and still pursued by the tourists of the twenty-first century, are in many cases the ruins of Hadrian's power and personality. To piece together the story of Hadrian's final years, to put flesh on the bones and round out the picture of this extraordinary reign, it is necessary to go beyond the ambiguous fragments of texts and to travel as he did, through a landscape of wonders and history that was already ancient in Hadrian's time.

Gibbon summed Hadrian up: '*He was in turns an excellent prince, a ridiculous sophist and a jealous tyrant.*' For the background to Hadrian's decline from excellence into tyranny, we need to turn to the events of his long last journey through his eastern empire.

1

The waiting game

We have stated that the stars are attached to the firmament – not assigned to each of us in the way in which the vulgar believe and dealt out to mortals with a degree of radiance proportionate to the lot of each – the brightest stars to the rich, the smaller ones to the poor, the dim to those who are worn out; they do not each rise with their own human being, nor indicate by their fall that someone's life is being extinguished. There is no such close alliance between us and the sky that the radiance of the stars there also shares our fate of mortality. When the stars are believed to fall, what happens is that owing to their being overfed with a draught of liquid they give back the surplus with a fiery flash, just as with us also we see this occur with a stream of oil when lamps are lit. But the heavenly bodies have a nature that is eternal – they interweave the world and are blended with its weft; yet their potency has a powerful influence on the earth, indeed it is owing to the effects that they produce and to their brilliance and magnitude that it has been possible for them to become known with such a degree of precision, as we shall show in the proper place.

PLINY THE ELDER, NATURAL HISTORY, 2, 28–31

From the memoirs of Julia Balbilla, Baiae, July 138

So, the dream is over. The emperor who brought Rome the peace that always eluded her, who turned divers fulminating or enslaved nations into one great compliant empire, is dead. Here he lies, his body still warm in this heavy heat. For many days we have become accustomed to the silence of his deathbed, the hushed voices and the straw in the yards muffling approaching footsteps, but with his death the villa resounds with the noise of life: the ring of metal, shouted orders, slaves running, hammering. We are on the move again. The horses are bridled, the guard mounted, the priests and the troops assembled – and soon the new emperor takes his place to accompany Hadrian on his last journey home to Rome.

This sweltering town is the place of dreams, founded by an early traveller, one of Odysseus' brave crew, and now the focus of elusive pleasure and rich men's fantasies. Baiae, the last resort of the incomplete and the desperate. They travel for three days from Rome to the coast in search of a cure, their desire for health equalled, if not frustrated, by the physicians' yearning for wealth. Or they seek the perfect woman or youth – one whose skilled attentions might offer an afternoon of oblivion and inspiration for some pretty poetry. Or they purchase the rarest fish, fresh and tender, to feed their insatiable hunger for novelty. They bring their doctors and their procurers and their cooks, they lie in bewildered dissatisfaction in the courtyards of one of the endless glorious villas that form a second mountain range along the shore from one cape to another, and they wait for night.

By day Baiae is a pretty place, with just the whiff of sulphur borne on the singular breeze that ruffles the myrtle groves and the vines. Equally, it is a rare current from Rome which disturbs the patrician sweating at his leisure like any stone-clearing peasant in a field. In the finest houses the fountains pour into the pools, but as the searing days turn into night the revellers gaze out into the haze of the ocean, where sea becomes vapour and their hopes shimmer into infinity. As night falls, the sunsets fill the bay. Then, sometimes, a wind gets up and the heat, and life, becomes tolerable.

So, Baiae, and for him, and for us all, the great dream is over. Some say that at the end he who had the power to snap the thread of a life found himself powerless when faced with the seemingly interminable unravelling of his own. That last terrible journey to the coast, the emperor largely delirious, muttering in Greek or the rustic accent of his childhood, calling for those long absent from his life or recoiling from some malign but invisible foe. Outside, his ageing court were anxious and the younger men fawned round Antoninus, priming their affections to be simultaneously transferred with the now inevitable succession. The fussing physicians determined that although he must die he must be seen to do so in dignity, at whatever cost to the emperor's ease or wish. There was to be no repetition of the furtive death in an unheard-of foreign village that had overtaken Trajan. Hadrian must hurry to Baiae before death arrived.

Nor was death to be accelerated by the hand of any other than fate. Poor Antoninus, finding that the private audience was a matter of the emperor begging him to assist in advancing his death, then in resentment and pain accusing him of ingratitude when he demurred. After that, neither the heir nor Hadrian's favoured servants were left alone with him. It was an impossible situation for them. To calm him, only two or three were allowed in his rooms; enough that people could not subsequently say, as they did of Tiberius' last hours, that the emperor was sent prematurely on his way.

There are no valedictions in music or words; there is no one left with the appetite to hear them. Nothing for Hadrian who remembered so many others. Hadrian who made sure he would not himself be forgotten in buildings, in laws and in dedications. There are young men now clambering the lower slopes of ambition – eager tribunes, junior senators and those serving the necessary time in less amiable provinces – to whom the word 'emperor' is synonymous with Hadrian. For all their sentient lives he has directed their energies, their expectations, their tastes; the terms of their world were set in stone by the man who grows cold in the villa at Baiae.

As for the new emperor – he seems a decent man, finding it harder to convince himself than anyone else of his translation into power. Yet here is that stolid Roman, long past youth, standing a little taller already. Not easy to be a second choice. Not perhaps a man to change the world, Antoninus Pius, but then Hadrian would never have wanted any man to surpass his creation. Nor is he a visionary, our new emperor – where Hadrian, for all his faults, encompassed the empire, poor Antoninus looks ill at ease even at Baiae, what with the fleshpots and the invalids and the women and the men playing at being women and the strain of being emperor. Antoninus finds that Rome, even in summer, has everything he requires; how relieved he must be that there need be no more expeditions.

As for me – I am an old woman and hardly have the heart to travel back to Athens. But when my time comes I should like to die among my last friends and be laid to rest near my brother. It is less than ten years since I came to court, yet so many have gone now, so many who were once young and hopeful and lit up with promise: Commodus the ailing prince, silly young Fuscus, even the living statue that was Antinous. They are gone with those more timely dead: Sabina, Vibia, that foolish old man Servianus, loyal Turbo, Apollodorus, the dreadful Juvenal and the irrepressible survivor Suetonius.

There is the matter of Hadrian's memoirs and my promises to consider. Of course, mine is not the only copy; but mine is the one destined for the place nearest to his heart. Will I take it? Will I deliver it, this justification, this testament to reputation whose pages I have read and endorsed admiringly, whose author I have agreed to become so that its message may appear more convincing? Hadrian, who never fixed his own name to any of his great buildings, counting that their very brilliance would announce him, now demands that his last and most imaginative construction

11

should enter posterity bearing my name upon it. Could with-holding it lessen the chances that Hadrian's version of the last sixty years should become the way that those to come will see and judge us? Hadrian's library, Hadrian's history, Hadrian's truth.

But perhaps I shall lodge it with my own journal and the fragments of Sabina's letters and diaries that I have kept by me. Her heart was never really in it, of course; the empress was ill-educated, though not the stupid woman so many assumed. She would write for a few days, never risking dictating her grievances – which were many, if largely justified – to a servant. But she had no real literary instinct; in her head the ideas were all there, vivid, silently but acutely observed, but on paper she faltered as often as not, told too often that her views were of no importance. Hadrian seldom faltered; lack of confidence was not one of his character-istics. What she had to contribute to history was not her negligible poetic skill, nor her untried opinions, but an account of her quiet scrutiny. Often ignored, eventually unnoticed like a competent slave, Sabina saw everything: a glance, a clumsy guiltiness, excite-ment, boredom. Sabina watched, she remembered and she concluded.

So our secret history may equal his public one, and I may take a passage to Athens. It is time for us all to return home; the great journey is over.

On a stifling summer day in Rome the Palatine Hill, above the stagnant traffic of the narrow city streets, is a slightly cooler haven which even in the hottest months of the year catches the occasional breeze. On some evenings the heat is broken by purple thunder-clouds which roll in from the west as they have always done, and for just a few minutes the small plateau and its famous pines are noisy with rain as the water runs fast over the ancient cobbles before it evaporates, almost as quickly, into mist.

Even two thousand years ago it was quieter and more comfortable on the Palatine. It remains a commanding position, with wide views of the further hills across the Forum, the ancient heart of the city. Here, in the Renaissance gardens, are the still remarkable ruins of the imperial palaces of the first and second century; further back still, according to legend, it was here that Romulus and Remus were suckled by a wolf. Long dismissed as myth, the story of the origins of Rome has been reinvigorated by recent excavations on the Palatine which have revealed traces of simple huts dating back to the ninth century BCE. Rather fewer tourists explore the gravel walks and roofless enclosures of this quiet hill than wander in the confusing and popular ruins below; but here on the Palatine are the broken walls, courtyards and vaulted terracing of the house of Augustus and the house of his wife, Livia; the palace of Tiberius, extended by Caligula; and the palace of Domitian. Here too are the palace of the Severans and the foundations of the temple of Elagabalus. Nero's notorious Golden House, now a black and damp cave under the Esquiline Hill, is just across a small valley and connected to the Palatine by a surviving underground tunnel.

This was always the city's most desirable quarter, lived in by the rich and the influential from Cicero to Catullus to Caesar Augustus. In this small area of Rome the greatest men in the world negotiated for power, started and concluded wars, and celebrated their ambitions and achievements. In these palaces they intrigued and regrouped, lived, fought, murdered, hid and died. There is no palace of Hadrian among the remains, although its absence was a matter of deliberate and significant choice; but in the second century this was still the centre of Hadrian's world.

Publius Aelius Hadrianus was born into the Roman aristocracy, the son of Domitia Paulina and a young senator, Aelius Hadrianus Afer. It has been suggested that Hadrian could have been born in Spain, his ancestral home, but opinion is generally in favour of Rome as his birthplace; indeed, he was almost certainly born in the vicinity of the

Palatine, as appropriate to his rank. It was the ninth day before the kalends of February, and the empire was in the wise care of the Emperor Vespasian. It was by no means predictable that Hadrian might one day rise to become the ablest, most inspired and most controversial emperor of Rome. It was by no means predictable, on a cold winter's day in second-century Rome, even among the most affluent of families, that the squalling infant would survive at all. And if childhood disease, service on the battlefield, or finding himself on the wrong side in a court intrigue did not prematurely curtail his life, then Hadrian's background certainly reduced his prospects of highest office. Social standing at this time was defined less by birthplace than by descent, and both his parents had origins in southern Spain, Paulina in Gades, present-day Cadiz, and Afer in Italica, a town near modern Seville; thus the new baby was a provincial, an outsider, from the cradle. Hadrian's father may have been a senator, but although his son was born into the most privileged class of the most successful nation in the world, there had never been a provincial Roman emperor.

Hadrian spent periods of his youth abroad, perhaps to avoid the endemic disease of the city. It is entirely possible that some of his early childhood was also spent following his father's postings, but we know nothing of the boy's life between his birth and his father's death ten years later. It is only at that point that Hadrian suddenly appears in ancient histories, as writers began to consider the unsteady course towards a possibly glorious future that was beginning to unfold for the senator's now fatherless son. The boy's care was shared between two guardians; one of them was a cousin, Trajan, at that time a high-ranking army officer, a carefully bluff but ambitious military man who also had Spanish connections. Trajan's meteoric rise to power was to drag Hadrian with it.

At fifteen Hadrian was sent back to Italica, where his

family held estates. It was appropriate for a young aristocrat to know his roots; but if it was a happy stay – and if we are to judge from his future treatment of his home town, it was not – it was certainly not productive; Trajan summoned his ward away from Spain, where it was rumoured that he was spending too much time hunting. All his life Hadrian was to seek out heroes, either to admire or to copy, but Trajan was a problematic role model. As Hadrian later found, dead heroes were more amenable. It is noticeable and may well have been confusing to an adolescent that where Hadrian emulated Trajan's interests he seemed to misjudge his powerful guardian. Trajan's passion had made hunting respectable – he was the first member of the nobility to show such enthusiasm for an activity not hitherto considered an aristocratic pursuit – but he was no more delighted to hear that the young Hadrian was neglecting his more serious studies to hone his hunting skills than he later was to discover that his ward was pursuing the same boys at court that the emperor had singled out for himself. The emergence of interests in hunting, whether boars or boys, was to gain greater significance later.

Many years afterwards, Italica must have hoped for great things from its generally expansive native son, but the affection of city and emperor was evidently not mutual. The wide-travelling Hadrian never returned to his ancestral city as emperor, and the snub was the more marked because he did return to Spain on one of his early journeys, only to ignore his family home. Nevertheless, from early stories of Hadrian being mocked by the senate for his provincial manners it is understandable that, once in power, Hadrian should have wished to rearrange his personal geography. He would not be the first to put Spain well behind him. The country had produced many cultured, creative men – Seneca, Lucan, Quintilian and Martial – but all headed for Rome. Spain provided a comfortable existence and the country was rich in natural produce, but it was not at the centre of things. Unlike

Hadrian, Martial retained a sentimental attachment to his home country and briefly returned there in the last years of his life; but, the most urbane of men, he soon tired of the leisured rural round he evoked so beautifully and yearned for the filthy streets of Rome. The country was a good place for poetry, but life and power were to be pursued in the city. Hadrian never showed any interest in the country life, beyond time spent hunting, and Italica was forgotten. In time the emperor was to create his own sophisticated pastoral vision within the great villa complex he created at Tivoli; but that had nothing to do with the provinces or the land, or indeed nature, and everything to do with creating his own cosmos, complete with internal gardens, pools and groves in which his collections could be displayed.

After a period undertaking official work – an occupation which had some prestige but was undoubtedly boring for an active young man – a hardier life was soon arranged, and Hadrian was posted first as tribune of the Second Legion in Pannonia, south of the Danube, and then to Moesia, in today's Balkans. Thus he, like Trajan, was well away from Rome as the tensions mounted that were to culminate in the assassination of the current emperor, Domitian, on an autumn afternoon in 96 CE. Domitian was swiftly replaced with the elderly Nerva, a caretaker emperor, and in 97 Trajan's, and by association Hadrian's, fortunes were significantly advanced when Trajan was adopted by the childless Nerva, with a degree of coercion, to lend youthful and heroic lustre to his reign. A provincial now stood in line to be emperor of Rome. It had always been unthinkable; but now it was not only possible but about to happen. Just a few months later, Nerva died in Rome. It was midwinter and Trajan was at his command in Germany, at what is now Cologne. Hadrian, serving as a tribune in another, nearer part of the province, heard the news and for the first time showed his instinct for the dramatic, and possibly advantageous, scene. He was determined to seize the opportunity to be the first to break the news to Trajan that he was now emperor. His commanding officer Servianus, who was also his brother-in-law, was equally determined to prevent such a *coup de théâtre* and sabotaged Hadrian's carriage; but Hadrian went off on foot into the bitter night and arrived before the official messenger from Rome. Hadrian was duly rewarded for his efforts – as, in his way, was Servianus, who had fallen foul of a man uniquely able to sustain grudges. Decades later, when Hadrian had been reigning for twenty years, he was to send the old man to his death.

With the vigorous but childless Trajan a popular emperor of Rome, his young cousin Hadrian's prospects began to be taken seriously. Having been treated with some contempt both by his peers, who mocked his clumsy speech and found him a charmless young man, and by his senior officers, who criticised his spending and self-indulgence, he found himself on the receiving end of a pragmatic shift in attitude as his eventual power became a clear possibility.

Yet this nebulous enhancement of status was in its way a curse. There was no point in his life at which Hadrian was clearly heir-apparent. The route to supreme power was conventionally through adoption, not blood descent, and although close relatives were likely to be in the running there were always other contenders. Hadrian himself clearly articulated the advantages of this system towards the end of his reign:

I, my friend, have not been permitted by nature to have a son, but you have made it possible by legal enactment. Now there is this difference between the two methods – that a begotten son turns out to be whatever sort of person Heaven pleases, whereas one that is adopted a man takes to himself as the result of deliberate selection.

Thus by the process of nature a maimed and witless child is often given to a parent, but by process of selection one of sound body and sound man is certain to be chosen.[1]

The disadvantage, for the potential successor, was the delicate business of treading the very fine line between permitting an assumption of status yet not seeming to be too eager, nor becoming implicated in rumours of plots which might seem to threaten the existing emperor. For Hadrian it was a matter of the subtlest diplomacy, keeping Trajan's support, making the right political moves, securing a power base in the army and the provinces while not falling out of favour with the senate or seeming to pre-empt the incumbent's decision as to his heir. Hadrian sustained this joyless balancing act for year after year, with no clear future, and in doing so perhaps acquired some of the skills (and indeed some of the failings) that were to mark his own tenure of power.

Nevertheless, Hadrian had cause to hope. Indeed, the conduct of his life was predicated on that hope and its substantiation. Hadrian had always been drawn to the supernatural, to magic and astrology as means by which he uneasily sought to understand his future. He was not alone in this; contemporary histories were full of the bizarre and ambiguous heralds of disaster or triumph, military and political decisions waited for good portents, and pontifical rites examined the livers of slaughtered animals for favourable signs. But as an eminent patrician, a member of the imperial family, Hadrian's attempts to discover the future were risky; in the past, consulting fortune-tellers had been seen as a direct threat to imperial power, exposing a hungry ambition. Indeed, towards the end of his reign, he was himself to destroy a young relative for just such over-keen anticipation. Yet Hadrian seemed to find fortune-tellers irresistible, despite the risks and the deceptions, and his repeated return to them provides one insight into the position of impotent desperation in which he found himself. Most emperors, once in power, conceded that their progress had been bolstered by some alarming indications of their future fortune. Vespasian was delighted when a dog brought a human hand into the dining room, heralding, all said, his eventual succession. The portents for Trajan's rule were more privately, and more safely, revealed to him in a dream. However, to be found seeking this reassurance when not yet in power was a different matter.

Hadrian started young. It was perhaps an interest fostered in childhood when his great-uncle, a master of astrology, predicted the boy would one day succeed to immense power. On different occasions he was told repeatedly, although the details are vague, that auguries had indicated his eventual triumph. As a young military commander in the Balkans, Hadrian was still seeking out predictions for the future and finding them, as yet another fortune-teller repeated the claim. Shortly afterwards, when one of a series of mild disagreements left him apprehensive of his crucial relationship with Trajan, he sought the advice of the famous Virgilian oracle. This impressive-sounding process consisted simply of opening Virgil's *Aeneid* at random and reading a message in the text, and on this occasion it provided him with a gratifying combination of images: an olive wreath, a mighty realm, a greying beard and a regeneration of Rome.

So years, a decade and more, passed while Hadrian watched for a sign, waiting for the definitive statement which might clarify his status. It never came. Beyond soothsayers, his hopes were sustained by what seems a troubled mixture of tiny phenomena and small gestures of preferment – losing the cloak of an inferior rank, or, more promisingly, being given a diamond by Trajan which he had in his time received from Nerva.

As an investment in his own future, marriage to Trajan's great-niece, Sabina, in 100 CE must have seemed an ideal move for an ambitious man. Sabina was Trajan's nearest surviving blood relative and her roots were, like Hadrian's, in Spain. But the couple had little else in common, and the match, arranged by Trajan's wife, was to bring no joy to either party. For both Hadrian, in his mid-twenties, and Sabina, who was probably around fourteen at the time of her marriage, the union was unsatisfactory – but Hadrian at least had the advantage of political consolidation. Of Sabina's thoughts we know nothing. She was only just out of childhood when she was given to Hadrian as a bride, and died in her fifties, a few years before her husband. Hadrian's willingness to accept Sabina was at least in part a ploy to reinstate himself with Trajan after a squabble over some page boys. It was not an auspicious start to the marriage. Within months, Trajan's unofficial would-be heir-apparent, newly appointed to the senate, returned to military service as trouble stirred again on the borders with Dacia. The couple never had children and the ancient writers largely repeat the claim that Hadrian found his empress uncongenial, although surviving inscriptions and images show that she was treated with the respect accorded to her rank in life. In later years he was reported to have said that if he had not been emperor he would have divorced her, and even after decades together the relationship between Hadrian and Sabina was so visibly poor that when she died it was rumoured that she had been poisoned by her husband.

It was not of course considered necessary or even desirable that there should be an affectionate bond between a high-ranking couple, and any kinswoman of an emperor could expect little beyond disposal in a strategic alliance. Even for a man within those circles, marriage was invariably a tactical move. When Augustus was emperor he peremptorily ordered his adopted son Tiberius, who was, unusually for the time, much in love with his first wife, to divorce her and marry Augustus' wayward daughter Julia. Tiberius, a difficult, taciturn man, was given to following his first wife, unable to surrender her completely and trapped in misery with his new and adulterous partner.

Although Sabina travelled with Hadrian, she shared few of his intellectual pursuits, and he was without doubt emotionally far more bound up with his mother-in-law than with his wife. The conventional age gap of a decade or more between husband and wife meant that Hadrian was probably nearer in age to Matidia, Sabina's mother, than to his bride, and when the elder woman died he was distraught. More importantly, Hadrian nurtured a close relationship with another slightly older woman: Plotina, the emperor Trajan's wife. She was to promote him throughout his life, being the prime mover in his useful marriage to Sabina and in his accession as emperor on Trajan's death. In both crucial moves forward in Hadrian's career, Trajan's own views seem to have been equivocal. There were inevitably rumours that Hadrian was romantically, and possibly, though less plausibly, sexually involved with Plotina. Despite the subsequent belief in his homosexuality, and some hints that he had been Trajan's sexual partner, early gossip suggested that the rather friendless young man had always been attracted to married women. Plotina was an intelligent, politically adept woman, and shared more of her interests and abilities with Hadrian than either can have done with their spouses. Despite a possible diminution in their closeness in later life, when Plotina died in the mid-120s Hadrian pronounced a period of unprecedented mourning and erected a splendid basilica in her memory at Nemausus, now Nîmes in southern France, then one of the leading cities of Gaul and on the main route from Italy to Spain. It may well have been the relationship between Plotina and Hadrian which condemned Hadrian and Sabina to their arid marriage. Given that marriage was an inevitable step in the life of an upper-class man, it is all too plausible that Plotina chose a young relative whose status would assist the man she cared for into office but whose personality and level of sophistication were unlikely to distract him from his relationship with herself.

Once Hadrian became emperor the unfortunate Sabina followed, or was taken, on most of his travels; possibly her mother, who was a widow, came too. In her portraits Sabina has a dignified beauty, with thick hair, even features and a solemn face, as she poses in the Greek styles which reflected her husband's taste. In court circles she was said to have a sour disposition, yet that was not all there was to her; her friend Julia Balbilla, who accompanied her to Egypt, described her prettiness in poetry, and evidently both enjoyed her company and felt protective of her. It has – perhaps inevitably – been suggested that there was a sexual element in Sabina and Julia's relationship.[2] As a story it is a tidy complement to the notorious involvement of Hadrian with the Greek Antinous, but ultimately it is probably just fantasy.

Trajan was healthy and well-liked; his reputation, unusually, remained intact both during his reign and after his death. There was no reason to expect that he would not live into old age, although Rome had been surprised before and Trajan spent much of his life leading his armies in sometimes hard-fought campaigns; indeed, in his one battle in the east he narrowly missed being hit by an arrow which killed his bodyguard, and he came close to death in the terrible earthquakes at Antioch in 115. But with the years stretching ahead of him, he, at least, saw no need to consider the question of succession. Trajan lived on for nearly two decades, the model of a Roman emperor, strong, brave and forthright, asserting the supremacy of his empire in an uncomplicated manner which made him popular with army, senate and people. He was a vigorous campaigner in Parthia and Dacia and pushed out the boundaries of the empire, reflecting back to Rome the image of itself as an invincible, omnipotent force, that it most enjoyed.

Yet the reality was not quite as it was filtered back to Rome. Defending an increasingly long and contested frontier was expensive and apparently unending. As one conflict followed another, Trajan found himself locked into continual warfare. His popularity was founded on his reputation as a soldier, yet the expansion which his campaigning achieved was constantly in need of military action to defend it. Increasingly,

Trajan responded to any confrontation by mobilising his forces, hurrying from one war to another. Even as Rome congratulated itself, the long boundaries of the empire trembled under the strain.

Meanwhile, Hadrian maintained his political balancing act of loyalty and patient ambition and rose through the ranks of a political career – at the normal speed: there was no sign of preferment signalling him out for accelerated progress.

Hadrian had entered middle age and was governor of Syria when Trajan finally fell ill while fighting in an unsuccessful engagement at Hatra in Mesopotamia. Simultaneously there was further disturbance on the northern frontiers, and news reached the imperial headquarters of serious Jewish insurrection in north Africa. It was later calculated that in the subsequent reprisals nearly a quarter of a million non-Jews were killed and the Jews were almost entirely displaced from Cyrene and Egypt, moving to further outposts of the east. With the periphery of the empire crumbling, provincial dissent mounting and the costs of continual warfare escalating, the ailing and dispirited Trajan turned back for Rome.

The imperial party probably travelled by ship, but by the time it reached the coastal town of Selinus in Cilicia, now southern Turkey, Trajan was seriously unwell and they were forced to drop anchor and go ashore. Only small towns now lie on this length of dramatically beautiful wooded and fissured coast, although several resorts cater to tourists, but the masonry that seems randomly abandoned on its hillsides hints at a previous busier existence. In the second century it was a place of fine Seleucid towns along a coast which had traditionally been plagued by pirates and was now heavily fortified. Here in early August 117 CE, in what is now Gazipaşa, the imperial party landed. Their situation was becoming difficult. Trajan's health was deteriorating; he was partially paralysed, with circulatory failure and generalised oedema. It was increasingly obvious that he was not going to get back to Rome. Messengers were sent urgently to the senate and to Antioch, where Trajan had set up his imperial residence and where Hadrian had remained while the emperor travelled on. Illness made the great soldier frightened and paranoid; Trajan believed he had been poisoned, although his neurological symptoms were consistent with a stroke. He had no designated heir, for the crucial final step of adoption, which would ensure that the 41-year-old Hadrian would accede, had still not been taken.

At Antioch, Hadrian was soon aware of the events unfolding only three hundred miles away. Whatever his personal feelings for his kinsman, he had waited a long time for this moment. Now middle-aged, he must have remembered his youthful, opportunistic dash to be the first to break the news to Trajan that Nerva had died and that Trajan was emperor. But for Hadrian, even now, success was uncertain; unlike Trajan at the same point, he had not been named the unequivocal heir, nor was he a popular hero; indeed, although the army might be counted on to support him, he was not particularly popular at all, especially back in Rome. Were the succession to be left to senatorial choice, as some rumoured, Hadrian stood little chance of selection.[3] Nor was this just a matter of seeing his ambitions thwarted; an alternative new emperor would almost certainly remove such a blatant rival from office. Hadrian's hopes of high position, and possibly even his life, would be at an end.

As the hot Syrian summer days passed in waiting for the sound of horses bringing news from the west, the tension was unremitting. Antioch was no mere provincial garrison; Trajan had restored the city handsomely after the terrible earthquakes of 115 and had made it in effect a capital second only to Rome, from which he could pursue campaigns in the east.[4] Here, in the comfortable imperial quarters of Trajan's city, Hadrian waited, unable either to carry on campaigning or to make any further move to consolidate his position. It is hardly surprising that he had disturbed sleep, claiming that in a dream on the very night of Trajan's death a lightning bolt struck him from a clear sky, yet passed right through his body without injuring him. It was a very personal, and unverifiable, portent. In the distant province of Egypt, where many years later Hadrian's fortunes were to change again, there were alleged sightings of the mythical phoenix, although he did not know it yet. Hadrian's officers and troops were loyal; he had been assured of support throughout the legions; he was occupying Trajan's own power base in the east – but he could do nothing more to influence the outcome. He had, however, determined allies in the empress Plotina and his other guardian, Attianus; and both of them sat in the dark, shuttered room beside what was now evidently Trajan's deathbed, looking beyond the pale, immobile body of the expiring emperor to the creation of the future.

The exact circumstances of Trajan's last hours and acts are confused, possibly deliberately so. Some time during the emperor's last days a letter of adoption was finally drafted and sent to Antioch and to the senate in Rome. This announcement of the adoption that Hadrian had waited so long to have confirmed was followed swiftly by the public declaration of Trajan's death – the first provincial emperor was also the first emperor to die outside Italy. Hadrian, relatively close at hand, would have received the news of Trajan's decline within perhaps three or four days, but the normal government routes to Rome took couriers two months.[5] In an emergency communications would be speeded up, using constant changes to fresh horses and the fastest riders, but it could still have been the best part of three weeks before Rome heard what Hadrian already knew. At Antioch, Hadrian was proclaimed emperor with the full support of the armies he commanded. Then he travelled west to pay his respects to the late emperor's body before its cremation. Trajan's ashes were placed in a golden urn and taken on to Rome. By the time the news of Trajan's death reached the senate, Hadrian's accession was a *fait accompli*.

At least, that was the official version of events. There were already rumours that release of the news of Trajan's death had been delayed to allow the crucial and legitimising letter of adoption to reach Hadrian and become public first, with an acceptable interval before the announcement of death that would permit him to claim power. There were wilder rumours that the empress had encouraged an impostor to pretend to be the failing emperor, closeted in a dark room, and to dictate his final letters in a frail, and therefore unrecognisable, voice.

It was, and was not, everything Hadrian had ever wanted. He was emperor; but not by consensus, and not yet securely. It would be hard for the senate to oppose the endorsement of the army or question the legitimacy of the procedures of adoption, but it was not impossible. There were those in the senate who would be vociferous in their doubts and quick in latching on to any irregularities in the succession. Meanwhile, although Hadrian had succeeded to domestic stability, the potential for trouble was neither forgotten nor far away. The problems of the troubled provinces and the wars of Trajan's years were unresolved. Hadrian did not have the option of letting the dust settle; there were instant military decisions to be made close at hand, and the senate back in Rome to be placated and convinced. Now was the time to put into action the strategies and moves that would make his position impregnable. He acted decisively with a speed which suggested a long period of forethought.

In the newest provinces Hadrian appeared to be facing a critical situation which could jeopardise his personal security. He proceeded with dramatic measures. In what appeared to be a direct reversal of Trajan's policies, Hadrian withdrew from what he believed were the unsustainable borders where Rome was weakened by continual warfare and moved to consolidate a tighter, more manageable empire. He negotiated with previously hostile kings; he withdrew troops from inconclusive engagements; he settled the demands of small enemies. He quoted the venerated old republican Cato, saying that those who could not be held subject should be set free.[6] (It was not a policy he was later to extend to Judea.)

It was undoubtedly a sound decision, and it was one that the hero-emperor Trajan himself had slowly been coming to accept as the only way forward. Its timing, however, did little to endear the new emperor to influential Romans living far from the battlefields of the disputed territories. Personal interest as well as imperial pride was involved: those whose ambitions included the appointments to prestigious foreign posts necessary for career progression now found the empire a smaller place with fewer opportunities for advancement. It was also a risky gambit in that a perceived departure from Trajan's agenda could be fuel to political opponents disputing Hadrian's claim that he was Trajan's obvious and intended successor. Coins were issued which showed Trajan and Hadrian hand in hand over a globe, affirming a consistency of direction which real-life events were swiftly contradicting.

Although written some decades later, the seemingly slight tale of Trajan's Bridge is a scarcely disguised metaphor for the succession, told by the partisan Greek who had become a Roman senator, Cassius Dio. The history of this crossing spanned the turbulence not just of the River Ister but that between civilised and barbarian Rome and between the reigns of two famous emperors; the bricks and mortar of this remarkable construction carried as many messages as it ever did troops and equipment.

Trajan constructed over the Ister a stone bridge for which I cannot sufficiently admire him. Brilliant, indeed, as are his other achievements, yet this surpasses them. For it has twenty piers of squared stone one hundred and fifty feet in height above the foundations and sixty in width, and these, standing at a distance of one hundred and seventy feet from one another, are connected by arches. How then could one fail to be astonished at the expenditure made upon them, or the way in which each of them was placed in a river so deep, in water so full of eddies, and on a bottom so muddy? For it was impossible of course, impossible to divert the stream elsewhere . . . this too, then, is one of the achievements that show the magnitude of Trajan's designs, though the bridge is of no use to us; for merely the piers are standing, affording no means of crossing, as if they had been erected for the sole purpose of demonstrating that there is nothing which human ingenuity cannot accomplish.

Trajan built the bridge because he feared that some time when the Ister was frozen over war might be made upon the Romans on the further side, and he wished to facilitate access to them by this means. Hadrian, on the contrary, was afraid that it might also make it easy for the barbarians, once they had overpowered the guard at the bridge, to cross into Moesia, and so he removed the superstructure.[7]

The Ister – the modern Danube – is Europe's second longest river, laden with mythological associations: it had carried Jason and the Argonauts westwards into the Adriatic Sea. Bridging its difficult waters was an astonishing feat of engineering and military strategy; Hadrian's disabling of the bridge destroyed the point of Trajan's heroic work, and this account carries hints of both cowardice and filial disrespect. In Dio's eyes, Hadrian had transformed a symbol of aggressive empire-building into a purely visual and useless ruin; an act typical of the apparently soft, defensive agenda of the new emperor.

Hadrian's delay in returning to Rome, dictated by the need to deal with the military situation in person, left the political situation in the capital unresolved – but it also postponed the moment of direct confrontation and, as it turned out, allowed deeply unpopular moves to be forced through in his absence by his cadre. As was always to be the case with Hadrian, one difficult situation could be turned advantageously into a solution for another. The pressing need to sort out the empire's borders also provided an excuse to stay away from Rome until he was in a stronger position and less likely to face open rebellion. He was not without supporters in Rome who continued to promote his interests, but the senate was still angry that Hadrian had pre-empted their decision. The belief that Trajan's dying acceptance of Hadrian had been a devious manoeuvre by Plotina and the new emperor threatened to ignite, if not an open challenge, certainly a whispering campaign, and this belief was entrenched when the letters of adoption which were received by the senate turned out to be signed, for the only time in Trajan's reign, by the empress. Although Roman conspiracy theories are a central feature of ancient histories, the allegation that this succession was stage-managed is given some credence by its being recounted by Cassius Dio, whose father was governor of Cilicia at the time and, it might be assumed, would have been in contact with the imperial party when Trajan's terminal illness halted it in the province.[8]

Faced with potentially virulent disaffection, Hadrian moved fast, ordering the removal of those he thought were unreliable, receiving intelligence as to which men were dangerous to him, and putting his known supporters into key positions before returning home to Italy. His strategies worked. By the time Hadrian returned to his capital in summer 118, having spent just under a year moving round the recent battle zones of the central empire, restoring peace, the senate, essentially a pragmatic and conservative body, had been persuaded to accept the inevitable. The new emperor was welcomed by letter; coins bearing his image had been issued; and Trajan, his adoptive father, had been declared a god, the standard honour awarded to a dead emperor but an important move which also elevated the living emperor, Hadrian, to son of a god.

But there was one other incident in the transition which

was to haunt Hadrian. Within weeks of Trajan's death the senate was coerced into agreeing to the summary execution of four alleged plotters against Hadrian's life. Neither he nor the senate ever forgot it, and the senate never forgave him. The deaths also appeared to contradict the new emperor's own stated intentions for his reign. In his first letter as emperor, while still well away from home, Hadrian had written to the senate in firm but conciliatory terms apologising for his hasty acclamation by the army but justifying it as essential to suppress any potential disturbance following Trajan's death. He could have stopped there; but he also promised to rule fairly and put no senator to death without trial. If the senate was temporarily persuaded of his benign objectives, the effect when Hadrian's ally and former guardian Attianus demanded the deaths of Nigrinus, Palma, Celsus and Lusius must have been shocking. The move may have been made with the intention of intimidation. The four powerful men, all known personally to Hadrian, were accused of involvement in various plots. It was said that they planned to kill him, either when as high priest, vulnerable and unarmed, he was involved in the rituals of sacrifice, or on the pretext of an accident while he was out hunting. The accusations were specific, the defence unheard. The four were never brought back to Rome for questioning but were sought out and killed wherever they were found: two on their estates, one at the seaside resort of Baiae and one while travelling. Dio states that it was widely believed that they had in reality been killed because of their wealth and, more convincingly, their influence. Ultimately their crime was that they were Trajan's men.

Hadrian, still keeping away from the city, disingenuously denied any involvement in their convenient removal. For Attianus, who was on the spot in Rome, and who had also been a party to whatever transpired at Trajan's deathbed, Hadrian had little gratitude: blame for the deaths was firmly attributed to a unilateral decision by Hadrian's old friend. As

Hadrian's long-term supporter, Attianus may well have done the necessary dirty work to ensure a smooth succession, but after this episode Hadrian hastened to put distance between himself and the man who had now become a liability.

It was a traumatic episode for the Roman elite, used to the domestic mildness of Trajan. Memories were long, and twenty years later this early bloodbath was still cited as one reason for Hadrian's unpopularity. Now Hadrian's early reign was compromised not only by a lack of clarity over the process of accession but by this immediate and violent action against four leading opponents. The implications looked bleak. Such an affair might have seemed less surprising had it been initiated by any of Hadrian's predecessors. But Hadrian, the consummate strategist, was seen as a milder man, less prone to the arbitrary removal of opponents. It was even more incomprehensible in that it directly contradicted his own statements made to the senate as part of his campaign of persuasion straight after Trajan died. Could he be trusted? Who would be next? Was there another Domitian in the making?

Hadrian was both much more robust and much more politically adept than Domitian. Despite the abiding unpopularity of his action, this removal of key opponents undoubtedly helped secure Hadrian's position, and history did offer some justification for the swift moves against the senators. Julius Caesar's clemency, which left troublemakers alive to foment opposition, played a part in his downfall, whereas Augustus' bloody and extensive proscriptions ensured his long and unopposed reign. The tensions of imperial reign were always difficult to negotiate, and never more so than early on in a reign, when the fault-line of power was exposed. The evolving tradition of adoptive heirs, which in theory permitted the most suitable candidate to move into position, also meant that at times the succession was unclear and the assumption of power might be challenged. Hadrian's background and education had caused him to be wary and ruthless; he swiftly developed an effective *modus operandi* and remained firmly in control of every aspect of his reign until the last years.

The key to Hadrian's behaviour, and to the subsequent integration of a style of rule, may be found in his relationship with the past. He was a broadly read man and a passionate, if nostalgic, historian, and the innovations of his reign as well as the strategies he adopted to consolidate power were all consistent with his pervasive sense of the past. His own immediate experience, infused with a broad knowledge of Mediterranean history, shaped the future of his empire. Hadrian had lived through the reigns of five very different emperors: Vespasian, Titus, Domitian, Nerva and Trajan, among whom only Domitian and Trajan, arguably the worst and the best of them, ruled for any length of time. The differences between them, and between those who triumphed and those who were overthrown, were often slight – a matter of public perception of personalities rather than their acts. The dilapidated tenement housing of Rome caught fire on many, many occasions; only Nero was thought to have rejoiced in it. Disease hit the itinerant population of the overcrowded city with terrible regularity; only Domitian was said to have deliberately infected his people. Such occurrences in the reign of a 'good' emperor were invariably used to his credit: plagues and conflagrations were seen as opportunities for Vespasian, Titus and Trajan to show their paternalistic strengths and generosity.

The peaceful empire Hadrian inherited was by no means long-established, and the recent past provided both lessons for would-be tyrants and examples of successful, survivable, rule. At the time of Hadrian's birth Rome was ruled by the benign and thrifty Vespasian, whose most notorious deed was taxing urinals. His reign brought a period of peace and growth after a tumultuous period in Roman politics, while his two sons promised dynastic continuity. Such an apparently peaceful political state (and it turned out to be an illusion) was the exception; from the emergence of, in essence, a dictatorship under Augustus, at the end of a revolution which swept away not just the republican state but hundreds of Augustus' adversaries, power had always been bought and maintained at great cost. From Julius Caesar onwards, assassination had, time and again, resolved the tensions of autocracy. The emperor's power was not infinite but, crucially, nor were its limits known. Autocratic and absolute, it was also, to a degree, experimental. The political structures were relatively young and still evolving. Behaviour which might be tolerated in one ruler was unacceptable in another, and a reasonably long reign might suddenly be rendered insecure by a shift in balance between the several vested interests which kept the emperor safely in power. The need for resident government in distant provinces permitted the growth of power bases from which serious challenges to the status quo might be mounted. The senate, the army and the families of the emperor had all at one time or another been implicated in the death of Rome's rulers. Even the long-lived, long-reigning, long-married Augustus might have been poisoned by his wife, or so some whispered. Long re-invented as a benevolent autocrat, father of his nation, with his bloody purges of civil war and the legal and semantic manoeuvrings that brought Rome from republicanism to absolute power far behind him, the ageing emperor liked to walk in his orchards each morning, plucking fruit from his tree like any solid Roman farmer. Seeing this, so the murmur went, his wife Livia painted a pear on a more accessible branch with poison – and the emperor succumbed to its fatal effects.

Whatever the reality of Augustus' demise – and it could hardly have been considered premature for a first-century man in his seventies – the imperial deaths that followed were bloody, brutal and blatant. Caligula, trapped leaving the games, was run through by noblemen who then hacked at his genitals and in their ferocity may even have gorged themselves on his flesh. His wife, one of the few people Caligula loved, was murdered on the spot and his infant daughter, so a narrative of chilling verisimilitude relates, was picked up by the feet and had her brains dashed out against a wall. Nero, on the run from mutinying troops, displayed a ghastly combination of wit, cowardice and bravado as he drank from puddles, crawled through thickets and made half-hearted attempts to kill himself rather than face the protracted and humiliating end his enemies had planned. Famously, his last words were *qualis artifex pereo*: 'What an artist dies with me.' After his death emperor followed emperor at such speed that there were four in the year 69 alone. There was the elderly Galba, whose brief reign ended in butchery, his severed head being tossed around the military camp, and Otho, his successor, who killed himself to pre-empt execution. The cruel, greedy and partly crippled Vitellius suffered a protracted and sadistic death at the hands and blades of soldiers who, having dragged him through the streets to the abuse of the crowd, tore him apart before throwing his corpse in the Tiber.

But although in Hadrian's childhood the political climate under Vespasian had – or so it appeared – finally found some sort of equilibrium, the natural world eddied in turbulence, which to the Romans was an ominous suggestion of disruption to come. There were rumours that great giants had been seen wandering about the countryside and even entering the city or flying through the air. Strange droughts and earth tremors had been a source of anxiety in the area around Vesuvius, although the inhabitants were unfortunately oblivious to the most obvious likely source of imminent disaster. Vespasian died when Hadrian was three and was succeeded by his elder son, the handsome, if opportunistic, soldier Titus, who once in power showed every sign of continuing his father's constructive ways. (Dio provides a rumour that Titus poisoned his elderly father and gives Hadrian as the source of this otherwise unsubstantiated story.) But the summer of Vespasian's death saw the catastrophic eruption of Vesuvius and subsequent engulfing of Pompeii and Herculaneum. Then, in an echo of events under Nero, fire struck Rome again in a conflagration which destroyed so many temples that some believed it was divinely ignited. Confirmation that the gods had turned their face away from Rome seemed to come when the apparently robust Titus fell ill and died just over two years and two months after his accession, having reigned for a short enough period not to have outlived his early promise. He was succeeded by his much more complicated and introspective brother, Domitian, and the atmosphere at the imperial court became more troubled and more dangerous.

None of these emperors was an appropriate model for Hadrian. Domitian's reign had ended in disaster, his record and memory officially obliterated in the notorious *damnatio memoriae* visited on disgraced emperors after death. This removal of all depictions and visible manifestations of the deceased from public buildings and monuments had the unsought effect of emphasising the target where figures were removed from group statuary or names in the middle of inscriptions. Modern variants include Stalin's doctored photographs and the cementing over of Mussolini's name on inscriptions in Rome. Still, the vigour with which it was enforced could be cathartic:

It was our delight to dash those proud statues to the ground, to smite them with an axe, as if blood and agony could follow every blow. Our transports of joy – so long deferred – were unrestrained; all sought a form of vengeance in beholding those bodies mutilated, limbs hacked in pieces and finally that baleful fearsome visage cast into the fire.[9]

Domitian was the emperor most like Hadrian in his intellectual tastes and his psychological complexities, but he was hardly a man Hadrian could openly emulate. He could, however, learn from him. The reign of Domitian lasted for fifteen years from 81 CE, when Hadrian was a child of five, until 96, when he was a serving officer in the Roman legions aged twenty; thus it formed the backdrop to Hadrian's experience of imperial life. Domitian, hated by the patricians, had been the target of unsuccessful attempts on his life early in his reign, and although there are records to suggest that he was in some ways a conscientious ruler, he lived the remainder of his life in a state of increasing paranoia, expressed in pre-emptive and imaginative sadism. Rome was an uncomfortable place to be in these years, and there was in effect, if not by decree, widespread censorship; yet Domitian was not uninterested in the arts, particularly architecture and statuary, although the *damnatio memoriae* has reduced what survives. His effect on Hadrian is apparent not least in the latter's admiration of his building schemes: only twenty-five years after his death it was Domitian's extravagant palace that the usually sensitive Hadrian found most congenial and that he chose as his official residence when in Rome. But Domitian is an important figure in Hadrian's life primarily because the choices and assumptions Hadrian was to make about how to be an emperor were undoubtedly influenced by the experience of living within the tensions of Domitian's reign.

Crucially, in Hadrian's personality there are traces from the first of Domitian's awareness that the emperor is always alone, can never, ultimately, trust anyone. Though Domitian was always respected by a loyal army, among whom Hadrian was serving at the time of the assassination, the reality was, and always had been, that no emperor could be free of the fear that others might make a bid for power at any time.[10]

Even the contemporary sources recognise that Domitian's fear made him cruel, and the more cruel he was, the more he had to fear; to an educated Greek or Roman, in his sadistic paranoia, Domitian displayed the characteristics of the eponymous Greek tyrant Damocles. The massive rooms of his palace were designed to intimidate, their perspective and size disorientating the apprehensive visitor; the galleries of this labyrinthine palace were lined with reflecting stone so that Domitian might always be alert to potential assassins.[11] (A similar strategy, this time auditory, can be seen in the Harem of the Topkapi Palace in Istanbul; here the bathroom floor is articulated so that the fabric of the room rattles if a stranger approaches the sultan at a vulnerable and unguarded moment.) Nobody conjures up more potently the distorted tensions of Domitian's mental disintegration in the palace that had become his prison than Gibbon: *'Domitian, trapped in his palace, felt the terrors he inspired.'* The portents of death clustered around Domitian, even as he had the prophesiers of doom punished or killed. Like Hadrian in years to come, Domitian was counting down the days to some pre-ordained date when it had been foretold he would die. He took desperate measures to propitiate the omens, executing fortune-tellers, scratching at a wart to draw his own blood, hoping it would be enough to fulfil the prediction, but died at the hand of his intimates – his chamberlains, his valet and possibly his wife – as he prepared to take an afternoon siesta. It was a grim tableau of a reign gone wrong; of an emperor completely isolated at the centre of his empire and his family. Domitian summed up his own predicament succinctly: *'Nobody believes in a conspiracy against a ruler until it has succeeded.'*[12] His death was a justification of his beliefs; and it was the justification for Hadrian's later hostile action against the four senators.

The Roman legions under Trajan were unequivocally loyal to their emperor and had continued to support Hadrian, who had less need than his predecessors to listen for the footfall in the night, or watch for the sudden movement in the crowd. But Domitian too had succeeded a popular soldier-emperor, and he too had been liked within the army; yet it was only twenty-one years since Domitian had been bloodily despatched in his own palace. As with Domitian, so Hadrian discovered an intrigue against him soon after he acceded. For Domitian, the plot was a fatal catalyst for his descent into a lifetime's oppression which ultimately brought about the very destruction he feared. It was a lesson for his descendants. Hadrian realised that such a plot need not necessarily be disastrous; for a more pragmatic political player a plot, or an *alleged* plot, could be strategically useful; it could permit the removal of known opponents with minimal objections, demonstrate the likely reaction to any hint of intrigue and justify the enforcement of otherwise unpopular measures as a reaction to unarguable risk. Faced with a major threat to his incipient rule, courage, political astuteness and ruthlessness were called for – and in Hadrian they were not found wanting. The personality of the new emperor was beginning to emerge, as was the vast task ahead of him.

Domitian's brooding presence still falls over Rome today. His ruined palace is a forbidding cliff of incomprehensible masonry, its walls, many metres thick, standing high above traffic hurtling along the Via del Circo Massimo. Tourists wandering up towards the orange groves of the Aventine, and boys kicking a football across the dusty park that follows the shape of the ancient Circus of Maximus, do so under the shadow of dark remains that still cover much of the Palatine.

Further afield the second-century restoration of Spanish Italica is presumed to have been grudgingly commissioned by Hadrian *in absentia*, but this has never been confirmed; although it does seem likely that he gave money for the construction of an elaborate baths complex there, and for a temple dedicated to the dead Trajan, his heart was never really in it. In France, the basilica of Plotina at Nemausus which Hadrian erected to honour Trajan's wife, a figure who was so crucial in his political advance, has disappeared, swallowed up by the subsequent success and development of Nîmes, although a tentative identification has been made with part of the ruin more usually known as the Temple of Diana.

Plotina's ashes and those of Trajan were interred under the remarkable 38-metre column that bears his name and still stands in the centre of Rome as one of its most famous monuments. The intricate detail of the spiral sculptural reliefs on Trajan's column which depict the soldier-emperor's brutal campaigns in Dacia has been a source of endless fascination and invaluable information concerning the logistics of the Roman army. It seems likely that the reliefs were added by Hadrian after Trajan's sudden death; they include a depiction of the bridge over the Ister which in reality symbolised the disconnection between the policies of the two emperors. When it was built the column was a triumphant declaration of Trajan's achievement, and from its viewing platform Trajan's other gifts to the people of Rome could be seen, notably his forum and the gilded roof of the law courts of the Basilica Ulpia. Surmounting the column was a bronze statue of the emperor himself.

The reliefs of the column, which so vividly conjure up the martial spirit of early second-century Roman life, can be viewed today as casts in the Museo della Civiltà. Trajan's column still stands intact at the foot of the Quirinal Hill, although it is no longer possible to ascend the internal staircase to the platform. Where the emperor's statue once looked from its top over pagan Rome, that of St Peter has been claiming the city for Christianity since 1587. Of Trajan's forum only rudimentary remains survive; the same is true of the basilica, which is currently being excavated. His markets, built by his architect Apollodorus, a man whose uneasy and ultimately fatal relationship with Hadrian nevertheless resulted in some inspired buildings in both reigns, still stand close by. The Temple of the Deified Trajan, which Hadrian built as an act of pious recognition of his adopted parent, and which was implicitly a statement of his own legitimacy, was the only one of his buildings in the city which is known to have borne Hadrian's name. Only one granite column remains, lying on the ground by Trajan's column. The rest of the temple complex is buried somewhere under the sixteenth-century Palazzo Valentini off the Via Santa Eufemia.

Yet another temple dedicated to Trajan lies above modern Bergama in western Turkey, in the impressive remains of the Hellenized city of Pergamum. The ruins of the largest temple on the acropolis are those of the Trajaneum, built in the already thriving city during the reign of Hadrian. Long gone are the colossal statues of both emperors which once dominated the temple precincts.

Many miles to the south-east, on the Turkish side of the Syrian border, and on the west bank of the Orontes, splendid Antioch, where Hadrian waited to become emperor, has become modern Antakya, its narrow streets leading down to the river and the remnants of its city walls still following the shape of the ancient settlement. Of the capital city of Syria, which once possessed a two-mile-long colonnade considered the greatest thoroughfare in the empire and numerous beautiful public buildings, virtually nothing remains, although some lovely second-century mosaics are now on display in the town museum.[13] The present provincial town is a fraction of its ancient size and there is little else left of note; in the thousand years after the fall of Rome, successive natural and military catastrophes obliterated a city which was in its time surpassed only by Rome and Alexandria. In the far south of the country, Gazipaşa, on the long Mediterranean coastal road, is unremarkable, its history vanished with its former names. Before it was Gazipaşa it was called Selinty, before that Trajanopolis, and originally it was Selinus, the place where Hadrian's accession was finally assured when Trajan died, far from Rome, in the summer of 117.

Traces of Trajan's bridge are still just visible on the Ister/ Danube as it flows swiftly through Romania to the west of the legendary Iron Gates rapids – *Potile de Fier* – where a modern barrage now controls the flow that Trajan's engineers brilliantly overcame and crossed. The bridge in its original splendour is represented on Romania's coat of arms. The lands of the Marcomanni, Quadi and Sarmartian tribes and the Roman-created provinces of Dalmatia, Upper Moesia, Macedonia, Dacia and Pannonia which were the focus of recurring warfare throughout the centuries of the Roman empire correspond to today's Balkans. Conflict continues to dominate the region.

2

A travelling court

They say that in the reign of Lysimachus the folk of Abdera were stricken by a plague that was something like this, my good Philo. In the early stages all the population had a violent and persistent fever right from the very beginning, but at about the seventh day it was dispelled, in some cases by a copious flow of blood from the nostrils, in others by perspiration, that also copious, but it affected their minds in a ridiculous way; for all had a mad hankering for tragedy, delivering blank verse at the top of their voices. In particular they would chant solos from Euripides' Andromeda, singing the whole of Perseus' long speech and the city was full of all those pale, thin seventh-day patients ranting 'And you, O Eros, lord of gods and men'. And loudly declaiming the other bits, and over a long period too, till the coming of winter and a heavy frost put an end to their nonsense!

LUCIAN, HOW TO WRITE HISTORY, 1

From the memoirs of Julia Balbilla

I should like to tidy up my memories as I would if they were to be constrained by the formality of text. I should like to be able to say I remember when I first saw the emperor, just as countrywomen mark out their lives by a calendar of childbearing or fine harvests, earthquakes or fevers. What blurs my recollection I think is that he was borne to me on wings of reputation so long before I saw him clearly that when I did see him it was just a matter of clarification. Many others later found that a man could never quite fulfil the expectations of an unknown emperor. In some ways even then the *idea* of Hadrian, from his golden hair to his bad poetry, being as it were the first to arrive, was also the most lingering guest of my imagination.

In reality his hair was more brown than golden and the poetry rather better than the wits gave him credit for. It was the same with his alleged cowardice in the wars and his womanising. I know nothing of his behaviour in action but I always observed that, whatever his past as one officer among many, as emperor he was at his best among military men; patient yet exacting, he understood their concerns and they respected him. As for women, again I was not privy to the campaigns of his youth, but his intimates – and they seemed to act as sisters rather than lovers – were older women and the rest of womankind almost invisible to him. Certainly he appeared oblivious to the process by which his wife Sabina turned from an awkward child into a fine, serious woman with a beautiful complexion and unusually pale grey eyes. Others were not, of course.

His appetites I would say were quite differently directed from the repetitive compulsions of the flesh. His rage was legendary, but until you had seen it it was hard to imagine such a breach of his customary control and deportment. Many were caught out; those who, one minute conversing animatedly with the emperor on some mutual enthusiasm, were so surprised by the shift from an equality of passionate discussion to the fury of a tyrant thwarted that they thought it a joke, and took it as such, found

45

their lives irretrievably changed for the worse. His drinking was little spoken of, yet it was a habit maintained and increased throughout the time I knew him.

He was clever. Men doubted it because of the necessity for the emperor to expound upon matters to prove it, but he was as able in diverse skills as he was immodest in declaring them. He was clever, though, in the way of open confrontation and competition; there was never a man less able to achieve his aims by the more subtle or devious ways of flattery, concession and insinuation. Nor did he recognise when he was the victim of such an assault and was oblivious to the more adept bending him to their will. In this way he was, for all his sophistication, an innocent.

He was not instinctively a cruel man, though cruel things were done in his name, but he could be a cold one. Like most men, fear made him cruel, and he was crueller to those nearly his equal than to the simpleton or the peasant whose path crossed his for a moment in time. To his distant followers he was a paragon of kindness; those who had least to do with him being most persuaded of what he might accomplish to help them. He was not cruel to Sabina, although she felt cruelly done by. If he had a fault it was that he did not smile enough. When he did – and that I do remember – when he was briefly happy he was more handsome than a man half his age and with none of his burdens of duty.

He has set down his own memoirs of his life, but great men who celebrate their great lives do not deal in what they regard as small matters in case they should be diminished by having noticed them. Nor do they look back upon themselves, but rather contemplate their effect, as they perceive it, upon their world. Those that follow may list physical qualities, but whether they assemble them from tradition or re-animate portraits in stone they cannot conjure up the living man.

Those who never saw more of the emperor than his picture on a coin, and only knew that it was him because no other emperor had worn a beard, still talked about him as if they had met him. It was the same with rumours of his visits – they were always there. Hadrian hovered about our business and our thoughts; never was an absent emperor more omnipresent. He was always about to favour this provincial city or that; someone would have heard from the wife of their cousin, who was very close indeed to a certain influential freedman in Rome who worked in the commissary, that the maps were out. Wherever you travelled in his lifetime there was a whisper at a grand dinner or in the marketplace or from the exasperated factor of a powerful man, that next year or perhaps the one after the emperor would arrive. Time to extend villas into palaces, turn perfectly good gardens into fantasy water-kingdoms, scour the countryside for fine stones or plump song-birds; to force begrudging peasants to think beyond short-term rewards, to set artisans to work on stone, to send out ships to fill the granaries with golden corn. All this just for a rumour. Were more men ruined or blessed merely by the idea of Hadrian?

For this reason I try to remember how he looked, as I saw him, briefly, many years before he became what all men now know. It was at Athens; I walked into a courtyard and there for two or three minutes I stood and he was. He was singing; his choice was some rousing military chorus but he put a light-hearted spin on it, changed the words perhaps to laugh at the deprivations of service. Not yet an emperor, every gesture heavy with conscious gravity, nor bearded – though he told my brother later that it was in Greece he had determined to let his beard grow should he reach full power – his face reflected a life full of hope and possibility.

He was something over thirty years old and had a fine voice. I have said that his hair was brown, and certainly he did not stoop to the affectation of others who, while holding barbarian ferocity in contempt, liked to imagine they were as blonde as the tribes of the north. No gold dust was artfully scattered through his curls, although his hair – for those who came close to him – could be seen to shine with oils and his skin smelled sweetly of cinnamon and balsam.[1] In summer his habit of going with his head uncovered meant that his thick hair was shot through with reddish streaks, and there was something of the lion about him. He was of a good height, moderately well-built, with strong limbs and long-fingered, mobile hands. His face, like those of so many who had survived the Roman fever of Domitian's time, was marked, but that served to his advantage; the plague had proved the most lethal of enemies among the legions, and the scars marked him as their own. His eyes were grey and he departed from handsomeness in that they were too closely set, but he was otherwise a well-made, if unexceptional, man.

That day it was possible to see the Roman clearly; he never again travelled with such a small retinue (whatever they tell you, he did not, even then, walk freely about the people taking note of their ordinary troubles). He had a few companions with him and, of course, Sabina, who had fewer still, and her mother with her small household.[2]

Sabina was younger than Hadrian by perhaps ten years. She had been married to him then for some time, and her face was already masked by the look of defensive disappointment which spoiled her natural beauty. She too was well-built, moving from the slenderness of girlhood to maturity. Her hair was thick and glossy, she was simply dressed and her garments were of fine cloth but ordinary in cut. It was her bearing that was most noticeable. She too was tall – almost as tall as the future emperor – but she stood well, gazing about her when she thought no one was looking yet when in Hadrian's presence, or tolerating interminable speeches of welcome or plays in archaic style, quite simply turning into a statue. It was a performance in itself. Her eyes would remain open, but virtually unblinking, her gaze fixed on some invisible point, her chest – I watched in fascination – hardly moving up and down and her hands, settled loosely in her lap, never trembling. If a strand of her hair was moved on to her face by the current of a slave's fan, or sweat ran down her skin, or a fly settled on her brow, she appeared not to feel it. She did not look bored. She did not look interested. She was, I believe, just not there; it was as if she fell into a trance. It was her greatest weapon. It was what enabled her to survive. It was what, in the end, enabled her to triumph.

Later I would discover that she could laugh when she thought herself unobserved and that she enjoyed pantomime, verse which rhymed and was in Latin not Greek, wild birds, fine clothes and being sung to; they were not negligible pleasures, but she believed that Hadrian's scorn could be best averted by her having no interests whatsoever. She was probably correct; like many clever men, his wit could be as wounding as it was considered. Enthusiasms, of which he had so many himself, were in others a particular target of his conversational pursuit (there came a time when to be introduced as 'Sappho in repertory' became embarrassing not just to me but to all who had heard the quip so many times).

Sabina's amusement was of no great concern to Hadrian; if she was possessed of enough understanding to respond in the appropriate fashion in public, that was all that was required of her. Hadrian's own pursuits were what set him apart; in the early days he would be excited and invigorated with his passion for a new subject and in searching out the best-informed and bravest practitioners in whatever art had caught his fancy. It is wrong to say, as people do now, that he was only a dabbler – he had a breadth of ability that in any ordinary man would be counted remarkable. Had he pursued just one course, what could he not have achieved? But it is an emperor's duty not to linger in one occupation, and so he moved on – and in time, I think, became jealous of all those who, not having an empire to mind, might study to their heart's content. In later life he invested passionately in many things which seemed to bring him little immediate pleasure. Hunting was an exception.

So the emperor laughed rarely – but he did so with my brother, my beautiful brother Julius.[3] Everybody laughed in Julius' company. Julius was a witty man, uncomplicated, with no hint of the melancholy which suffused Hadrian from the first. Julius liked people, parties, plays, loved his adopted city, Athens, loved Hadrian from their first meeting in Rome. Julius was a true friend. Though young, he was already sick, puzzled by fatigue, when he met Hadrian. He knew there was no advantage to come should

Hadrian gain the imperial power he denied considering but was so passionately desirous of. Anyway, Julius was a king, in name at least, and had no need for any preferment. All that he wanted he had. He, unlike me, had long forgotten the hope of real power, had no unease with an empty kingship. The Romans wrenched our kingdom away from us: Commagene, which did not go quietly like other, more powerful nations; Commagene, whose armies, men, young boys, grandfathers, even, it is said, women, drew themselves up to face Rome. Commagene, the most beloved of lands, extinguished in a moment. The Romans took the mountains where the light shifted from brown to purple as the days turned, the fertile valleys, the small insistent rivers, the monuments, the traditions and the pride. Men in Rome who could not have found our country on a chart swept it away as it went about its business with nobility, swept it away, not for its beauty, not for its amenities but because it lay in their path.

Now he lies under his great mausoleum and those who can read stone can read of the dynasty of which Julius was a last and glorious son. Dying a happy exile among his friends, he numbered gods as intimates and guides. When there is nobody left to remember once-proud Commagene, passers by on the Hill of the Muses may stop at Julius' tomb and wonder who was this mighty king.

The emperor had become a great man when the invitation came to me, but it was made, I believe, in memory of those early days in Athens when Julius had reached the apogee of his hopes: a Roman consul, the most eminent of Athenians, loved by all who knew him. Julius did not live impotent and nostalgic in exile, but made exile his new-found land. About Julius there was an air of amiable indolence; he was constantly demanding but easily pleased. This was never so with Hadrian, who at that time asked for little but never seemed quite content. He was a restless man and even at leisure, teasing Julius, enjoying his wines and table, he was never quite relaxed. He could be charming, he was a great recounter of anecdotes, he had a prodigious knowledge of ancient stories and of the customs of the world – but he had the alertness of one who must live by his wits and who was always hungry for more.

The future emperor, also a consul, lived in thrall to hope in those days. Julius laughed, not unkindly, and said that like so many ambitious men Hadrian was the victim of an 'understanding', the clarification of which dominated his thoughts and endeavours. This understanding was a promise never made explicit by his guardian, Trajan – a promise Hadrian, perhaps unwisely, confided to Julius, for whom all secrets were just currency for contracting new friendships and for the entertainment of the old. His guardian wished – all things being equal – for Hadrian to succeed, but, being as yet a man in the prime of life, was disinclined to consider formal recognition. The congenial state of certainty which might transform Hadrian's life and facilitate his advance was not granted him. It was Julius' lack of discretion on this, as on all matters, which may have promoted his friend's invisible status to a point where the aspirant was treated with respect – or at least with self-interest – by those at his service.

While Julius was elevating his oblivious friend to the rank of prospective prince in the eyes of Athens, Hadrian, for once, had forgotten the elusive glory that might or might not lie ahead. He had come from the philosophers and was elated by their discourses; Epictetus mingled wit and honesty, he found, and was afraid of no man. He had studied the ideas of the Stoics and Cynics from boyhood, but to see the famous man dispensing his wisdom to the curious and the learned gathered around him from all the countries of the empire and beyond was a different matter. Possibly he considered that one day he might style himself a philosopher-emperor. It was impossible, of course. Emperors are soldiers. Or so we thought then.

Julius' misplaced confidences were matched correctly with confidence in Hadrian. Hadrian's dreams were realised; at least all the ambitions he believed himself to have held since boyhood were realised. Once he grasped power, he united the energy and determination of Trajan with the glittering rituals of the eastern kings of old. In just over ten years, by the time he sent his emissary to Athens, he had made the ill-used words 'Roman peace' a prosperous reality. He had crossed the empire, welcome in every province. He had assuaged his own curiosity and that of his people. Some thought him a scrupulous diplomatist, but they misunderstood; he was in his own way as strong and implacable as his fathers. Like them, he got what he wanted. The philosophers now come to Hadrian, and his days are full of the counsels of the wise – and the not so wise.

They were already talking of an incessant, greedy curiosity. He was compiling a lexicon of outlandish words and a handbook on the mathematics of stone-vaulting; he claimed to have copies of the works of Ennius and Homer and other long-dead men, written in their own hands. Later he showed me poetry written on papyrus so fragile that even the eye's gaze caused it to fade from the page. It would take its place in the library he planned for the centre of his new palace that would be the greatest assembly of manuscripts under a private roof. Like any rich man he collected statues from Greece, furs from the Danube, jewels and horses from Arabia, unguents and spices from Asia minor. He even had the best of our Athenian coffins despatched to Rome. But he also treasured and preserved sea creatures and old weapons and stones in which shells and beetles had been petrified. All these were laid in cabinets as if they were carved in silver or lapis. Around him he gathered the cleverest men of our age from every city of the empire. Nothing like it has ever been known or imagined, and the ardent already called it the Golden Age, hoping that if it were not, naming it would make it so.

So the invitation arrived – it was of course more of a command than an invitation, but nicely put. First there were discreet enquiries as to my health, my disposition, my responsibilities here. Answer: first, good; second, amenable, though I might have replied 'realistic' to any other than the emperor's agent; third, few – I tend my brother's tomb, I live and write and am amused by my friends. The enquiries were not so discreet that when the emperor's suit was pressed it was any kind of surprise. He was planning another and more ambitious voyage. Sabina required a companion, Hadrian required her to be accompanied. A woman of my abilities would be an advantage; the emperor remembered my poetry from Athens. So it went. He had of course never heard me speak, neither poetry nor dinner gossip, but I admired the thoroughness of his secretaries.

In Athens it was a wet, grey winter, the streets slippery with rain and animals, the skies heavy over the citadel. It was not just a matter of the emperor and empress; like a vortex, he drew the greatest and most luminous minds of our times around him. Who would not want to escape and travel in such company and be gilded by association? So I took ship in Athens with Sabina some time in the following spring and we set off through Asia to the provinces of Syria, Arabia, Judea and Egypt, intending then to return to Greece. It was also possible, but tantalisingly unclear, that while in Syria we might cross into Commagene. I could not pry into the exact route for fear that my loyalties might be called into question and the emperor reconsider the gift of his offer. But possibly he has forgotten that that sliver of land and the great River Euphrates was ever paramount to an entire people. No emperor could permit himself to comprehend that to be free within a small country of mountains and forests is a better thing than to belong to a mighty empire with all its amenities. To my grave I remember Commagene, of whose royal, pious house I am the last descendant.

But while we travelled we would all live like kings. Kings not of Commagene, or Rome, or Athens, but of a caravan court, a court with no frontiers; a travelling academy, a nation of poets, musicians, architects and pantomime actors. We would explode into the lives of cities with our masks and our speeches and our gold and our music. We were all to be on stage and knew our words. I was to be the well-connected poetess. He was not the poet he believed himself to be, or he would have known that although our greatest historians and architects may soar to the heights of achievement in later life, the poetic gift dies early. Poets do not age well. I still knew how to play the role, but the art of poetry was far behind me even then.

Julius would have been glad of my inclusion and would have urged me to live in Hadrian's magnificent empire, not my own geography of dispossession. Julius was a pragmatist, and happier for it; he was just incapable of looking back, even so short a distance as forty years. He was an infant when Commagene fell and history held no lessons for him. For Julius the King life was good and, like a generous man distributing the favours of his most beautiful mistress, he ensured from the first that Athens would be good for his friend Hadrian. Perhaps in displaying Athens to Hadrian as an irresistible and amusing diversion, never dreaming that it would become the inspiration for a reign, Julius changed the world at one remove, more powerfully than were he a rightful king on his own throne.

Trust no one, Julius said, and live without fear; love and torture make betrayers of us all.

He didn't want to die. Nobody, of course, ever wanted to die. But when an emperor – *the* emperor – doesn't want to die, the consequences and ramifications are likely to prove more wide-ranging. When an emperor nods, the sword falls, the army advances, the walls come down, the city is put to the flame.

Hadrian didn't want to die. And once he became emperor, he was in a position to do something about it. He was, as we can deduce not only from his actions and by reading between the lines of his biographers, but also from his own writings, a man of an almost modern sensibility: intelligent, aesthetic, insecure in himself, given to that particular form of nostalgia that the Portuguese call *saudade* – the longing for a past happiness one never really possessed. So to understand Hadrian as a figure in history, we must first understand him as a man inhabiting a history of his own.

Hadrian's dispositions, nurtured for good or ill in his

childhood, in his sense of himself as a provincial outsider, in his backward-looking longings for a golden past and in what must have been the agonisingly uncertain wait for Trajan to legitimise his succession, had formed his character long before he ascended to imperium and power let them shape an empire. And the same dispositions, rooted in his nature, were to express themselves in three crucial aspects of his character which shaped his reign and his reputation, and on which were built both the best and the worst aspects of his career.

He was clever; he was a Hellenophile; and he was a traveller.

In his travels he was fascinated by magic, by heterodox religious practices, by divining and fortune-telling. These were common preoccupations for sophisticated Romans, who conducted their daily lives – in their private concerns as much as in affairs of finance or state – against a background of sacrifice, augury, omens and prophecies. Animals were offered on the charcoal brazier, statues venerated, libations poured out, entrails examined as keenly as the flight patterns of birds. Yet much of Roman religion – a broad and tolerant paganism – was conducted more as a matter of observance than of internalised faith.[4] It was certainly no formalised theology offering the promise of divinely democratic judgement followed by an afterlife.

Such a theology might have been welcomed by a man like Hadrian, who throughout his life was possessed by an intermittently troubling spirituality; his own writings reveal his fretful speculations about the afterlife, a sense that although something of him might go on, it would be a lonely something, and if any sensibility remained, it would be an awareness of missing the action. And in what was probably his last letter, he explicitly asks to be judged as he was. Perhaps the already evolving Christian doctrines would have held out some appeal for him. But he did not have that option. All he could do was impose himself on the world and hope for good report. And to do that would require, as well as good fortune, control: control not only over the empire to which he eventually acceded, but (or so he hoped) control over his standing (in the shadows of the past) while he lived, and over the judgement of the future after he had gone.

Clever. A Hellenophile. A traveller.

The latter two characteristics, bound together and fuelled by the first, dictated how he set about his task. He travelled his empire, assiduously as he believed, recreating a lost Hellenistic earthly paradise, where his buildings stood not only as a reminder to his subjects after he had gone but as a memorial to his beloved Greece, to exceed his predecessors and as a legacy to the posterity which would judge him. He used art to bind his empire with his own past and an unknown future. This was the great imaginative task of Hadrian's life. To understand its impact on both him and his subjects, since the imagination of an emperor is not confined to his own head but works in blood, in stone and in human lives, we need to understand something of the context and consequences of his times, and of Hadrian's sense of himself within these times.

The earliest and most abiding influence on Hadrian was his love of Greece. It is here, and with Hadrian's intention to create a new golden age, that the uniqueness of his reign and legacy begins. The Romans had an uneasy relationship with Greece. Rome had finally conquered Greece at the battle of Actium in 31 BCE – over a century before Hadrian was born and almost 150 years before his accession to the imperial throne. Yet it remained the case that, in matters of taste and sensibility, educated Romans saw Greece as an unequivocally superior entity. Rome's artists, even at their best, borrowed their themes and techniques from Greek art. Greek drama and philosophy, medicine and science were all pre-eminent; Greek cities like Athens and Alexandria were superior, in appearance and organisation, to Rome. Greek intellectuals dominated the world of ideas. In the first century Horace had expressed the conundrum with his customary incisive wit: '*A captive Greece has conquered its savage captor and taken civilisation to barbaric Latium.*'[5] For Roman pride it was at times intolerable.

The cultured Roman was faced with a dilemma: how to incorporate – and emulate – the best of Greek culture, while simultaneously clinging to the republicans' determined belief that Greeks were decadent and effete. Had they not, after all, allowed themselves to forgo their autonomy? The Greeks possessed, it was conceded, creative genius. But what the Romans felt they lacked in philosophical and artistic adventurism, they made up for in their self-aware pre-eminence in the military virtues: courage, self-discipline and moral stature. They also had the power. Conservative Romans thought, as have conservatives ever since, that there was something unmanly about overdeveloped aesthetic interests. They exemplified what might be called a 'muscular paganism' – a cast of religion that was to resurface, notably, in the nineteenth century, this time with Christ, not Jupiter, as its figurehead. The aristocratic young Roman might take a grand tour of the older civilisation, just as his British and American descendants would travel to Rome in the eighteenth and nineteenth centuries. But anyone with an eye on a senatorial career also undertook several years of military service.

As in individuals, so in the state at large. Petronius, writing a few years before Hadrian's birth, mercilessly lampooned the catastrophically rich freedman Trimalchio as a man of wealth and power and, indeed, far-reaching enterprise, yet so utterly without cultural underpinnings that he becomes an object of grotesque, vulgar buffoonery.[6] In Trimalchio it was possible, not too fancifully, to see the fate awaiting the Roman culture were it to lose its hold over the cultural patrimony of the conquered Greeks. Hadrian, as it turned out, had a natural inclination towards this view, for an inextricably complex constellation of reasons: personal predisposition, childhood experience, cultural pressures, ego and political expediency. But to understand the sheer pull of Greece we need first to look at the reasons for its extraordinary pre-eminence in the Roman imagination.

The position of the Greek world, both as territory and as ideal, within the Roman empire is rooted in the long and complicated history of Greece's own domination of the Mediterranean world. It is impossible in a condensed account to do justice to its extraordinarily successful expansion, but a brief outline will give a hint of its scale and scope.

In the late second millennium BCE the early Hellenes had responded to incursions from outside by themselves moving outwards, settling first on what are now Greek islands and then moving east, eventually reaching Anatolia, now part of Turkey. Although there was some exchange of culture with the existing populations, the Greeks flourished and the east became firmly Hellenized. As centuries passed the successful immigrants spread inward, and the new communities in their turn sent out colonists all over the Mediterranean. These settled in what is now Sicily and in parts of Italy to the west, and as far north as the Black Sea. The flowering of Greek culture which followed was an artistic and intellectual explosion which has probably never been equalled and which reached its zenith in the fifth century BCE.

Like all colonists, the Greeks did not achieve their upward and outward progress without confrontation; eventually, they were beset also by terrible internal conflict. By the seventh century they were under threat both from native Lydians and from the Persians, and in time came under control of first one and then the other. Persian rule was brought to an end only after a series of legendarily bloody battles in the fifth century BCE, notably Marathon, Athens and Salamis. For a while the Greeks of Asia minor were contained within the Athenian empire before being ceded to Persia after the Peloponnesian War. Caught between the demands of Athens and the predations of Persia, the Asian

Greeks were finally rescued by Alexander the Great, only to become part of his Macedonian empire. When Alexander died in his early thirties, the territories of Asia minor entered a period of autonomy as independent states dominated by the powerful city of Pergamum; but by the second century BCE Pergamum capitulated to unavoidable reality and gave way to the increasing might of the Romans.

It was a wise move, despite the surrender of autonomy it entailed. Within the Roman empire, communities of Asia minor eventually entered a prolonged period of peace and subsequent prosperity. For the Romans, giving Greek interests and priorities pre-eminence over those of any other sector of the empire was not just a whim; at the time of Hadrian's accession more than half the peoples of the empire had Greek as their mother tongue.[7] The Greeks dominated not only in cultural terms but in numbers.

Throughout their history, and despite continued conflict and their wide dispersal, the Greeks retained a remarkable cultural coherence which, from the very beginning, was expressed and reinforced most clearly in their dazzling architectural achievements. Under the Roman republic, as the demands of the conquerors ate into Greek resources and energies, this vigour had faltered; but once the principate was established, Greek communities began to flourish again, with individual Greek men acquiring great fortunes and becoming assimilated into the higher levels of Roman politics, such as the consulship. So by Hadrian's time, the Roman imagination was firmly held between the two tines of the Greek pitchfork: their cultural and intellectual patrimony on the one hand, and their all too real, and vocal, presence both in the empire at large and in Rome in particular on the other.

In some ways, the Greeks were so much a part of the Roman world that, in the surviving texts, they are often more visible by the shadow they cast than by their actual written presence. Often that shadow is tainted with a malice which, by the very fact that it is thought worth writing down, reveals their cultural importance; nobody wastes time complaining about the insignificant, the pointless, the losers. Pliny the Elder, the indefatigable encyclopedist of the *Natural History*, has barely a good word to say for them, and even that is expressed in the negative, as when he comments that '*Of the Greek sciences, it is only medicine that the Romans have not followed, thanks to their good sense,*' or that '*amber provides an opportunity for exposing the false accounts of the Greeks. My readers should bear with me patiently, since it is important to realize that not everything handed down by the Greeks merits admiration.*'[8] Elsewhere, he more shamelessly castigates the Greeks as '*progenitors of all vices*', on the rather innocuous grounds, one might have thought, that they '*have diverted the use of olive-oil to serve the ends of luxury by making it available in gymnasia*' – with a hint, we may confidently assume, at undisclosed and unspeakable practices – and announcing sternly that '*It is astonishing how far Greek gullibility will go. There is no occurrence so fabulously shameless that it lacks a witness.*' It must be said that, within the context of the *Natural History*, a vast work which has been enchantingly (and accurately) described as '*a catalogue of unreliable wonders*', Pliny's sniffiness sits rather ill-at-ease among his accounts of one-legged men (with one giant foot they use as a sunshade), magical snakes and the two-inch goby fish which can hold a ship back by the power of suction. But just in case his readers were to be left in any doubt, he announces that '*Undoubtedly the one race of outstanding virtue in the whole world is the Roman.*'[9] That tension – between Roman virtue and Greek sophistication – was one of the many that Hadrian would, with varying degrees of success, attempt to resolve in his life and in his reign.

Hadrian seems to have developed his preference for the Greek way of life while still young. Even as a boy he had acquired the nickname *graeculus* – 'Greekling' – an ambiguous soubriquet which was at least partly derogatory. Those with long memories could also recall the fact that the great Augustus had once been called 'Thurian' with equal disdain, although Thuria was at least Italian, albeit provincial. Laughed at for his rustic accent when he first read out one of Trajan's letters to the senate as a teenager, Hadrian persevered with perfecting delivery of his native language, though doing so brought its own risk of further ridicule: as with Mrs Thatcher and the alleged elocution lessons, socially ambitious Romans were damned (for lack of sophistication) if they failed to improve on their provincial accents and damned (for pretension) if they did. But though a command of Latin was necessary, Hadrian's real passion was for the study of Greek.

The second pair of tensions which Hadrian would, in due course, have to attempt to reconcile were more purely Roman, and specifically connected to the very nature of imperial power. History looks back on the Roman emperors and divides them, conveniently and appealingly, into good emperors and bad. It is this dramatic simplicity which has made them such irresistible subjects for novels and films. The 'good', such as Augustus, Vespasian and Marcus Aurelius, are possessed of every Roman virtue; the bad – the majority, in the retelling – have a capacity for derangement exceeded only by the imagination of their biographers. Tiberius, Caligula, Nero, Vitellius and Domitian became bywords for perversion, madness, decadence, greed and sadism; one historian commented wryly that *history is a gallery of pictures in which there are few originals and many copies.*[10] Hadrian was to be the first emperor to survive his biographers with the lasting reputation of a man of more realistically mixed abilities; and so he is the first ancient ruler to move beyond caricature. While it is sometimes difficult to grasp that emperors such as Tiberius, Nero and Domitian did in fact rule for many years – the inventories of their atrocities flattening any sense of trajectory –

with Hadrian an uncertain start, followed by a strategic recovery and the gloriously successful central part of his reign, fleshes out our picture of the man, and makes the disasters of his later reign a tragedy. That term is indeed peculiarly appropriate for the events of Hadrian's later reign, for it derives from the Greek word for 'goat-song', while the genre has been defined as being concerned *de casibus illustrorum uirorum*, with 'the fall of great men'; on both accounts it has a curious appositeness.

Hadrian was to take as his conscious model the masterly consolidator of imperial rule, Augustus. Most emperors did – to say nothing of would-be emperors such as Mussolini. Rome had chosen to forget the bloody wars, the terrible proscriptions and the thousands dead which were the cost of Augustus' power. Augustus had brought peace, firm government, prosperity and order to Rome after a long period of domestic chaos, and ruled over a largely grateful populace for more than forty years. Like Augustus, who had left his architectural mark, rebuilding the war-stricken provinces but also triumphing in the city of Rome itself, boasting that he had turned a city of brick to a city of marble, Hadrian would promise a golden age of Roman renewal.[11] Unlike Augustus, who fought his bloodiest battles abroad but brought the rewards back to Rome, Hadrian would discover in himself transforming ambitions which went far beyond Italy, and in these, too, his own personality would assert itself: clever, Hellenophile and, above all, a traveller.

Travel itself was not so unusual. The early careers of young patricians intending to become senators followed an established path which involved military service overseas and usually the governing of an imperial province. By the second century, too, wealthy private citizens were certainly travelling widely for the purposes of sightseeing and collecting; upper-class travellers followed reasonably well-established tourist itineraries and complained in familiarly modern terms about the cost, the shoddiness of souvenirs, exploitative innkeepers and filthy conditions. Hadrian's guardian Trajan had spent a considerable part of his reign abroad. Indeed, it was Trajan's extended stays in the east, as a base from which he could subdue various uncooperative client states, that laid the foundations for Hadrian's travelling court.

But before Hadrian, when emperors visited their empires it was largely for the purpose of further conquest or to maintain existing control in the provinces. To do otherwise might be seen as evading duty. The reclusive and bleak Tiberius was much criticised for the indulgence of his self-imposed exile in Capri in later years, and the one emperor who had clearly enjoyed, if not preferred, time spent in Greece, and had spent it in artistic rather than warlike pursuits, was Nero. Nero's insistence on entering himself in singing competitions and athletic contests, where being awarded the supreme prize was a surprise only to him, was perceived as undignified. Emperors sponsored games; they were not supposed to become part of the spectacle.

So the precedents were slender and not felicitous. Emperors who travelled abroad fell into two categories, and Hadrian would find himself fitting into neither. The virtuous emperor travelled, but not to amuse himself. Soldier-emperors like Augustus and Trajan had battled in the provinces, their agenda one of public service, even if self-aggrandisement was an indissoluble part of their campaigns. More clearly self-indulgent emperors such as Nero embarked on voyages which were perceived as essentially frivolous, putting the desires of the individual before the demands of empire. They were criticised and destroyed, either in reality or in reputation: Tiberius was always emotionally distant from Rome; Nero brought down on himself contempt and ultimately civil war following his aesthetic pilgrimages to Greece and his predatory acquisition of public city territory on which to build his splendid folly, the Golden House.

Hadrian was to create a third and new category which was closest to that of a roving diplomat – but a diplomat with immediate access to the power and resources to make and implement policy. In the difficult period of uncertainty while he was waiting to see if Trajan would legitimise his succession – a particularly demanding period for a man only too well aware that the absolute avoidance of loss of self-control was the highest of the classical Greek virtues, and who was so determined to control not only himself but his posterity – Hadrian had ample time to contemplate what sort of emperor (were he to succeed) he would be. What he became was, in every sense, a truly great Master of Ceremonies, deploying the arts of peace – building, image-making, great acts of public sponsorship, and above all the ubiquitous reality, and memory, of his own vivid presence – as much as the arts of war. And for the majority of his reign, he mastered his ceremonies with precision and style.

That Hadrian's profound Hellenophilia and his love of travelling, the two major driving impulses of his reign, were closely linked is clear. That his early experiences of Greece were formative in a different way – one which was to have considerable resonances for his spiritual curiosity and what was perhaps an innate predisposition to melancholy – is less well known.

On Hadrian's very first visit to Athens as a young man, long before he became emperor, he visited Epictetus, the famous Stoic. Philosophers, like emperors, lived outside the structures inhabited by ordinary men. Unconstrained by fear or need of patronage, both might speak their minds. Inevitably their collisions were treasured by those who heard of their exchanges. Epictetus was a performer, prepared to inveigh on any topic from beards to the unattractive characteristics of the Olympic games – but he was particularly notorious for his sarcastic reflections on the questions and lives of his famous visitors. His honesty was part of his appeal, for those who visited him lived in a society where ease with flattery, rhetoric and ambiguity might be a matter of life and death, certainly of success. Quite undaunted by fear of repercussions, Epictetus would put into words what an upper-class Roman might hardly dare let into his thoughts. His philosophical beliefs were enduring, typified by the dictum: 'Seek not what you want to happen; seek to want what happens.' To the idealistic young aristocrat, in search of intellectual and spiritual direction, this was a fine sentiment; but it was almost directly antithetical to the personality of the emperor Hadrian came to be. Their encounter would later be echoed in a darker, more ominous meeting between Hadrian and another philosopher: Secundus the Silent.

On that first visit, too, Hadrian became immersed in Greek religion. He was welcomed into the cult of Demeter, celebrated at the dramatic mysteries of Eleusis, near Athens. Introduced to the cult by Julius Antiochus Philopappus, brother of Julia Balbilla, Hadrian was to revisit its rituals on every return to the country. But his initiation into the cult functioned as more than just an expression of his personal and restless spirituality, for religion was entwined with status. Leaving aside what, to modern eyes, seems their lack of theological substance and their almost exclusive concern with outward observation, the second-century pagan religions were by no means democratically inclusive. Religion was for the ruling class; religious and political authority were synonymous. The emperor was the chief priest of Rome; initiation into rites abroad was an honour and a mark of respect. Celebrants were invariably aristocratic and inclusion was a matter of bonding; the ceremonies were secret – so secret, indeed, that the details of rituals are still not entirely clear, though it is evident that their performance was also an impressive way of proclaiming authority. To be a religious man in the second century was to be a man of power, not of self-denial and a democratic spirit. (Hence, in part, the eventually perceived threat of the cult of Christ – and to others, of course, its attraction.)

Here too, then, Hadrian's experience of Greece showed him a means of reconciling opposing factions of his own role and personality: in this case, the man of intellect and spiritual curiosity with the statesman. The answers to the inevitable questions of how to rule, how to measure up to his predecessors, how to continue the central process of the early principate – which can perhaps be defined as the invention of power: all seemed to be found, for Hadrian, most readily when he was away from Rome. Everything he did, or aspired to, derived from his belief in the pre-eminence of Greek values. Later, claims of homosexuality and antisemitism were to become the most enduring features of his reputation. But, although probably accurate by modern standards, as accusations they are anachronistic. Now, they are matters of harsh and glaring definition. Then, they were not seen as discrete entities, let alone flaws in personality; and they were inextricable from Hadrian's broad, deep-rooted and increasingly obsessive immersion in the Greek world.

And so his reign took shape.

The new emperor was a complex, immensely cultured man. He could display great personal charm or irritable melancholy. He was a man of letters, a collector with a creative drive, a philosopher and a poet. He had a wide-ranging intellect and a famously retentive memory; he was stubborn and competitive; and yet, although notoriously quick-tempered, he showed little of the cruelty that tainted so many of his predecessors. Perhaps his worst characteristic was that he was changeable, both in his mood and in his interests.

In many ways he was a practical, modern man, an internationalist who pursued the advantages of peace within his borders and was fascinated by the latest techniques of engineering and design. But he was also drawn to the arcane and the supernatural; in times of crisis, particularly in the difficult circumstances of Egypt and in the uncertainties of the end of his life, this predisposition would come back to overwhelm him. It is unsurprising; his was a time of superstition, when portents and fortune-telling were ways of attempting to understand and control a capricious world. But Hadrian, dogged by bouts of ill-health and unspecified fears, attempted not just to assert his power over geographical territory but to gain knowledge of the supernatural, and it was rumoured by contemporaries that he sought the secret of eternal life. He studied magic, followed esoteric religions. He was a man, some contemporary commentators said, who wished to know things that were better left unexplored.

All these strands – the intellectual and aesthetic intensity, the probing of the occult and his own stubborn, untrusting and impatient character, which would in fact serve him well for many years – were to come together disastrously on Hadrian's last great journey. But in the early months and years of the reign he set about establishing the style and tone of his rule swiftly and decisively. His actions already indicated, despite his statements to the contrary, that it would be a vastly different matter from the years of Trajan. It was also immediately clear that he was aware of the personal and political disaster that might await an emperor whose rule struck too idiosyncratic a course.

With accession assured, and the tougher, more contentious actions of transfer completed, Hadrian immersed himself in a programme designed to court popularity and – in the tradition of his forebears – to assert the wealth, strength and taste that qualified him to become, and to remain, emperor. But his agenda became far wider than anyone could have imagined possible at the beginning of his reign. There were obvious advantages to succession by a mature and experienced man, and certainly the most serious disasters of the previous century had been exacerbated by the youth of emperors at their succession. An older incumbent would have the experience to navigate these dangerous waters, though weighed down, inevitably, by his own history, prejudices and agenda. Over the next two decades Hadrian controlled the empire in a way which had no precedent. What he did, at first perhaps by instinct, but later almost certainly as a calculated and largely successful policy, was to take the established dynamics of imperial rule and aristocratic behaviour and expand them beyond anything that had been seen before.

The whole mood of his reign and his policies for maintaining power differed significantly from those of any previous emperor and any who followed him. No emperor before Hadrian made such efforts to consolidate the empire, not by aggression but by meeting the reasonable demands of his provinces – and, above all, by being *seen* throughout his empire. Hadrian's vision and his restlessness shaped the cities of his empire and the creativity of the first half of the second century, but his was also a calculated, innovative and potentially risky style of ruling a vast territory; and it was more than a thousand years ahead of its time. What seems at first to be a cosmic caprice may actually have been a fine strategy for unification of an eclectic empire. Probably, for Hadrian, it was a convenient combination of both political acumen and natural inclination. What may have begun in curiosity and acknowledgement of necessity – the boundaries of the empire were urgently in need of ratification when Trajan died – evolved into a system that suited the emperor, the times and the empire's unique problems.

First, although it is the consequences of his artistic choices that have come to be seen as Hadrian's greatest legacy, he asserted himself as commander-in-chief of the army. Astute and mentally agile, he saw that manipulation of the army, and the place of the army as an idea in Roman consciousness, was central to his success. Hadrian was no natural soldier, and as a junior officer had not been particularly liked by either his cohorts or his commanding officer. But he had served his time as a tribune with some credit, had been decorated, and remained a fit and active man. Though his military service had been a conventional step for a young man seeking a career in public life, it had been no sinecure, being undertaken during a long period of war; and thus Hadrian was well respected in his subsequent dealings with the legions.

His very first moves on becoming emperor were concerned with securing the army's loyalty, and in his late fifties he returned to campaigning in the field when it became necessary. Even sources which are generally tinged with hostility towards him comment on the high standards he demanded from his military forces. Most importantly, if the army was not to be seen engaged on the battlefield, it was crucial that its very existence was perceived as an effective deterrent to assault or insurrection. Even the coinage, carefully manipulated by Hadrian throughout his reign, showed almost as many military images as it did those of peace. His agenda was clear: peace through strength or, failing that, peace through threat. Touring his provinces, Hadrian watched field exercises, maintained exacting standards of weaponry and imposed strict regimes on bases. He never let it be forgotten that he had served his time in battle, nor forgot himself that it was the army which had initially acclaimed him as emperor.

Military expediency aside, how did the new emperor appear to his subjects? Experience, inclination and natural intelligence had made him a polymath, though the demands of his role as emperor, and the infinite resources available to him, left him open to accusations of dilettantism. This charge was unfair; he was unusual in that he genuinely wanted to become adept in many areas himself, rather than simply be served or amused by the ability of others. Throughout his reign his understanding was gained either by direct observation or by the development of skills that he admired in others. Poetry, architecture, music, philosophy and mathematics all intrigued him and he was patron of them all, surrounding himself with men of genius: the poet and satirist Juvenal, the architect Apollodorus, the historians Tacitus, Suetonius and Arrian, the writers Pliny the Younger, Pausanias and Plutarch.

He was also, famously, interested in athletics, though possibly predominantly in their performance in the politically important Greek games. Games, along with religious ceremonies, were an integral part of Greek life – an institution – not just as amusement but as part of social organization and national definition. The appeal of athletics, with its surviving pottery images of muscular young men wrestling half-naked, has often been used to ornament claims for Hadrian's homosexuality; but he was more prosaically concerned with the embrace of all things Greek, with his usual shrewd eye for the alchemy of power.

Above all, Hadrian's favourite sport was hunting. With the diminution of continual warfare, and the possibilities offered by exploring very different terrains, hunting offered an attractive test of masculine skills, and one which Hadrian knew he could invariably pass. The dramas and challenges of the hunt gripped Hadrian's imagination. He was fearless and agile, pursuing bears, boars or lions in the many countries in which he found himself, on one occasion saving the life of a friend attacked by a lion, on another breaking his own rib and collarbone. Hunting also inspired some of his surviving poetry, including a touching verse on the death of his favourite horse, Borysthenes. (Alexander the Great had set a precedent in naming an entire city after his racehorse, Bucephalus.) The man who found human relationships invariably problematic built a tomb for this much-loved animal at Apt in southern France, then Apta Julia in Gaul.

Borysthenes Alanus,
the swift horse of Caesar,

who was accustomed to fly
through the sea and the marshes
and the Etruscan mounds,
while pursuing Pannonian boars, not one boar
dared him to harm
with his white tooth:
the saliva from his mouth
scattered even the meanest tail,
as it is custom to happen.
But killed on a day in his youth,
his healthy, invulnerable body
has been buried here in the field.

Above all, Hadrian was a magnificent showman. The great Roman historian Ronald Syme described the subtle tensions that directed the ambitions of the seeker after power: 'the true glory of a Roman aristocrat [was] to contend with his peers for primacy, not to destroy them.'[12] In this he echoed Augustus' claim (rather disingenuous – he had, after all, removed his opponents in their thousands before re-inventing himself as father of the people) that he was (only) *primus inter pares*: first among equals. The tyrant eliminated rivals with violence; the complete emperor merely placed himself so far above his peers in achievement and wealth that his position was impregnable. It was a pretty theory, and after opening as a tyrant with the crude but possibly necessary executions of his first weeks in power, Hadrian placed his primacy beyond doubt by using the traditional methods employed by his predecessors to an extraordinary degree.

Although Roman emperors enforced a rigid autocracy, ended only by natural death or violent intervention, they maintained residual republican traditions of courting the people. To an extent this was a cosmetic exercise, for no emperor was ever at risk from the masses in the way that he was from the senators, the army, the praetorian guard or indeed his intimate circle; but the vast numbers of poor who congregated in the empire's cities could genuinely be considered a general factor in civic instability if not placated. It has been estimated that only one in four of the empire's citizens lived above subsistence level,[13] and a rural population had become increasingly urbanised. While a rural life of self-sufficiency and simplicity was still held up as the ideal, the reality for a large number of second-century Romans was an impoverished and dependent city existence. Certainly, providing for and manipulating the teeming urban hordes was an opportunity for the rich to display a sometimes gloriously excessive command of wealth; it was also an opportunity to provide daily labour for the poor. But the Roman elite had no concept of charity; the ambitious building schemes that were an essential component of any public benefaction, along with days of entertainments in the arena, free corn and distribution of financial help for the children of the destitute, were not disinterested assistance but were intended to reinforce their authority and status.

While financial measures may have been a long-established duty, and the provision of games an enjoyable routine, for Hadrian, when it came to buildings, he was – unusually for an emperor – closely involved with the concept and design of those erected in his name, to the extent of drawing up his own plans for innovative projects. Again, we see Hadrian placing clear water between himself and his predecessors: Augustus may have transformed Rome, Trajan may have built massive utilitarian structures, but under Hadrian the programme of imperial restoration and elaboration took off to the extent that, throughout the lands of the Mediterranean, many of the ruins of ancient Rome that modern travellers encounter are Hadrianic in both commission and inspiration.

And once again we return to the crucial observation that the energy which gave Hadrian's reign its astonishing momentum and took it in a new direction was drawn from his relationship with Greece. As his reign proceeded, it became clear that Hadrian believed not only that Greece was intellectually and aesthetically superior to Rome (the old tension again), but that its heritage suggested ways in which the diversity of the empire could be its strength (and thus the tension resolved). By the time of his death, his implicit rejection of many traditional Roman values and a commitment to and admiration for the older culture had imposed a lasting Greek renaissance on the greater part of the empire. To Hadrian, it was the ultimate imperial triumph: a fine and realistic use of the resources of a conquered power and a glorious fusion of two great cultures. To other Romans, however, it was an act of submission – to some, it even seemed the ultimate cultural victory of Greece over Rome – and their objections showed themselves in a number of ways, some serious, some apparently so trivial as to be almost risible.

First, there was the matter of the emperor's beard.

This was an immediate visual sign of his Greekness, and it was displayed to every citizen on the imperial coinage. And it mattered. Every Roman emperor since the great Augustus had been clean-shaven. The practice required a daily and protracted toilet – Romans shaved without lather or oil, being groomed by their slaves simply on wet skin – yet (or possibly because of this) it was such a crucial marker of Roman-ness that elite citizens never considered the advantages of a well-manicured beard. Beards were for Greeks, particularly Greek philosophers. (Equally, Greeks viewed their clean-shaven countrymen as submissive to the Romans.) Among Romans, beards were worn by men of lower status. But, significantly, in the magnificent detail of Trajan's column are tough, bearded generals in the thick of the fighting. Whether these officers' hirsute faces were a reflection of the hard military life or of exposure to eastern culture is unknown, but the synthesis of military experience and pro-Greek sympathies that a beard could convey was irresistible to Hadrian's self-invention. Nevertheless, the mockery that his pretensions always seemed to attract pursued him: 'If you think that to grow a beard is to acquire wisdom, a goat with a fine beard is at once a veritable Plato,' wrote a contemporary, Lucian.[14] There was the occasional whisper that the imperial beard was not so much a symbolic choice as an effort to cover up facial blemishes, but all the same, after Hadrian the beard became fashionable, and for the next 160 years the emperors who succeeded him are always depicted as wearing them. The risk that Roman coins might thereby seem to display not just non-Roman values but perhaps a Greek king was offset by the fact that – as we shall discuss shortly – Hadrian was seen in the flesh by so many more people than any of his predecessors.

But there were more serious matters at stake than art and beards. Hadrian's political favours, his rumoured homosexuality, his unsympathetic attitude towards the Jews, the history he chose to emphasise and the breadth and focus of his travels – all stemmed from his uncompromising determination that his empire would be one in which the best of Roman and Greek alike would be integrated. It was to be a very modern shift from Roman dominance by force and threat to a spirit of internationalism. And it would be seriously breached only once in twenty-one years of rule. From the start, despite his popularity among the army, Hadrian's own strategy was one of peace; and if he was unrealistic in his hopes for a return to a more gracious past, his refusal to prosecute incessant border wars enabled him to distribute money directly to the people and to build public amenities in the many cities of the empire. Under Hadrian, even the poorest were able to share in an increased prosperity.

Hadrian made less effort to enforce the spirit of the new age in Rome, or in those western provinces which had already adapted to Roman *mores*, but travelling around the eastern lands of his empire he became increasingly bound up in his

Hellenistic re-creations (or inventions). And in this pursuit, he developed perhaps the most extraordinary characteristic of his reign.

Hadrian was already an outsider. He was only the second emperor to have his roots in the provinces, and when his Hellenophilia combined with his geographical preferences and, indeed, a certain unease he seemed to feel in Rome, to dictate his whereabouts; when his actual physical presence, and, of course, the imperial court, started to follow, literally, his cultural tastes; then the world was set to change. What Hadrian, in practical terms, invented was a travelling court: one which disseminated not images and ideology, but the presence of the living emperor.

There had always been a tradition for emperors to display themselves at public ceremonies, particularly the Roman games. In the stands of the arena the emperor was, at least theoretically, accessible to the people. It was important that he be seen, and contemporary writers were quick to criticise emperors who misplayed their part: Augustus who signed letters, Claudius who had a penchant for topless women gladiators. There were occasions on which the emperor was heckled, and wise emperors accepted this with restraint, though some, like Domitian, responded by throwing members of the audience into combat in the arena, and it was recorded that people pretended to die just so they could escape Nero's interminable recitations.

The games were such an important showcase that they were rigorously controlled by imperial laws, and they were the subject of numerous colourful or bizarre anecdotes. Decapitated ostriches, simulated rape of a female criminal by a bull, dwarves, galleons floating in artificial lakes, deranged gladiator emperors, exotic creatures from every corner of the empire and myths bloodily enacted with condemned protagonists – all were ingredients in the brew of constant novelty provided for the crowd. In the sense that these were imaginative diversions, they were violent precursors of the masques which preoccupied the courts of Europe in the sixteenth and seventeenth centuries; but unlike those, which were primarily exclusive and played out for aristocratic amusement, the excitements of the Roman arena were, crucially, *inclusive* entertainment – and instruction – for all Roman citizens. So the idea of spectacle as an appropriate environment in which the emperor could reveal himself to his subjects was firmly established; but perhaps Hadrian's greatest strategic innovation was to take this idea and extend it beyond the confines of Rome, so that he appeared in great dramatic set-pieces throughout the world he ruled.

It was a triumph – a great conquest, perhaps his greatest – of, above all, the imagination: to understand, from the start, that the emperor *as an idea* would always be more potent than any flesh-and-blood manifestation. There was anticipation, then appearance, and then, after his departure, permanent commemoration in stone and marble, the spirit of the emperor captured in gold and spectacle and largesse. If the emperor was going to reveal himself to the world at large, it was essential that he and all his works should appear superhuman. Hadrian may well have enjoyed playing Pericles or Alexander; but his was also a powerful statement of political supremacy.

And so – marked out from those who preceded him and those who followed (in other words, from the heritage and posterity he wished to control) – Hadrian travelled extensively around his empire, anticipating by more than a thousand years the progresses of medieval monarchs and of rulers such as England's Elizabeth I. It is tempting to draw comparisons, between Hadrian and the great Renaissance princes, themselves also collectors, patrons and iconoclasts. But this would be a mistake; despite the trappings of wealth and culture, Hadrian was in no sense a modern historical ruler, although his journeys were used strategically to similar effect.[15]

Seen in hindsight, Hadrian's travelling court was an extra-ordinary, and extraordinarily effective, innovation of rule. As his autobiography has long disappeared, and the writers of the time merely commented on the fact of his journeys, we can only conjecture as to his motives. But whether it was for reasons of policy, as a means of escape, or merely a way of life which evolved to suit both the emperor and his times, travel became Hadrian's default position. The periods he spent back in Rome, moreover, were increasingly affected by the experiences and sights gathered on his travels; like a sort of cultural merchant, he exported Roman values to the provinces, but – despite the innate conservatism of the Roman elites – he also *imported* back to Rome new ideas, new images and, above all, an integrated vision of power unknown since the time of Augustus. Increasingly, too, he seemed ill-at-ease in Rome, returning only to consolidate those political foundations which permitted him safely to leave the capital again. In his absence the city was left in the trusted hands of the prefect of the praetorian guard, while the serious business of the empire was following Hadrian.

Curious and engaged with novelty, he roamed his empire, controlling and uniting his world. The title *pater patriae* – 'father of the fatherland' – had seemed ludicrously inappropriate when bestowed on the deranged Caligula (though perhaps no more so than 'Caligula' itself, a childhood soubriquet best translated as 'Bootsie'), the impulsive and immature Nero or the reclusive Tiberius; but it was entirely appropriate for a ruler who went out to meet his subjects and was clearly – magnificently – seen to do so.

It was the nature of imperial power that enabled Hadrian to travel so widely. While Rome remained the symbolic centre of the empire, government followed the emperor. Of course, day-to-day administration took place locally, in Rome as it did in the provinces; what was in effect a vast civil service kept the business of the empire moving; but one of the advantages of absolute power was that it was vested in one person and, as long as he retained that power, it was as mobile as *he* elected to be. The emperor *was* Rome.

Roman emperors had been involved in incursions overseas and in border wars for so long that their absence from the seat of power was a well-established practice. Few emperors had not been called to war; a few others chose to go – or, in Tiberius' case, to remain – outside Rome. Systems had long evolved to transport the military and the freedmen, who comprised the bulk of imperial administrators, with the emperor. Though the senate continued its deliberations in the city, and there was some risk in the growth of factions hostile to the emperor developing there, equally Hadrian's presence in the provinces, particularly with his energies unencumbered by war, diminished potential problems outside Italy.

Most of the important holders of symbolic and executive power were at the emperor's side. A constant stream of correspondence emerged from the travelling court directing the activities of the empire. Despatch riders were a crucial aspect of government communication, their activities speeded up by improved roads and safer conditions at sea. Indeed, among the surviving texts for Hadrian's reign are several documents settling disputes, assigning cases to lesser authorities and generally dealing with the business of power. Throughout the journeys – which, even buffered by every available amenity and service, must have been gruelling – between the rituals and the spectacles, the restorations and the dedications, Hadrian had to find time to deal with the mass of imperial administration. There were appointments, civil and military, to be made, legal judgements to be delivered, allocations of resources to be decided. It was an arduous process. No doubt the long city stopovers, usually in winter, were to facilitate all this as much as to rest the court.

Hadrian was fortunate that for much of his reign he had an indispensable and indefatigable supporter in the Rome city prefect, Marcius Turbo. Turbo, who replaced the equally sound Annius Verus in this crucial role, occupied it for over fifteen years. As guardian of Hadrian's interests in Rome, Turbo impressed all who saw him as

a man of the greatest generalship . . . Prefect or commander of the Praetorians. He displayed neither softness nor haughtiness in anything that he did, but lived like one of the multitude; among other things, he spent the entire day near the palace and often he would go there even before midnight, when some of the others were just beginning to sleep.[16]

It is one of the baffling acts of Hadrian's last years that the emperor turned against the now elderly man who had served him for so long and enabled him to travel for years on end by maintaining Rome's stability in the emperor's absence.

However, despite the refined legal and logistical structures that enabled the empire to be governed effectively in the emperor's absence from Rome, there is a hint in the historical sources that Hadrian also employed secret police – the *frumentarii* – to investigate significant individuals.[17] The activities that are recorded are trivial (although undoubtedly this was not always the case), but it is not inconceivable that an emperor who attempted to see into the future and to master many skills might also be curious about any secrets kept by those around him. It is not impossible that the phrase used of him, that he wanted to know things that should not be known, might apply to the private lives of his courtiers as much as to the magicians' arts. Knowledge – of whatever sort – was power.

The logistics of Hadrian's twenty-year reign, over half of which he spent travelling, are almost inconceivable now. The impact and demands of the imperial court on relatively small communities must have had an effect which lasted years. A visit from the emperor was never going to be forgotten. Estimates that Hadrian travelled with an entourage of 5,000 are likely to be correct, although as his consecutive journeys were themselves unique it is hard to find comparisons except in army records and those of later travelling monarchs such as Elizabeth I. Roman armies did not, of course, have a requirement for comfort or entertainment comparable to that of the Tudor court, and Elizabeth was travelling within a much smaller area, among her own people and nearly fifteen hundred years later. One analyst believes that when travelling in Britain in 122, in a period of instability, Hadrian may have been accompanied by as many as 8,000 soldiers, as well as a large detachment of his personal bodyguard and the administrative and domestic personnel of the imperial household.[18] It is likely that the entourage even included designers and builders; there is enough similarity among Hadrian's buildings to suggest a central corps of expertise.

The most likely scenario is that numbers fluctuated according to the destinations chosen. A (still large) central group of courtiers, administrators and guard may have undertaken local journeys while the great body of the retinue remained based in the nearest city. Nevertheless, despite the hospitality of some of the richest and most powerful men in the empire, the pressures on provincial communities required to feed, house, amuse and protect the emperor and a retinue of thousands must have exhausted their resources. Whether or not food was diverted from Rome, calculations on the few details that have survived of provisions requested in Egypt suggest that the poorest, usually subsistence, farmers must have found the burden intolerable. But – again in contrast to the sixteenth-century Elizabeth – complaints were few, or if they existed, have not survived – though there is an acceptance that the burdens were too onerous in the reasons given by Hadrian's successor for not travelling in this way.[19] It is possible that the advantages of Hadrian's visits and the prestige they conferred outweighed the vast demands on the host communities. It is also possible, indeed probable, that those who celebrated these gains were not the same as those almost invisible, and certainly silent, farmers who suffered.

Conventionally, Hadrian is said to have completed three major journeys: broadly, to the north and west of the empire, to the southern Mediterranean and to the east. In fact these were interspersed with numerous smaller journeys to destinations closer to home. Indeed, the first part of his reign was spent in moving swiftly around the crisis-stricken area of what is now central Europe. This, as noted earlier, had the triple benefit of resolving inherited disputes over various contested territories, reviewing the troops and ensuring their support, and keeping out of Rome until, with the army firmly behind him and certain murky political removals undertaken in his absence, he could return with minimum threat to his claim as emperor. Throughout his reign, Hadrian resorted to travelling to solve many of his problems, both personal and political.

Hadrian's first long journey lasted four years and was very much one of duty. Geographically ambitious, it took him to the northern, western and eastern peripheries of his empire. He visited his homeland of Spain, Gaul and the northern frontier of Britain, where he travelled the long and bleak line of the *limites* – the extreme edge of his empire – and commissioned the defensive wall which bears his name. This was a journey which bridged the gap between the militarily motivated travel of previous emperors and the aesthetic revival which was to be the focus of Hadrian's later explorations. From the choices he made when his power was assured and he was enjoying the security of the central years of his reign, it can be assumed that he took little personal pleasure in the western part of his empire, with its cooler climate and largely Romanized barbarian culture. But the composition of this first journey was essential; thereafter Hadrian, having ceded problematic border territories, could begin his uniquely mobile reign not in retreat but as a strong ruler reviewing and consolidating the new and more solid borders of the empire.

Importantly, the emperor could still be seen in military contexts, but without the need to expend money and energy, or indeed put himself in danger, either in battle or as a result of the unpopularity consequent on humiliating defeat. Like a modern dictator, Hadrian could wear the uniform of a general, line up his military power, and impress or coerce both those loyal to him and the potentially hostile.

It was in the central years of his reign, when he was in his prime and at his most politically secure, that personal preference began to shape his itineraries. His second journey was a smaller affair, largely concentrated on north Africa, but his third was to his preferred eastern empire, which had kept more of its own idiosyncratic characteristics. Over the next few years the emperor's ardent convictions, combined with his extraordinary wealth and power, allowed him to model himself increasingly as a Hellenistic king and to immerse the Roman world in a Greek cultural and artistic revival. Inevitably, what Hadrian re-created was an idealised ancient Greece; it was thus the ultimate conquest of its culture rather than the ultimate concession. Hadrian's Greekness was not that of authentic contemporary Greece but an imperial creation.[20] Such a nostalgic view of the Greek past acquired all the florid trappings that second-century Romans associated with the cultural apogee of Greek antiquity. For example, the elite took on the now rather uncomfortable affectation of prizing archaic Greek rather than the contemporary language. Like the Victorian English with their poetic embellishments of 'thou' and 'wert' and 'e'en', so the Hadrianic circle wrote in Aeolic dialect for a refined effect; it was a marker of inclusion in the inner circle. This uneasy juxtaposition of enthusiasm for an idealised 'ancient' civilisation and a distinct lack of enthusiasm for its present-day descendants has its echoes in the problems that the American and European Grand Tourists had with Italy, whose geography and ancient remains they loved – were it not for the drawback of its current inhabitants.

Second-century elite culture and nineteenth-century romanticism were both heavily vested in a nostalgic golden past.

But not all Hadrian's destinations were so congenial, nor were all his observers so starry-eyed. One of his few close friends, the poet Florus, wrote to him in terms which, though we now read them as ironic, actually paint a ruefully admiring picture of a hardy, dutiful Hadrian which would have pleased propagandists. The three surviving lines (freely translated) read:

> I don't want to be Caesar
> Plodding round Britain,
> [. . .]
> Freezing my nuts off in a Scythian midden

Hadrian's matching riposte conveyed wit and affability and a side of his personality that he was eager to project:

> I don't want to be a Florus,
> Crawling round pubs,
> Skulking in pie-shops
> Bitten by bugs.

This slight exchange shows Hadrian as more human than in most other fragments of biography. It is a small insight into the person which makes it all the more distressing that Hadrian's own autobiography has been entirely lost. We can make some reconstruction of the early second century from histories, biographies, inscriptions, coins and papyri; but the scholarly bones of biography, where they exist for Hadrian's reign, are corrupted, evasive or tantalisingly incomplete when it comes to dealing with Hadrian the man. The more interesting information is often to be found, as in the case of Florus' verse, in the apparently inconsequential anecdotes – the word itself deriving, appropriately, from the Greek *anecdotes*, or 'unpublished' (though of course they were). (It is pleasingly symmetrical that Procopius' *Secret History*, telling the 'hidden' and, by implication, 'true' story of the Emperor Justinian, was also originally published under the title *Anecdotes*.)

The anecdotes which historians repeated, however slight, nearly always represented some aspect of the public relationship of Hadrian to his subjects or the exercise of power. Usually they show the emperor caught out and then, through power or insight, retrieving the situation. Historians are enthusiastic in assembling what might be regarded as a compendium of The Wit of the Emperor, and the small cameos are much more important than they might at first appear. In the retelling they are astonishingly stolid tales, but they are informative. For example, a woman in the street petitions the emperor over some minor mystery and Hadrian brusquely brushes her and her complaint aside with the excuse that he is too busy for such minor matters. When the woman calls after him, 'Stop being king, then!' he returns and listens to her, the humblest of subjects.[21] Hadrian finds a man scratching his back against a post in the public baths and donates a slave to perform the duty for him, and money to keep him; on his next visit the emperor finds a whole group of old men hopefully rubbing their backs on posts, and confounds them by genially suggesting that they scratch each other. A man whom Hadrian assists financially disguises himself by dyeing his hair from grey and returns with another petition. Hadrian, amused, claims to recognise a family likeness and remarks that he has already given a favour to the man's grandfather.

All these anecdotes portray an emperor who is, primarily, extraordinarily accessible to ordinary people; the inevitable courtiers, bodyguards and soldiers are all invisible as the emperor interacts directly with his humblest subjects. These anecdotes also suggest that Hadrian is continually at risk of being duped by his dishonest, greedy and, above all, stupid subjects, and that he responds to these assaults on his natural generosity with good humour and tolerance. But of course, what may seem irrelevant or trivial detail can often turn out, in retrospect, to be highly significant. And it is in one apparently peripheral story that the triumph of Hadrian's reign begins to unravel.

In late 128 Hadrian set out from Rome for Greece. He had visited almost every corner of his empire, he had enjoyed the usual rewards of Athens, and was in the process of elaborate plans both to ensure the Greek city's future and to beautify it beyond any city in the empire, save Rome. Ahead of him lay his first visits to two of the more challenging provinces, Judea and Egypt, but there was nothing to suggest he would not captivate them and bring intelligent and open-handed solutions to their individual problems. Confident, healthy and successful, he was at the height of his career.

Then a strange story began to circulate. It was said that while in Athens, in an overt demonstration of power, Hadrian had threatened a man with death not for acting against him, nor for arguing with him, but simply for keeping silent. It seems an improbable account but it was a remarkably persistent tale, elaborate, vivid and quite different in style from anything else written about him, although, like the other stories, it has at its core a simple example of the differences between men and emperors. In the curious tale of Secundus the Silent Philosopher, the most bitter of confrontations was purely Greek in location, in style and in precedent. Though variations on the story of Secundus and Hadrian have branched into the literary traditions of several cultures from Greek to Arabic, and may even have inspired tales within the Arabian Nights, with Sinbad a derivation of Secundus,[22] Hadrian's beloved Greece was implicitly at the centre of the tale.

To set what follows in context, it should be understood that apocryphal altercations between emperors and philosophers were set-pieces happily relayed by contemporary writers. In the battle between men who had everything and those who had nothing to lose, the philosopher invariably triumphed. Of the main schools of philosophy prevalent at Hadrian's time, Stoics were anti-materialistic, believers in fate, the pre-eminence of reason and the freedom of human action; Epicureans believed that man was mortal, that there was no god, that only life in the present counts and that pleasure lay in desire, not in the search for resolution; Cynics found virtue in extreme poverty and asceticism, but also defied the social conventions of the time. Hadrian, who was eager to keep company with philosophers of all schools, nevertheless led a life diametrically opposed to the value system of any of them. When inconceivable power, wealth and experience were pitted against the intractable beliefs and considerable intellectual wiles of a philosopher, the contest was compelling but the outcome assured. It is not surprising, then, that the enormous populations of the Roman empire, who owed their welfare and indeed their continued existence to the structures of Roman rule, and thus ultimately to the emperor, would eagerly pass on tales of anyone getting the best of the emperor and surviving. For example, the doctor and writer Galen gives an account of an irritable Hadrian lashing out at a servant with a pen and blinding him. On realising the extent of the man's disability, Hadrian insisted that he ask for a compensatory present from the emperor; the injured man asked for an eye.[23] In the law of retribution this would, of course, have been not the impossible request for a new eye, but the demand for the unthinkable: the emperor's own eye – but the emperor was beyond such laws.

The philosopher Secundus was already renowned for his silence and it was probably inevitable that Hadrian, a connoisseur of the esoteric experience, would seek him out. His taste in this respect was not unusual. Travelling Romans seem to have pursued the grotesque and the phenomenal. Like the Victorians so many hundreds of years later, they were anxious to gratify their curiosity as to what lay within their imperial boundaries, and gullible when novelties and strange tales were provided for them. Pliny, the famous and interminable compiler of natural history, records monsters and improbable prodigies alongside conventional lists of races, creatures and geological phenomena. There was a tradition of presenting freaks of nature or animals of extraordinary size to important men of the day. It was no doubt a potentially profitable one, the guides being rewarded for their introductions; but was not without risks. Hadrian, for example, was shown, among other things, a woman who had surviving quintuplets, and a strange serpent; he, of course, was gracious in acknowledgement, but others did not always receive the gifts in the spirit in which they were presented. One aristocrat was shown a captured sea monster which he failed to treat with respect; the more gullible were delighted when he was subsequently shipwrecked. The always suspicious Tiberius was given an enormous fish and promptly beat the fisherman about the face with it. The fisherman, in thoughtless simplicity, responded with the comment that he was glad he hadn't given the emperor the oversize lobster he had also collected.

Secundus was an oddity fit for a collector of experiences as well as artefacts, intellectually compelling and an open challenge to the emperor's power. The meeting of the two men must have been a happily awaited diversion. Yet if altercations between philosophers and emperors traditionally had equivocal outcomes, confrontations with Hadrian seldom ended well. The architect Apollodorus was killed, it was rumoured, as revenge for a long-remembered criticism of Hadrian's designs. An intimate member of Hadrian's circle, Favorinus, left court rather than argue with the emperor over a grammatical error. Those familiar with Hadrian knew how to handle him, and themselves.

But Secundus was an innocent. Or so it appeared.

The context of Secundus' life was probably publicly known. The story went that, as a child, he had lost his father and then been sent abroad. After many years' travelling, having become a Cynic philosopher, he returns home and, realising that no one recognises him, decides to put his mother to a test by bribing her maid to arrange for the apparent stranger to seduce her mistress. Unwittingly, Secundus' mother agrees, although she is a little surprised when, having got as far as her bed, Secundus fixes his eyes on her breasts, the symbol of maternity, turns over and goes to sleep. In the morning he reveals his true identity and his mother, the victim of Secundus' moral experiment, hangs herself. Secundus himself decides that it was talking too much that had precipitated this tragedy and takes an immediate vow of lifelong silence.

There are implications for Hadrian, the almost permanent traveller, even in Secundus' history: the dangers of leaving one's homeland for too long, of non-recognition, of the risks of testing trust.

And so Secundus the Silent and Hadrian the Emperor meet. The one-way audience begins with Hadrian asking Secundus to explain the basis of his philosophy. Secundus refuses. Eventually Hadrian asks a tribune to force Secundus to speak. When Secundus remains obdurate, the tribune declares that the philosopher will be executed for his refusal to obey the emperor; but as the philosopher is led away, Hadrian, in a slippery piece of manipulation, indicates to the officer in charge that he must continue to entreat the condemned man to reveal his secrets; if Secundus *does* speak he is to be beheaded . . . but if he does not, then he is to brought before Hadrian again.

Secundus, silent as ever, duly appears before the emperor and a superficial compromise is achieved; the philosopher maintains his vow, and the emperor never hears him speak; instead, Secundus is induced to write down responses to twenty questions posed by the emperor. Both have lost and, at this moment, both have won. In itself, this was a fairly standard literary formula; but the diatribe with which Secundus prefaces the answers to Hadrian's questions is an apt and potent revenge. The emperor gets his answers, but his pretensions are struck hard, and his fears mercilessly exposed.

You too, Hadrian, are a human being like all the rest of us, subject to every kind of accident, mere dust and corruption. The life of brute beasts is even such. Some are clothed with scales, others with shaggy hair; some are blind, some are adorned with beauty with which they are born and which nature has given them. But you, Hadrian, as it happens, are full of fears and apprehensions. In the bellowing wind of winter you are disturbed by too much cold and shivering, and in the summer time you are too much oppressed by the heat. You are puffed up and full of holes like a sponge. For you have termites in your body and herds of lice that draw furrows through your entrails; and grooves have been burned into you, as it were, like the lines made by the fire of the encaustic painters. Being a short-lived creature and full of infirmities, you foresee yourself being cut and torn apart, roasted by the sun and chilled by the wintry wind. Your laughter is only the preface to grief, for it turns about and passes into tears . . .

Think not lightly, therefore, O Hadrian, of what I am saying. Boast not that you alone have encircled the world in your travels, for it is only the moon and stars that really make the journey around it. Moreover, do not think of yourself as beautiful and great and rich and the ruler of the inhabited world. Know you not that, being a man, you were born to be Life's plaything, helpless in the hands of fortune and destiny, sometimes exalted, sometimes humbled lower than the grave. Will you not be able to learn what life is, Hadrian, in the light of many examples? Consider how rich with his golden nails was the king of the Lydians. Great as a commander of armies was the king of the Danaans, Agamemnon; during and hardy was Alexander, king of the Macedonians. Heracles was fearless, the Cyclops wild and untamed, Odysseus shrewd and subtle, and Achilles beautiful to look upon. If fortune took away from these men the distinctions that were peculiarly their own, how much more likely is she to take them away from you? For you are not beautiful like Achilles, nor shrewd as was Odysseus, nor untamed like the Cyclops nor fearless like Heracles, nor hardy and daring like Alexander, nor such a commander of armies as was Agamemnon, nor yet rich like Gyges, the king of the Lydians.[24]

The bitter energy of Secundus' written testimony must have lodged itself in Hadrian's mind. He was, we know, superstitious and pessimistic, and Secundus dismantled the emperor's self-importance and removed the illusions of comfort. Psychologically acute, this diatribe held little of the amiable malice which was half the entertainment of public exchanges with philosophers. Nor was it an aphoristic, one-line riposte by a witty courtier or a frustrated citizen. Secundus is addressing not just the emperor, but a man. What Secundus writes is not just the traditional recitation of the ephemeral nature of power and riches but is highly specific to Hadrian, mocking his passion for travel, diminishing his achievements. Secundus turns the golden ease of Hadrian's reign into a bleak harbinger of future misfortune. Hadrian, apparently at the peak of success, has nothing ahead of him but grief that all he treasures in his present life has been surpassed by greater men.

It was closer to a curse than a piece of rhetoric.

From Athens, Hadrian embarked for Asia minor, Arabia and finally Egypt. His specific route and intentions, as he swept in an arc round his eastern empire, are now uncertain; but his standing in the city of his departure is unmistakable. Hadrian had great plans for Greece, and in particular for Athens, and these were already under way: new buildings appeared, new festivals were inaugurated, honour upon honour were heaped upon the emperor, and he left Greece with the additional titles of king and Olympian. What followed could only be less satisfactory – but it was not just that he was leaving his favourite city (after all, he intended to return as soon as possible); something else had shifted in the emperor's confidence and judgement. In the next eighteen months, first in Judea and then in Egypt, he was to falter in his usual firm and agile handling of local exigencies, and his behaviour would become more recognisably touched with the pointless cruelty and irrationality of his predecessors.

That some time around this period Hadrian believed himself to have fallen under a curse was widely believed, although the details are vague. Was it in Athens, even as the Greeks hailed him as a god, that Hadrian felt the fates turn against him? Did he, in the dark years of the 130s, still remember Secundus' prophetic words?

The legacy of Commagene, the land of Julia Balbilla's family, is now a major tourist attraction near the large modern city of Gaziantep in eastern Turkey. King Mithridates founded his nearby capital, Arsemaia, now Eski Kâhta, in 1 BCE and the dynasty claimed roots going back to both Darius of Persia and Alexander the Great. The once pretty, fertile and short-lived kingdom, strategically sited near the Euphrates, is now a dry and rocky land destroyed by drought. But the great, even megalomaniacal, tomb of Antiochus I of Commagene, Julia Balbilla's paternal ancestor, is still an astonishing sight high on the peak of Nemrut Dagi, 2,200 metres above sea level. Here, where the air is always cool and the mists take time to clear in the morning, are vast crumbling terraces and the immense fallen heads of statues, representing the divine ancestors of Antiochus and the deified king himself.

The tomb of the heroic Borysthenes at Apt has vanished under river silt, but seventeen hundred years later another complex man, poet and Hellenophile, echoed the sentiments of Hadrian's monument to his horse in carving his own inscription to his dog. It can still be seen at Newstead Abbey in Nottinghamshire. It was unlikely to have been a coincidence. Lord Byron, too, was a man whose human relationships were always fraught and whose idealised passion for Greece was his downfall.

Near this spot are deposited the remains of one who possessed Beauty without Vanity, Strength without Insolence, Courage without Ferocity, and all the Virtues of Man without his Vices. This praise, which would be unmeaning Flattery, if inscribed over human ashes, is but a just Tribute to the Memory of BOATSWAIN, a Dog.

3

The shifting sands

Who knows not to what monstrous gods, my friend,
The mad inhabitants of Egypt tend?
The river-fish, cat, ibis some enshrine;
Some think the crocodile alone divine;
Others where Thebes' vast ruins strew the ground,
And shattered Memnon yields a magic sound,
Set up a glittering brute of uncouth shape
And bow before the image of an ape!
Thousands regard the hound with holy fear;
No one Diana. And 'tis dangerous here
To violate an onion or to stain
The sanctity of leeks with tooth profane.
Oh, holy nation! Sacrosanct abodes
Where every garden propagates its gods!
They spare the fleecy tribe and think it ill
The blood of lambkins or of kids to spill;
But human flesh — oh that is lawful fare,
And you may eat it without scandal there.

JUVENAL, SATIRES, 15

From the memoirs of Julia Balbilla, August 130

I was born between the mountains and the sea, and am used to hard, hot seasons – but the day we crossed the border was the hottest I can ever remember. Colourless and hazy from dawn, the hard blue sky cleared only when the sun was at its highest, while the heat shimmered in pools over the packed sand and the horses lathered at the mouth. Messengers set off in a flurry of sand and others returned exhausted, the saddle-cloths under their riders patched dark with sweat. The journey from Judea had numbed the body and the senses so that the excitement of finally reaching Egypt seemed unreal. Although it was foolish to believe it, we had half expected a dramatic transition from rock and near-desert to a vista of the mysterious Nile, and that the border be marked by battered colossi of lion-headed women. The Egypt of our imagination was such a mighty continent. In the event the border passed almost unnoticed. The sand remained, the sun still shone, the same sea was still distantly visible.

A party – the fortunate, it seemed – went ahead to prepare the prefect for our arrival. The rest of us lingered a little on the road in what shade could be found, intending that the emperor's entry from Judea might be made in daylight and at a propitious hour. Once the caravan was brought to a standstill, and even the draught of movement ceased, it was soon impossibly uncomfortable. Hadrian dismounted but Sabina lay in the litter, the curtains let down to prevent the sun. We suggested she step out and join her ladies in some food but it was too hot to eat, too hot to do more than lie back halfway between sleep and waking. Sabina felt unwell, she said; with her eyes open her headache worsened in the glare, with her eyes closed thoughts and images leaped through her mind like a nightmare. I felt each breath thick, as if I was inhaling through a veil.

I got down at one point; giddy for a moment, standing on the solid earth after so many hours swaying on the tracks, I could see the broad road edged with its uneven clusters of attendants, crouched under what protection they could find. Awnings had been put up near at hand, but as the road stretched away from the small hamlet, those unlucky enough to have missed the sparse shelter of the trees were forced into sitting behind the small shade provided by their horses and donkeys, motionless so that they looked like so many scrubby bushes along the road edge. To my right – far, far to my right – there was sea; they had kept close to the coast for the last day in hope of feeling its cooler breezes, but the horizon was so indistinct that it seemed I stood between two deserts, one red, one grey. To my left, after the great sweep of sandy valley, it was just possible to see hills, but impossible to gauge their distance away.

This was supposed to be fertile land with the most hospitable climate, but it had been a bad year and the only sign of its usual richness were the date palms which intermittently fringed the road. That and the rocks which might have marked out some fields, and mile upon mile of dead vegetation, yellow and grey in the dust. The huts we saw seemed deserted, although wild men wrapped in cloth appeared on mangy camels as if from the sands – almost getting themselves killed in their approach – and offered turquoises from who knew what distant treasure trove beyond the mountains.

It was good to have left that terrible place where we slept the night. Rhinocolura – the place where they severed the noses of miscreants, though in truth, not to smell its foulness might be considered an advantage – lay mute in an atmosphere of hopeless-ness. Such a barren, salty town; even the sea which lay close at hand seemed dead and too still. It marked the border, but was thought too insignificant for our official reception into Egypt. Better that way, really, as it would have seemed an inauspicious start.

The dinner was obviously a brave attempt to make what the local chefs thought of as a Roman feast. The imperial cooks, who often did tolerably well with local ingredients, had become sick in Judea and the border town, though forewarned months ahead, still seemed surprised, even put out, at our arrival. It was perhaps that they could not conceive of the demands our brief stay would make upon them; that they simply prepared for the largest party they could imagine and that their efforts were quite inadequate to our needs. We had goat again and two kinds of fish fresh from the sea. The chef's assistant came in with a platter upon which the newly caught creatures were iridescent and muscular, but whether he apportioned a piece back to his family or let some burn in the fire, what came to us later was foul and slimy. For Hadrian they had devised something they believed approximated to his favourite dish. The original was composed of game, offal, ham and pastry; it seemed the Egyptians possessed none of these ingredients. To his credit he ate it. But the dates that followed were plump and sweet and even knowing that they would, in excess, be regretted the next day, hunger made us incautious. The rest of the household had to fend for themselves, and hunger did not improve their mood or their competence. That they found some resources seemed indicated by the surliness of the locals on the following morning.

Hadrian seemed oblivious to the general mood and was even-handed in telling jokes at the expense of others and against himself. The story of the man in the public baths who was scraping his back against a wall when the emperor intervened to give him the slave that his rank but not his fortune merited, then being greeted by a whole row of slaveless townsfolk, hopefully rubbing themselves up and down the tiles, and not flying into a rage at yet another example of the boundless greed of his citizens but suggesting benignly that they use the strigil on each other, had been refined since I first heard it. Where it lacked humour it provided a lesson for the empire, for those who could understand it. Others looked eager; if a humble citizen could be given a slave, then what rewards might await a consul with a back in need of scratching? The Greek boy laughed.

Now we are approaching Pelusium, growing like a rich fruit on a branch of the Nile, and its port, looking out to sea. I try to amuse the empress with stories about great men and the buildings and the ruins of kings and giants. She is well travelled, but no one seems to have told her where we are going or what she should know before arriving, beyond the necessity of maintaining a careful deportment. Hadrian is not a man to share his possessions, even knowledge. But Egypt, *Egypt*. This is not a gallery of art or another week of games; it is different from anywhere else in the world. It is a place of marvels and possibilities and deceptions. Like its great monuments, it is an enduring entity impervious to those who win it in some bloody struggle, who prevail, abide a while, are entertained, perplexed, struggle to impose their ways, fail and leave.

Sabina says that her throat is dry beyond thirst and the canteen water is tepid. A skinny child with dull black skin and sore eyes beats a fan over her head; it merely buffets the dust and the hot air about, but Sabina is unusually patient. In one hand she turns a small object between her fingers. I know what it is; it is a smooth, honey-coloured lump of amber with an insect caught for ever inside it. She showed me once; the creature had perished in the moment of flight, its fragile wings undamaged by the engulfing resin, perhaps as it alighted hoping for nourishment. It had a sting longer than a hornet, perfectly preserved. Hadrian gave her this curiosity many years ago.

After an hour or so, with the heat building, a flurry of horses brought back a little news and – much more precious – some sugar-coated nuts and blessedly cool water sent by the prefect from the very waters of the sacred Nile. The Nile water does not only quench thirst but is possessed of other remarkable properties which ensure long life, fertility, protection against your enemies. Sabina was in need of its more mundane qualities; once she had drunk deeply, I soaked linen in it and pressed it to her brow. Water trickled down her temples and ran like tiny tributaries behind her ears. When I drank myself I could feel the water cutting a cold channel inside me. I try to tell Sabina of the country that awaits her, of its mysteries and wonders; all the stories my grandfather told me. But in truth what we all want now is not to be entertained but just to be comfortable, to be clean, to be still. The mysteries can come when we have bathed and eaten.

Ahead is Pelusium, gateway to Egypt. Already they will be assembling their troops, the crowd clambering on to the stands, the street traders and the thieves calling down blessings on the emperor. Among them the merchants of plausibility sell aspirations: badly struck coins of The Imperial Entry, or a balcony seat, or a lead curse – just fill in the name of the beloved or your enemy – or a phial of Nile water, guaranteeing fertility, or freedom from bladder-stones or scrofula. The musicians will be trying out their instruments, squabbling over the notes, and the child singers, dressed as little gods, already fainting under their canopies. It is the same everywhere. It will be the same, only bigger and louder, in Alexandria. Sabina has been told that he intends to enter that great city on an elephant-drawn chariot. (Not with her, he's not, she says redundantly.) Is he teasing his adjutants, who know he is entirely capable of demanding such a spectacle, insisting that it is not he who wants it but the crowd, who need their emperor to be extraordinary?

Nevertheless, after so many visits he is practised at arrivals and delivers what is expected; indeed, part of that delivery is to exceed what is expected. There is something magnificent in the performance and the inexorability of ceremony. However tired, however long the journey, he walks with dignity and, when all is said and done, majesty. So it will be here, entering by the Gate of the Sun between the trumpets and the troops, the prefect at his side, the guard and the priests accompanying him: he will enter his city, coming like a bridegroom to an unfamiliar bride. He will see her with the certainty of possession, she him with wonder, curiosity and fear. So Hadrian will walk up the dizzying white steps to the temple, slowly but without pausing for breath, always standing forward of his retinue so that the crowds may see him – not so far forward that they may *reach* him, but near enough that they feel they could. However bright the sun, his gaze around him is level; he never narrows his eyes in the glare, nor covers his head in the dizzying heat. Behind the emperor, the empress, her plain but beautifully dressed sister, Vibia Matidia, and her ladies. Behind them, smiling at the people, his great-nephew, Pedanius Fuscus, so full of young promise and, like Hadrian all those years ago, so full of hope. Beside him, Lucius Ceionius Commodus, a little older, his beautiful features an ornament to any parade of dynastic ambition, and between them, rightly uneasy if he knows their feelings for him, Antinous, honoured not by birth but by selection.

After Egypt I can go back to Athens, my duty done. All I ask now is that the journey passes safely and calmly and the wonders create their effects. Here on this gritty border they sell paltry copies of their country's monuments which they have never travelled to see themselves. A hand's-breadth sandstone colossus, or a sphinx the size and appearance of a dormouse, which will turn back into the mud it is made from in the first rainfall. Still, the soldiers provide a willing market for such absurdities. Everything in Egypt is for sale, from camp-followers to the ancient myths peddled by mendacious vendors. Even Sabina longs to see the altar of the purple phoenix and feed the sacred crocodiles. Wise priests who charge for the honour of saving themselves the cost of provisioning their scaly charges.

My friends who have seen Egypt say that these people would sell a story as easily as they would an ass. More easily, in fact, because the stock of stories is dependent only on imagination and a tongue to utter them, whereas oats are in finite supply. They stand by their monuments, inscribed in a language which no ordinary man can read, and, seeing that the weary visitor, dirty and far from home, appears a very ordinary man indeed, gush forth a farrago of rubbish about heroes and magical birds. He who revisits may find quite a different story attaches to this inscription or that.

Hadrian looks well and strong, despite the alleged illness which obsesses him and mystifies his physicians. The Egyptians and Greeks will get a return on their expense; he is every bit an emperor. Every bit a pharaoh. He is a charm which attracts crowds to him; the Egyptians understand these things. This morning I saw him in his open tent, standing taller than those around him, his skin browned by the journey but like a military man not a peasant, his hair lightened by the sun and a little shorter than he wore it when not travelling, his beard reddish and tight-curled. He looked happy and, despite the journey and the heat, relaxed. He is excited at the array of new beginnings which lie enticingly ahead.

And there too was the cause of his happiness. Never far away, when I glanced over, he was standing in the full sun, and he looked bored, picking up small stones from the track and skimming them at a small bird, then absently rubbing a groove in the sand with the toe of his foot. The new boy, same as the old boys – healthy, young, beautiful and almost certainly stupid. Or clever enough to keep his mouth shut and know that opinions are not required of the emperor's intimate companion. Those who talked least lasted longest. This one, with his thick, light brown hair, the tall fit body, the averted eyes, looked promising. I suppose he was the age Hadrian's son might have been. Harmless enough. He had walked to the horses where they stood in their shelter and he was suddenly animated, rubbing their muzzles, letting the beasts lower their heads and push against him, taking a handful of grain which he scooped from the bucket, straight from his hand. Sabina said he had been a groom. He was smiling now, the ordinary beauty of youth transformed into something more special, so perhaps it was true. It was a good thing he liked horses; he would need some friends. At that moment I saw the emperor's head turn across the earnest group of advisers and his eyes watch the boy as he stroked the animals. Perhaps this boy would do; would keep the emperor happy and occupied while they coped with Egypt.

Sabina says Hadrian believes that Egypt may provide a cure for his ills. They are simply the ills that beset us all, of course, the ills of passing years; but Hadrian wants to be immortal, and this becomes increasingly onerous, pitting body against will. Even as he sleeps old age creeps up on him, and the thought leaves him sleepless and tired. He wants to live for ever because he is so afraid of death. He is so afraid, I think, not of pain but that in dying others will finally triumph over him, will in outliving him see places and receive plaudits which should rightfully be his in perpetuity.

Sabina, on the other hand, greets advancing age happily. The usual benefits of youth – love, intrigue, children, a settled house – were never hers. Marriage reduced her portion rather than added to it. The empress in her jewels was destitute of what other women might take for granted. In middle age she is becoming quite reckless: she speaks out, though softly; she thinks about being indiscreet; dangerously, she makes much less effort to disguise her anger. She too, when not prostrated by heat, dreams of an Egyptian remedy, though she is not certain what it might be or where it might be used. Much as she may think she longs to soar free, she has never known liberty and were the cage to be opened, she would stand shivering at the door, having quite lost the memory of flight.

I have dreamed of Egypt all my life, of the chance to flesh out my grandfather's tales, yet now that we are here, the anticipation is touched with apprehension. I am frightened in part that the Egypt of my dreams and blood will prove too big, too extraordinary to allow this earthy Egypt to amaze me, and in part that I have left it too long and it is too much to encompass. I have written poetry to mark the visit, yet it now seems an impertinence to have done so. Why was I so excited? What did I think I would see? What gods must be placated? What scores might be settled in this place where the dead are so much present that the living fear to disturb them and go about their business overwhelmed by their small and temporary lives?

It is time to dress; to scour off the red earth which has covered everything, even behind the hangings of our litter. It is gritty in the hair, caught in the folds of our garments, yet the Egyptians will expect us to look as if we had passed straight from Rome to their borders. Sabina must play the empress. She will be dressed and be carried to Pelusium to walk at his side and be received by Flavius Titianus – a prefect who for once is nobody's cousin – and all the crowds who have never seen an emperor will marvel at his ease and elegance. How long we have all waited, in our different ways, to be here. This place has many marvels and many secrets and we bring our own to it.

In the summer heat of 130 CE Hadrian's retinue passed from Gaza in Judea along the Mediterranean coast, through Rhinocolura, the bleak easterly outpost of Egypt with its notorious penal settlement, to Pelusium. The moment of his arrival had been long planned on both sides, possibly with the intention that Hadrian should enter the kingdom at the height of the annual Nile floods, his presence a symbolic reflection of the fertility and wealth the waters brought to the country. The commemorative coinage had been minted, its imagery rich in compressed information about the relationship of the emperor and Egypt. He is shown arriving in state in Alexandria, as is Sabina. Many of the coins were largely religious in their symbolism – the range of gods a precursor of those whose statues would eventually fill Hadrian's villa back in Rome. Others portrayed the wealth of Egypt in terms of wheat and fruit being displayed or handed to Hadrian by personifications of the city or country; symbols of fertility abounded. This potentially pleasing cameo was a miscalculation – the first of many in Egypt – for the Nile could rarely be taken for granted and its fortunes were capricious; the 130 flood was proving to be inadequate and there was general unrest, presaging problems to come.

The coins were ready because the emperor's visit, and its obligatory success, had long been expected. The Egyptians had been amassing the food and resources to support a sophisticated modern ruler and his court; Hadrian had established a precedent of generosity in his earlier travels which ensured that he would be a most welcome guest, but before

Egypt could benefit similarly it needed to invest in the emperor's satisfaction.

The Greek population of Egypt prepared to welcome the most powerful of all Hellenophiles with considerable enthusiasm. At Alexandria the city was filling up with those wanting to celebrate or exploit Hadrian's arrival, and intellectuals, writers and artists flocked to take up residence, hoping to be included in the cultural revival that was charged by the emperor's presence. But the delightful prospect of profit and entertainment was not universal. Farming communities surveyed the year's poor Nile floods with bewilderment; the prospect was of a bad harvest, yet there were demands to increase a quantity of agricultural produce already eroded by the demands of Rome's domestic economy. Fragments of surviving documents from Oxyrhyncus hint at the quantities of food needed for even a short, local imperial visit: one year in advance of the emperor's arrival orders were submitted for 200 artabs of barley, 3,000 bundles of hay, 327 suckling pigs and 200 sheep. (An artab or ardeb was a Coptic Greek measure equal to approximately 5.62 bushels. The amount stipulated here would have filled a small barn and provided perhaps 100,000 loaves.)

Hadrian was received with great pomp as both emperor and pharaoh of a country which at the time of his arrival had been under Roman rule for just 160 years. Egypt was well used to foreign rule; since 525 BCE it had been dominated by the Persians, then the Greeks, then the Macedonian Ptolemies whose descendant, Cleopatra, had been defeated by the Romans in 31 BCE at the Battle of Actium. But Egypt was still a problematic and unfathomable province; a destination which could deliver reward or disaster with little predictability. The success or otherwise of Hadrian's visit might leave the local Egyptians facing either prosperity or ruin, but he too was vulnerable; for Hadrian, too, there was more at stake than a triumphant demonstration of rank and power. In Egypt, Hadrian had a personal as well as a political agenda to fulfil.

Egypt staggered under the weight of its own history. No second-century Roman, least of all the most powerful among them, could enter the province of Egypt merely as a sightseer. There could be no innocent, unencumbered appreciation of its geographical and historical wonders. Rome's extraordinary growth had encompassed some alien and perplexing cultures, but no part of the empire carried more symbolic freight than this most desirable and troubling of Roman acquisitions. Egypt was a precious possession, its fertility always one of its principal attractions to predators. The Greeks had not sought to deplete the country's assets, but under the Romans the agricultural prosperity of Egypt diminished as its wealth, particularly its corn, was shipped back to feed the ever-increasing demands of the population in Rome. In return, the Romans did what they were good at: set their armies and engineers to improving connections and restoring and extending the crucial irrigation that brought more land into use – land which would feed Rome. While the hungry waited for Egypt's corn, better-fed Romans were inspired by Egypt's distinctive imagery; the antique art and style of the new province were emulated enthusiastically back in Italy by the wealthy and the fashionable – just as they would be again by the British of the early nineteenth century, inspired by the growth of travel and the explorations of archaeologists. The famous Roman landmark of the pyramid tomb of the first-century BCE praetor Gaius Cestius, erected only a few years after the Battle of Actium, is a surviving relic of this cultural infusion. To the Romans, Egypt was exciting: incomprehensible, with a pleasing hint of malignity.

Egypt was geographically and spiritually unique. The life and wealth of a land which was in effect two broad river banks and a highly fertile delta, was entirely dependent on the vagaries of the Nile floods which, in turn depending on the amount of summer rain which fell far away in the mountains of Ethiopia, annually deposited a rich silt on agricultural land. Roman artists, architects and poets marvelled at the Nile's fertility:

Sluggish Nile pours forth her waters, and the lucky tribe of Pellan Canopus farm their lands, patrolling them in painted boats; where the borders of quiver-bearing Persis press close, and the river that flows all the way from the dark Indians empties through its seven mouths, making Egypt green with silt.[1]

Roman emperors and civil servants lived in less comfortable collusion with an esoteric set of rituals and appeasements enacted to ensure that the river would feed her people and, by extension, Rome. Rome found itself having to react to the vagaries of climate and topography in this alien land whose history and beliefs were both disturbing and challenging to Roman habits of thought and behaviour. The extraordinary architectural remains of the pharaohs, seen by Romans from the height of their powers, could be viewed as a threatening object lesson in the transience of even the greatest nations, much as the ruins of ancient Greece and Rome itself were to evoke melancholy, if appealing, uncertainty in European travellers of the eighteenth and nineteenth centuries. But there were political as well as imaginative tensions. Egypt, then as now, had been at the centre of political and violent conflict in comparatively recent history. Rome was continually aware that the strategic and economic importance of Egypt made it attractive to other predatory states, some of which were not so far away. Any independent power base in the east was a serious challenge to the authority of Rome and must never be allowed to arise. The memory of Mark Antony and his attempts to create a new eastern Hellenistic empire had not yet died. So sensitive was the situation under Augustus that the emperor prohibited independent visits to the new province by Roman senators and eminent knights.

Superimposed on Egyptian antiquity was the culture of the dominant Greek population who had colonized Egypt, creating the Ptolemaic kingdom after the early death of Alexander the Great in 323 BCE. The first Ptolemy was a Macedonian general and he maintained the character of the Egyptian nation, ruling as pharaoh; a subtle balance which the conquering Romans were to continue. The influence of the early Ptolemies had enriched the intellectual life of the country, but the dynasty had become increasingly self-indulgent and notoriously weakened by the established practice of sibling marriage. When Cleopatra VII failed in her bid to break away from Rome and re-establish an autonomous power with Mark Antony, committing suicide to avoid the humiliation of public display and retribution, her son became the last of the line. During the reign of the Ptolemies the powerful Egyptian priests were indulged with elaborate temples, but the Greeks also introduced their own cultural spirit and under their aegis fine cities and seats of art and learning had been established. Alexandria, founded by Alexander the Great in 331 BCE, was in the first century, in its amalgam of cultures, a more elegant, civilised and learned metropolis than Rome could conceivably hope to be.

For Hadrian, Egypt, particularly the sophisticated north, was undoubtedly an attractive destination. He had come with the intention of founding his own Hellenistic city at some time during his stay there, and the museum and libraries – in effect a university – at Alexandria must have been an irresistible attraction for a man who prided himself on his intellectual breadth. It also made political sense that from a comparatively stable atmosphere in Rome, Hadrian should visit the place where Rome's future had been fought over, where, the republic had died and where Augustus himself had both fought and travelled.

Most interesting of all, it is at this point in Hadrian's travels that it first becomes clear that the emperor had his favourite, a Greek adolescent called Antinous, with him. Antinous, never mentioned in the ancient histories until Hadrian's stay in Egypt, was to become central to the whole account of the emperor's time there. It was not, however, Hadrian's sexual choices that cast a shadow over his reputation; the question of his homosexuality became a problem only because of events in these few weeks which revealed the extent of his attachment.

Rumours of Hadrian's homosexuality surfaced quite early on in his life, and several named individuals have been suggested as his sexual partners. Suggestions of sexual impropriety and excess were commonplace in accounts of Roman nobility. Many of Hadrian's predecessors were recorded as having some or even exclusively relationships with men: Julius Caesar, Tiberius, Nero and Domitian were perhaps the most notorious. Others were equally enthusiastic but attracted less calumny. This sort of gossip was par for the course, and Hadrian's biographers made generalised but half-hearted assertions of both homosexual and adulterous diversions. Nevertheless, by the age of twenty-one Hadrian was apparently squabbling with the (otherwise virtuous) emperor Trajan over some boys, and it does seem that his marriage soon afterwards was undertaken at least in part to restore him to the emperor's good offices. As we have already seen, Hadrian's marriage to Sabina is widely believed to have been unhappy, but again, personal happiness had no great place within patrician marriage and there is no indication that sexual orientation had any place in their mutual antipathy. Hadrian had no children, but many emperors had barren marriages; where bloodline was not a necessary aspect of succession, and where adoption of adults as well as children was an accepted convention, the matter of an heir was less crucial than in the autocracies of other cultures and times. Sabina was, however, in Egypt, as she was on most of the emperor's travels. So too, now, was Antinous. What effect the arrangements had on domestic concord can only be imagined; but in any case it appears that by this time the emperor and empress were hardly on speaking terms.

In Greek society, sexual relationships between an older man and a youth were part of the fabric of society, accepted, even idealised. But Hadrian, whatever he might be coming to believe, was a Roman emperor, and Romans were less tolerant and more cynical about the beauty of homosexual passion. Nevertheless, it was commonplace in the army, and more widely it was not unusual for a man to have a variety of partners of either sex. There was no question of a man being defined, as now, by his sexual preferences, nor, as long as he was the dominant party, was there any conflict between homosexual practice and virility. However, whatever the public view of relationships between men – and public acceptance was certainly less institutionalised outside the Greek elite – involvements of this kind left Hadrian vulnerable to criticism. The moral issue was elusive; some emperors, like Julius Caesar and Trajan, had preserved their reputations relatively untarnished by associations with partners of the same sex. For others, notably Nero, Domitian and Elagabalus, and usually within a package of other baroque accusations of decadence, sexual indulgence undercut imperial authority. Discretion was crucial. So it is quite possible that, as with all his other Hellenic pursuits, Hadrian felt freer to indulge in such activities outside Rome, and that this was one motive for his incessant journeys outside the city. It is also possible that a homosexual relationship was more attractive to Hadrian simply as an *idea* than one with a woman; that it fulfilled an aesthetic as well as a sexual desire. Certainly his biographers reflect on his liking for all things Greek almost immediately before commenting on his pursuit of young men. Whatever his emotional or physical involvement with Antinous, the relationship itself was a decidedly Hellenistic accessory.

So Hadrian and Sabina entered Egypt. Their choice of route was not an obvious one. Pelusium took advantage of a fine logistical situation and was sited on the eastern mouth of the Nile as it branched into the wide delta, facing the sea. The fertile coastal strip was under cultivation; the town was laid out on a grid pattern and fortified. To the south, though, the land soon became gritty and arid, eventually rising into mountains. Why did Hadrian arrive overland through Pelusium, which meant that subsequently he had to cross the marshy tributaries of the delta? Why not arrive by sea into the city most fit to greet an emperor, Alexandria?

Once the party had decided to go overland – probably because it made the imperial progress more visible – Pelusium was quite simply the first stopping place of any charm or size in many days' travel. It was the main port at the north-eastern border of Egypt. However, the town also had several symbolic connections which made it inevitable that Hadrian would pass through it, and that he would take steps to make sure he would be associated with it in the future. For a start, Pelusium had been the place where the all-time heroic exemplar, Alexander the Great, had received the surrender of the Persians almost 400 years before. At Pelusium, Egypt had become Greek. But Hadrian's most explicit intention was to honour a more recent hero. His first recorded action in Egypt was to find the tomb of the Roman republican general, Gnaeus Pompeius Magnus – Pompey the Great – who had been murdered in 48 BCE, aged fifty-eight, as he arrived to an uncertain welcome in Egypt after the débâcle of the Battle of Pharsalus on the plains of Thessaly.[2] The dramatic and poignant story of Pompey's death was well known, and was retold by the historian Appian writing in the time of Hadrian. Its themes of danger, impenetrability, betrayal and violent death were the themes of Egypt as a whole. Egypt might feed Rome, but little good had ever come to any Roman who tried to rely on her.

For these reasons he sailed to Egypt, whence Cleopatra, who had previously reigned with her brother, had lately been expelled, and was collecting an army in Syria. Ptolemy, her brother, was at Casium in Egypt, lying in wait for her invasion, and, as providence would have it, the wind carried Pompey thither. Seeing a large army on the shore he stopped his ship, rightly judging that the king was there. So he sent his messengers to tell of his arrival and to speak of his father's friendship. The king was then about thirteen years of age and was under the tutelage of Achillas who commanded the army, and the eunuch Pothinus, who had charge of his treasury. These took counsel together concerning Pompey. There was present also Theodotus, a rhetorician of Samos, the boy's tutor, who offered the infamous advice that they should lay a trap for Pompey and kill him in order to curry favour with Caesar. His opinion prevailed. So they sent a miserable skiff to bring him, pretending that the sea was shallow and not adapted to large ships. Some of the king's attendants came in the skiff, among them a Roman named Sempronius, who was then serving in the king's army and had formerly served under Pompey himself. He gave his hand to Pompey in the king's name and directed him to take passage in the boat as to a friend. At the same time the whole army was marshalled along the shore as if to do honour to Pompey, and the king was conspicuous in the midst of them by the purple robe he wore.

Pompey's suspicions were aroused by all that he observed – the marshalling of the army, the meanness of the skiff, and the fact that the king did not come to meet him nor send any of his high dignitaries. Nevertheless, he entered the skiff, repeating to himself these lines of Sophocles, 'whoso resorts to a tyrant becomes a slave, even if he be free when he goes'. While rowing to shore all were silent, and this made him still more suspicious. Finally recognising Sempronius as a Roman soldier who had served under him, or guessing that he was such because he alone remained standing (for according to military discipline, a soldier does not sit in the presence of his commander), he turned to him and said, 'Do I not know you comrade?' The other nodded and, as Pompey turned away, he immediately gave him the first stab and the others followed his example. Pompey's wife and friends who saw this at a distance cried out and lifting their hands to heaven, invoked the gods, the avengers of violated faith. Then they sailed away in all haste as from an enemy's country.[3]

It was a sad and sordid end to a spectacular, if ruthless, career. Decapitated when the boat landed, the corpse had drifted in the wash at the beach edge. A substantial tomb was eventually erected by Pompey's family at Pelusium. (Although there is a monument known as Pompey's Pillar in Alexandria, this has nothing to do with Pompey's grave, nor even, possibly, with Pompey.) It was impossible terrain for a permanent memorial; like so much in Egypt it was soon engulfed by the sands, and the statues which marked the last resting place of the once powerful Gnaeus Pompeius fell, or were defaced or moved to other locations. In less than a century the monument had disappeared.

Pompey was not alone in coming to grief in Egypt during the unsettled first century BCE. Julius Caesar temporarily survived his relationship with Cleopatra, but Mark Antony, finding his reputation in decline and having failed to found his new world order at the side of his Egyptian queen, with no political options left to him committed suicide there.

Pompey had fought successfully to secure the east for the empire, initially as an ally of Julius Caesar and member of the ruling triumvirate, and ultimately in opposition to him. His head was taken back to Caesar as proof of his death; but it was not the triumph his murderers had expected. Caesar, once Pompey's friend, was appalled at the act of mutilation, even of an enemy. Pompey's head is still familiar today, for several statues and coins of him have survived, and his is an instantly recognisable face: broad, amiable rather than strong, with a puzzled brow and thick hair whose quiff to the front – known as *anastole* – was consciously modelled on the hairstyle of Alexander the Great. The images date from a time in which realism was a central part of portraiture, and Pompey's personality and aspirations are powerfully depicted.

Homage to dead heroes was a recurring theme in Hadrian's travels, and when he arrived at the site of Pompey's burial at Mons Casius, he followed his own precedent in taking a decision to reinstate the tomb. The sand was removed and the original decoration tracked down, and the restored tomb became a monument to both Pompey and Hadrian with, given the situation, oblique reference to Alexander. The emperor, much of an age with Pompey at the time of his murder, sacrificed at the spot and wrote an epigram to mark his reaction to the monument and, in passing, his own agenda: *'how mean a tomb for one so well-endowed with shrines'*. It was a fine gesture; but before Hadrian had even left the country, the sands were engulfing Pompey again. At the same time Hadrian's own mausoleum was being constructed on the bank of the Tiber back in Rome: a far from mean tomb, so vast that neither sand nor time would ever destroy it.

The recognition of Pompey had other resonances which gave a hint of troubles to come. Pompey was famed for his destruction of Jerusalem in 63 BCE and Hadrian's recent actions – establishing a brand new metropolis to replace the Jewish city – made this a highly sensitive area. The Jewish presence in Egyptian affairs was significant in the history of both peoples. The original twelve tribes of Israel had emigrated to Egypt when famine made life in their homeland untenable. As immigrants, they led miserable and impoverished lives and were led back to Canaan by Moses in the thirteenth century BCE. The Jewish diaspora under the Greeks and Romans saw the Jews scattered around the countries of the empire, leading lives whose conditions varied markedly according to the tolerance of individual ruling regimes. There are some estimates that at its peak, when Egypt was a popular place of exile, the population of Jews in the country numbered a million, many of them in Alexandria. Certainly Egypt had once had a Jewish population which was sufficiently large for both Jews and Greeks to feel a sense of mutual threat and to send emissaries to Rome to plead their respective causes. The Jews had felt at that time, in the reign of the otherwise notorious Caligula, that their pleas might be heard sympathetically by imperial Rome, and were represented by Philo in an audience with the emperor.

When the Jewish delegations from Alexandria arrived in Rome in 40 CE, they did so in response to the worst outbreak of violence against their people that had yet been known. The deteriorating conditions of Jewish life there had ultimately resulted in the first pogrom in Jewish history and it was, in effect, sanctioned by Rome. Caligula was not noticeably anti-semitic; he treated the Jews no worse than he did other envoys. Nevertheless, as the emissaries traipsed after the emperor while he amused himself by asking them why they refused to eat pork and demanding they set up a statue to him in the Temple in Jerusalem and recognise him as a god, they cannot have felt optimistic that their arguments would be given full consideration. It was not until the succeeding emperor, Caligula's ill-favoured but earnest uncle, Claudius, came to power that the position of the Jews improved. It was no coincidence that Claudius was an emperor whose actions and vision were almost entirely Roman in spirit. Caligula's assassination was followed by Jewish riots in Alexandria. Unencumbered by Hellenic interests, Claudius had the riot suppressed and its leaders executed, but shortly afterwards issued an edict which recognised the Jews' status as full citizens of Alexandria and their right to follow different customs from the Romans and Greeks.

Claudius' enlightened solution allowed peace to survive for a quarter of a century, further disturbances breaking out again only in the uncertain times of Nero. Firmness and tolerance: here was a model for how the Jews could be incorporated successfully into the empire. It was a combination the Jews may have hoped Hadrian would emulate ninety years later – and it was one which, in the event, he completely ignored.

In the early second century a Jewish revolt had spread from Cyrenaica, the province immediately to the west of Egypt that is now Libya, to Alexandria and beyond into wider Egypt and then to Judea. Trajan had quelled the riots forcefully, and the casualties and expulsions were such that the Jewish presence and influence in Egypt were virtually extinguished. The area around Pelusium, where Hadrian now honoured Pompey, the scourge of Judea, had been one of the centres of the Jewish uprising. Fifteen years later there were few Jews left in Egypt outside Alexandria, but the country bordered Judea and rumours spread fast. Thus it is not fanciful to see Hadrian's first action in Egypt as sending a disturbing message to the already troubled Jewish communities of the east. That he should do so is not surprising. Hadrian's early restorative moves had included making good damage caused during the Jewish revolt, but the intended statement was clear: he was not moving on in a spirit of reconciliation, he was making a formidable declaration about the pointlessness of Jewish resistance and the inexorability of Roman progress. Hadrian was denying their cause, not accepting it. The Greeks, invariably opposed to Jewish customs and influence, kept the fervour of antisemitism alight, and Hadrian was to espouse their cause as he did all things Greek. Of all Hadrian's Hellenophile stances, this identification was to have particularly disastrous consequences.

The details of what Hadrian saw and did in Egypt are vague. But here it is easier to speculate than in respect of other countries for which sources are sparse, as it was an established destination for wealthy travellers. Between the known destinations, where foundations or inscriptions confirm the emperor's presence, there are sights which all cultured Romans visited and some, like the tomb of Alexander, which

Hadrian would have found irresistible. Alexander was laid in state in the city he had founded. A previous imperial visit had not been a complete success; Augustus, passing his hands over the inspirational features of the conqueror's corpse, broke off his nose. Whether it was repaired or the emperor removed it as a relic is unrecorded. For the first weeks of his visit Hadrian intended to stay in Alexandria: the jewel of Greek cities, founded nearly five centuries earlier, the envy of the civilised world and the particular envy of Rome. The founding of coastal Alexandria, with its wide harbours, had signalled the end of the inward-looking world of the early pharaohs, with their capital, Memphis, in the centre of the country, and the birth of a great trading nation exchanging goods and ideas with the Mediterranean world. Alexandria was refined, economically successful, beautifully laid out and logistically unparalleled in situation. The sprawling city of Rome was larger, but Alexandria had no peer. In Alexandria were parks and gardens, palaces, shrines and a zoo. The city was rich in sights to please even the most jaded traveller, and its architecture laid out its cultural and intellectual claims to pre-eminence. The pharaoh-emperor's arrival was the most extraordinary occasion most Egyptians would ever see.

Contemporary coinage shows Hadrian entering Alexandria on an elephant-drawn chariot of a type that was normally pulled by four horses. It is possible that this was more than metaphor and that Hadrian did lay on such a dramatic spectacle; but it seems more likely that from Pelusium's port he took a ship westwards round the northern coast. The delta was still flooded and there was a prevailing custom prohibiting the passage of Egypt's rulers on the Nile in flood. Equally, there were superstitions regarding sea journeys: for instance, late in the month was not generally considered a propitious time to set out to sea, and it was moving towards late August. The twenty-fourth of August, in particular, was viewed as a disastrous date. But if the summer weather was good, despite the passage being against the prevailing winds, the journey could have been accomplished in less time than a journey across the flooded delta with its numerous tributaries.

Approaching Alexandria from the sea, the uniqueness of the city was proclaimed long before the details of the fine harbour could be made out. On an island connected to the mainland by a narrow, man-made isthmus was the great Pharos lighthouse, with a statue of the sea-god, Poseidon, resplendent on its summit. The light from the constantly burning fire in the Pharos lantern was magnified by a mirror which was capable of reflecting it for a distance of 35 miles out to sea. Erected in the mid-third century BCE and designed by Sostratus, a contemporary of Euclid, the lighthouse was an incomparable accomplishment, in terms of both visual impact and engineering. It was later to be accepted as one of the Seven Wonders of the World (the concept of the Seven Wonders was well known long before Hadrian's day, but the lighthouse was not included in the canon until perhaps the sixth century CE). It was the only one to have a functional as well as an aesthetic role; and by the second century it had already become a tourist attraction; important visitors could dine on a viewing platform offering a panoramic view of the city, its hinterland and harbours.

Alexandria's buildings reflected the breadth of its intellectual life. Here were the magnificent library and the Mouseion – in effect a great academy, unequalled throughout the empire, with its four faculties of medicine, literature, astronomy and mathematics; the obtaining of dining rights here was a fiercely contested honour. Among the presidents of the Mouseion had been Julia Balbilla's grandfather, Claudius Balbillus. The library contained half a million books and at its zenith it was said that it held a copy of every available manuscript in the world. Hadrian appointed various learned men to its number, but, in the company of so many great minds, was unable to resist the intellectual competitiveness for which he had become renowned. One biographer observed wryly: 'In the museum of Alexandria he propounded many questions to the teachers and answered himself what he had asked.'[4] All manner of gods were venerated in Egypt, and an enormous rise of steps led to the famous Shrine of Serapis on the heights of the city. Here the emperor too was worshipped, in the finest temple in Alexandria.

But Alexandria was not only for the high-minded. There was something for everyone. There was *everything* for everyone. The lure of the sensual and the arcane attracted Romans who believed that any service or experience could be bought there. The city nightlife was legendary; later that century a Greek writer was to describe the Street of the Blessed, where every conceivable vice and luxury could be obtained.[5] Alexandria had a reputation for materialism every bit as powerful as that for intellectualism. One less captivated visitor wrote, *unus illis deus nummus est* – they only have one god there: hard cash.

The Romans were both fascinated and repelled by what they perceived as the corrupt and bizarre aspects of Egypt. Egyptians, they observed, were simultaneously primitive and complex, brutal and sensual. These perceived contradictions persisted over the centuries, apparent alike in the oriental fantasies of nineteenth-century Europeans and the image of the relatively modern city of Port Said as stereotypical of infinite corruption. Founded in 1859 to service the Suez Canal, Port Said soon became a byword for eastern depravity and European susceptibility. In the second century Canopus, in the west of the country, was similarly considered the dazzling focus of excess and libertinage. With time to kill while the Nile floods receded, Hadrian went off to this notoriously louche resort to the east of Alexandria. It evidently delighted him – and, by implication, his young lover; it was later to be reproduced in stylised form at

Hadrian's villa at Tivoli, back in Italy. In Canopus the attractions and mysteries of Egypt were compressed. It was a place both of religious breadth and luxurious pleasure. In the town itself, in the famous Temple of Serapis, the sick in mind or body might sleep and undergo a dream cure; in the rows of inns and pretty villas alternative diversions were on offer. On the road to the town, running alongside the canal, the atmosphere was lively and untroubled. One moralising ancient visitor after another – Strabo, Propertius, Augustus, Seneca, Juvenal – condemned its contradictions in lubricious terms.[6] Just to go there was to be condemned by association. How could it be resisted?

It contains the temple of Serapis which is honoured with great reverence and effects such cures that even the most reputable men believe in it and go there either in person, or have others do it for them. Some writers record cures and others the virtues of the oracles there. But on the other hand there is the crowd of revellers who go down from Alexandria by the canal to the public festivals; for every night and day there are crowds on the boats who play flutes and dance without restraint and with extreme licentiousness, with each other and the Canopeans who have places close to the canal adapted to relaxation and carrying-on of this kind.[7]

For Hadrian, the combination of the esoteric and the sensual held compelling charm. Whether or not he spent a night in the temple in the hope of deflecting whatever malign fortune he felt threatened him is unknown. Possibly he deputed Antinous to represent him in sleep. It may even be from Canopus that Hadrian finally began the river journey which was central to his Egyptian visit. By mid-autumn 130, the floods had abated and the imperial party was finally able to embark on a flotilla which would take it on the long journey upriver to Philae, 886 kilometres south of what is now Cairo and was then Heliopolis.

From the beginning of the trip to Egypt there had been strange rumours. The dark anecdotes which make up much of the story of Hadrian's stay in Egypt nearly all reflect a deep unease and the gradual emergence of the negative aspects of the emperor's character. Despite the beautiful companion at his side, it seems that from the time he left Athens in 129 Hadrian was more introspective and more uneasy. How much of the account of the Egyptian tour has grown up as a dramatic framework to what happened next is impossible to clarify, but there was some kind of shadow hanging over the party and the tension was exacerbated by the volatile situation in Egypt itself.

It is perfectly conceivable that the suggestible Hadrian had taken Secundus' words as prophecy rather than rhetoric. It may have been that his casting of his own horoscope had revealed impending disaster; or that he had himself inadvertently predicted the hour of his death. So far, Hadrian's occasional explorations into the occult had been gratifying – he was, after all, emperor, just as the fortune-tellers had foretold; but when the signs began to look less positive it was hard for him to disregard less welcome results. If so, his actions may well have precipitated the very catastrophe the horoscope predicted. It is equally possible that the explanation may have been much more prosaic: that the emperor felt unwell after a recent illness, or that in passing through Judea he sensed – correctly – that the province was in a state of tension which might yet explode, damaging all that he had achieved in his reign so far.

Whatever Hadrian's pre-existing anxieties, the atmosphere in Egypt could only add to them. The Nile flood, on which the economic prosperity of Egypt depended, was always nervously awaited; poor floods brought poverty, starvation and unrest. The flood had been poor the year before Hadrian's visit, and it was poor again while he was actually in the country. The visit itself was draining local resources. It was a discouraging background to what was supposed to be a triumphant visit. In Africa some years earlier, Hadrian's arrival had coincided with the first rain for five years. In Egypt, uniquely among the provinces of his empire, Hadrian was considered to have supernatural powers; yet they were powers he was apparently failing to use to alleviate the problems Egypt faced.

Again, it is in discrete, vivid stories that the strange mood of the tour is made clear; again, the incidents they describe draw a broader, and stranger, picture of the emperor than the chronological histories.

The oases which sit among huge, rolling dunes to the west of Alexandria are rich with date palms, fruit trees and olives, but around them stretch hundreds of miles of sand and rocky plateau. The seemingly bare sands of the Western Desert sustained a variety of wildlife, and the terrain was a challenge to Hadrian. Some time before he set off on the journey down the Nile, Hadrian had a few days' hunting. At his side was the young Antinous. This moment of apparently innocent pleasure is captured on a carving on a tondo at Rome and in a scrap of poetry, commissioned by Hadrian and found in a cache of papyri in the desert. It is remarkable because there are no descriptions of Hadrian and the young man who was the supposed love of his life enjoying themselves together at any other time. There is no account of them being together at all – no accounts of games or plays, music or sightseeing, although there is an implication that Antinous was initiated into the mysteries at Athens with the emperor. Beyond that, either Antinous was unimportant or the biographers were exceptionally – and unusually – discreet. But in September 130 there they were, setting out together to pursue a lion in the deserts of Egypt. Whether Hadrian was still hunting regularly in his fifties we do not know; this is the last time his hunting is mentioned in accounts of his life. The impression of an ageing emperor trying to impress a beautiful youth is hard to dismiss. But the outing was not quite as straightforward as the heroic images might suggest; the value of Antinous' life was about to be made explicit.

There were rumours that the huge beast had been terrorising a neighbouring province. Here was an excellent opportunity for Hadrian to combine his passion for sport with a demonstration of imperial solicitude. Hadrian's skill and courage were undoubted; he had felled a boar single-handedly, and on another occasion had broken a collarbone and narrowly missed crushing his leg. A city near Balikeşir in modern north-western Turkey was named Hadrianoutherae – meaning Hadrian's Hunting Ground – possibly after a successful bear hunt. The bear is adduced from the coinage, which shows Hadrian striking her from horseback. Other coins had been issued in the past which showed the emperor in manly pursuit of wild animals. He was even called 'god of the chase' in one city – a soubriquet which can only have delighted him. It was a virile, youthful image which he now needed to live up to. It was to be an instructive outing.

A hunting party was drawn up and Hadrian and Antinous left on horseback equipped with spears, Hadrian's tipped with bronze, befitting his rank, and Antinous' with steel. Hadrianoutherae and its expanse of hunting territory were not far west of Antinous' homeland, so it is possible that Antinous had learned to hunt as a child; nevertheless he was immediately out of his depth in the Western Desert. A large and starving lion which had already killed several human beings was not the same test as a Bithynian boar. When the lion was finally tracked down and charged, Hadrian deliberately provoked it by inflicting a non-lethal wound. When the animal went berserk, foaming, tearing up the ground and then bringing down Antinous' horse, Antinous was insufficiently skilled to deflect its charge and Hadrian intervened to save the boy's life.

It was a spectacular piece of erotic power play. The dynamic of the incident was more like a bullfight than a spontaneous hunting trip; this was no casual escape from the routines of court life, but a further staged, almost choreographed, display. The experienced Hadrian did not just fail to kill his quarry with his first shot, nor did he merely provide an opportunity for Antinous to enjoy the glory of the actual kill. Part of the sport *was* Antinous. Hadrian acted as a traditional picador, injuring the animal without despatching it; the less-adept Antinous was cast unwittingly into the role of toreador, a role which he was quite unable to fill. At stake for the toreador are not just courage and skill but masculinity. It was a test Antinous publicly and humiliatingly failed. All was as it should be: Hadrian had displayed courage and the prowess for which he was renowned; Antinous had been reminded of his place.

Within days, Hadrian was involved in another strange piece of careful cruelty. His compulsion to seek out the esoteric may well have been heightened by his own sense of impending disaster, but it is possible that the pursuit of novelty was beginning to take him in ever riskier directions. In an encounter which has echoes of the chilling disregard for human life exposed in his exchanges with the Greek philosopher Secundus, Hadrian visited an Egyptian magician known as Pachrates (or Pancrates) in Heliopolis, south-east of Alexandria. In both stories the intelligent and generally benevolent Hadrian suddenly appears to have acquired the characteristics of a Tiberius or Domitian. In Heliopolis Hadrian paid, and paid handsomely, for the magician to destroy a man in front of the emperor, by magic. It is possible, though unlikely, that Hadrian was simply curious; given the nature of the performance put on by the magician, it is more likely that he was seeking a powerful charm himself, and with a degree of desperation. Not only was it bizarre behaviour for an emperor, but Hadrian showed his delight and relief at the lethal efficacy of the charm by paying Pachrates double for demonstrating his power.

Many hundreds of years later the strange and anomalous tale, dismissed as myth by many historians, was given substance when an ancient account of it was found. It was one of history's startling tricks; the substantial text of Hadrian's memoirs, an invaluable source had it survived, had disappeared into time, and the unprotected and apparently inconsequential fragment that was the spell had survived in the desert sands.

Take a field mouse and deify it in spring water. And take two moon beetles and deify them in river water, and take a river crab and fat of a dappled goat that is virgin and dung of a dog-faced baboon, 2 eggs of ibis, 2 grams of storax, 2 drams of myrrh, 2 drams of crocus, 4 drams of Italian galingale, 4 grams of uncut frankincense, a single onion. Put all these things onto a mortar with the mouse and the remaining items and after pounding thoroughly, place in a lead box and keep for use. And whenever you want to perform a rite, take a little, make a charcoal fire, go up on a lofty roof and make the offering as you say this spell at moonrise and at once she comes.

Pachrates, the prophet of Heliopolis, revealed it to the Emperor Hadrian, revealing the power of his own divine magic. For it attracted in one hour; it made someone sick in 2 hours; it destroyed in 7 hours, sent the emperor himself dreams as he thoroughly tested the whole truth of the magic within his power. And marvelling at the prophet he ordered double fees to be given to him.[8]

The details of the spell are almost culinary, so much so that the powers of the potion are almost incidental. The seemingly incomprehensible raising of small rodents to gods, merely by immersion in river water, presumably that of the Nile, is a tiny forerunner of much greater rituals of the dead to which Hadrian was to find himself party not long afterwards. But it appears that Hadrian bought not only a performance of magic but the spell itself. How he intended to apply it is a mystery. As emperor he already had power to order life or death – he had demonstrated that to Secundus, just as Pachrates demonstrated it to him – but in his greed to possess and direct the future Hadrian had moved from fortune-telling to necromancy.

Pachrates' display took place in Heliopolis. Long subsumed into the north-eastern part of modern Cairo, in the second century it was a cult centre, dedicated to the sun and full of priests and magicians. Anything could happen at Heliopolis, and it was no accident that Hadrian was drawn there to increase his knowledge of the dark arts. Heliopolis was the home of the mythical phoenix, the splendid bird which created itself and then at the appointed time built a funeral pyre of sweet-smelling woods and spices and voluntarily sacrificed itself, singing as it burned, with its body turned to the sun, only to rise again from its own ashes. Its story was strongly represented in Egyptian mythology; the cycle of its death and regeneration was supposed to coincide with the rising of the star Sirius, which preceded the rising of the Nile. After Hadrian's visit the bird was also occasionally shown on his coinage – possibly after he had been told of its sighting as he came to power, possibly because after his experiences in Heliopolis he had more reason to consider its message of transformation and resurrection.

The two stories, of the lion-hunt and of Pachrates' spell, were bizarrely linked by an extraordinary coincidence. From the end of the nineteenth century onwards numerous papyri were found at Oxyrhyncus in the Western Desert. These were not always complete, but they were unique, exciting, and marvellously preserved by the hot dry conditions. The finds included both familiar and hitherto unknown texts, mostly in Greek. Among the discoveries is a fragment of a work by the poet Pancrates which modern biographers believe is the same Pachrates who, to impress the emperor, arbitrarily summoned up a man's death. The poem describes the terrifying ecstasy of Hadrian's and Antinous' desert hunt – and is almost certainly written by the magician of Heliopolis who had the power over life and death.

Both spell and poem throw a disturbing light on the actions of the emperor in the few weeks before he travelled down the Nile and into calamity. Hadrian, tired, ageing, preoccupied by the joys and anxieties of his love affair, balancing the administration of routine affairs of state with the commissioning of ambitious development schemes throughout the empire, can only have been vulnerable to the unsettling effects of all that he was experiencing in Egypt. There was Greek rationality; but there were also the unfamiliar beliefs and superstitions of the Egyptians and the weight of a history which, unlike the Hellenic past, was not enlightening but static and oppressive. He had longed to go to Egypt; and yet the problems he found there seemed insuperable on both a personal and a political level. His energy was impeded and his curiosity had turned into apprehension. It is not surprising that the more aggressive and morbid aspects of his personality came to the fore in this period.

As he set off down the Nile, Egypt's traditional attractions lay ahead: the Pyramids, the ancient capital of the pharaohs and the home of the sacred Apis bull at Memphis, the renowned Sphinx. Maybe Hadrian felt confident that his new magic had armoured him against his fears; but disaster was to strike within weeks.

Just one hour's bus ride eastwards out of Rome, the appealing hill town of Palestrina has a typically medieval flavour, with its differing levels of terracotta roofs and its labyrinthine layout. The small squares are heavily shaded with trees and in the town centre is a statue of Palestrina's most famous son, the sixteenth-century composer of the same name. Stepped lanes wind in hairpin bends up the steep hill between tall, shuttered houses, finally reaching the curved front of the Palazzo Barberini. But the shape of the town is dictated by its former existence as Praeneste, and Palestrina is home to a wonderful survival of the ancient Roman fascination with Egypt.

Since the eighth century BCE Praeneste had been the home of a vast temple to Fortuna Primigenia, last rebuilt in 2 BCE. The terraces of the temple are now the foundations of the medieval town. In summer 1944, with the war in Italy drawing to a close, Allied aircraft bombed Palestrina. The goddess Fortune protected her own and the resulting damage usefully exposed a whole unknown segment of the ancient construction. In antiquity Praeneste housed a famous oracle, and excavations there have revealed several treasures, mostly of them on the site of the temple itself, and most of them since carried off to city museums, though broken columns and carved masonry can still be seen on the upper terraces. Undoubtedly the most prized artefact from Praeneste is the unique and extensive Nile mosaic. This exquisite piece, whose date is still debated but which was probably created in the late second or first century BCE, was found in the apse of the local archbishop's palace in the sixteenth century. Since then it has been subject to depredations, broken into segments, taken backwards and forwards to and from Rome, and partly crushed on the journeys. It was finally re-assembled and restored and is now displayed back in Palestrina, inside the museum housed in the Palazzo Barberini.[9]

In its original form the mosaic pavement was even more of a masterpiece than it appears today. It formed the floor of a nymphaeum – a shrine in a grotto where shallow water bubbled over the images. What was thought for some time to be just a delightful aquatic fantasy, with rushes, water creatures and all kinds of river craft, has been identified more recently as being, at least in part, a schematic map. It illustrates a Roman view of Egypt and Egyptian life that, although stylised, may also be informative. Full of long-extinct animals and plants, waterborne traffic, galleys, temples, columns, crags, trellised canopies and greenery, the Nilotic landscape is depicted as fertile and exotic. There are fishermen, musicians, drinking soldiers and a priestess performing her rites. Roman grandees alight from a boat.

The Nile delta of Hadrian's day has changed beyond recognition. There is little sign of the vigorous communities which lay along the route of his progress through this part of the country. There are a few remains, but in the Nile delta even the lie of the land has shifted and what ruins persist are hard to identify. Pelusium existed by grace of the Nile; it flourished when the unpredictable river bestowed her favours upon it, and died when that branch of the tributary dried up in the ninth century. The unostentatious settlement, which had a central role in the campaigns of Alexander and which was the seventh-century stopping-off point for the Muslim forces of Amr before they rode on to drive western rule from Egypt, is just discernible today, 30 kilometres north-east of Qantara, as an area of spoil heaps and rubble. The sands once again cover Pompey's tomb.

Following natural subsidence and several catastrophic earthquakes and tidal waves, the coastline of Egypt altered. Canopus, lure of the dissolute and the anxious, where Hadrian and Antinous, like Cleopatra and Mark Antony before them, amused themselves in 130, and which made sufficient impact on Hadrian for him to give its name to part of his palatial villa at Tivoli, also lay on a tributary of the Nile west of where the river runs today. From the fourth century onwards a series of natural disasters wiped Canopus off the map. The rise of Christianity had long destroyed the temples and removed the treasures of pagan religion, and the depravity against which both ancient and Christian commentators had inveighed came to a truly biblical end. The eastern arm of the Nile had already cut a new channel and the greater part of Canopus slipped slowly under the sea. In the First World War the last paving was removed to construct military roads.

For hundreds of years silt and sand covered what remained

of the fair and sacred sites of the eastern Nile, although occasional artefacts were discovered by unauthorised diggers. Since 2000 an extensive marine archaeological survey has pinpointed Canopus and is retrieving some wonderful artefacts: statues, gold and jewellery which the Christians and the sea left untouched. Hadrian's schematic Canopus at Tivoli, complete with its vaulted temple to Serapis, was excavated in the 1950s and is the central, and still puzzling, attraction of the beautiful villa complex there. In its original state the statues of Egyptian gods and goddesses lined the banks of a representation of the River Nile beside a sphinx and a stone crocodile. Several statues of Antinous were found nearby.

The much more substantial Alexandria survived the earthquakes but became a very different city. Part of the fabric survived under the sea; some was re-used, some was moved to different locations, much simply disappeared, and what survives does so in displaced fragments. One of the obelisks from Heliopolis which once stood outside the temple known as the caesareum, where the emperor was worshipped, now stands on the Thames Embankment in London, while a diorite statue of the Apis bull, commissioned by Hadrian, survives in the Greco-Roman museum in Alexandria. Like the burial place of Pompey, the site of Alexander's tomb has been forgotten. It was last heard of in 215, when yet another emperor, the malign Caracalla, paid the required homage. In the following 100 years bloody riots, invasions and earthquakes changed the face of Alexandria. The tomb was just one of many famous landmarks to disappear; its whereabouts is still a matter of constant speculation. More extraordinary is the fact that the Mouseion, the greatest centre of learning in the world, has also disappeared, thus far without trace.

The Pharos lighthouse finally collapsed in the fourteenth century, having survived the earthquakes that damaged so many ancient structures. The position of the Pharos lighthouse is marked by Fort Qaybey, a fifteenth-century fortress.

Around it, under the sea, divers have started to identify vast blocks of masonry that once formed part of the building. Deep inside the fort is a small mosque which, unlike other mosques, is not aligned to Mecca but follows the original alignment of the Pharos of Alexandria, along the points of the compass.[10]

4

Memnon laments

'I come because I have lost my Memnon, who took up arms bravely but vainly in his uncle's cause, and was slain in his early youth – for so you willed it – by mighty Achilles. Grant him some honour, I pray you, great ruler of the gods, to make his death less hard to bear, and so soothe a mother's wounded heart!'

Jupiter nodded his consent. As Memnon's lofty pyre collapsed, consumed by leaping flames, rolling clouds of black smoke darkened the sky, just as when rivers breathe out the fogs they produce, and prevent the sun from shining through. Then the black ash flew upwards and, packed and compressed into a single body, took on a definite shape: it acquired heat and the vital spark of life from the fire, while the lightness of the substance gave it wings. At first resembling a bird, and then in fact a real bird, it flew on whirring wings and countless sisters too, born from the same source, made the air noisy with their flight.

OVID, METAMORPHOSES, 29. 576–622 (TRANS. MARY INNES)

From the memoirs of Julia Balbilla, November 130

Even in Egypt by late November the hour before dawn is chilly. Summer's impossible heat has long departed, and the autumn warmth and glow that the sun brings to the monuments and cliffs of Thebes is yet to spread from the east. Horses and donkeys shuffle, grooms snigger and there are still attacks of coughing; illness has been rife since our arrival in Egypt in midsummer.

We wait and it is cold. It is dark in this time before dawn. We have been lodging near here for some days and wait to be told whether we are moving on south up the river or returning to Athens or Rome. Meanwhile we explore as expected. No one comes to this country, no one explores its ancient secrets without waiting, as we do, for a sign. Everyone comes, everyone expects a popular mystery. You come, you pay a priest to sacrifice to the gods, you pay a man to chisel your messages upon the hard stone and, if you are lucky, the statues sing to you at dawn. This, I know, is true – unlike so many travellers' tales. If we wait we shall not be disappointed. My grandfather came, my father came and here, I, Julia Balbilla, granddaughter of a king, wait for the morning.

Kings scarcely stir the dust as they move across history. Who later remembers the triumphs of this war, that conquest? Who counts their children, enumerates their laws? Even as the flesh shrivels on the bones, their tombs fall into desuetude, their reputations are corroded by contempt and fashioned to the purposes of others, their descendants partition the land and their names are forgotten.

But eminence endures in stone. Stones are the exultations of the mighty as words are the cries of the poet. Who may know in the end what deeds of merit or notoriety a king performs? Who may stand among the fragments and say, 'This was a wise king' or 'This was a cruel ruler,' still less, 'This was a good or cruel *man*'? But when they look upon his cities, his roads, his monuments, his statues, they may say, 'Here, once, was power.'

We have travelled to the tombs of great men – Pericles, Alexander, Pompey – and found them forgotten, decayed.

Through the power of another they are brought briefly to prominence; they are illuminated while his light glows brightly; and when he dies, they return to dissolution. To build beyond the reach of time's assaults and man's imagination, to build on so lavish a scale, to employ such skill, such material that even when the years melt away its purpose and form, a rough, untidy memory of power endures, is all that a king may achieve.

Only until the third generation will his descendants bear witness.

So here we stand, whispering instinctively, although it is unnecessary. Are we intimidated by these hulks of stone, featureless in the darkness, or the messages they bring? Or have we got into the habit of silence – talking furtively, watching for observers? Here we are on the crumbling edge of history. How can we know what lies ahead when we are so uncertain as to what has happened in our immediate past?

We wait here by rocks that in darkness might seem to be wrought by the hands of gods, not men, to be on this plain by accident, not design. Savagely assaulted by later, jealous generals, lying as fallen casualties of battle, they yet remain implacable; who knows how long they have remembered the short moment of one man's power? So it is on a hillside in that rich place I love, near another, more beautiful river than these sluggish, lethal waters and, so, too, high above the most beautiful city of the Greeks: the great are remembered. Their greatness is never forgotten, even as their history is smoothed away like the features on a statue. I have come to leave my mark – their mark – upon these stones. It is not enough that we should carve our names on the rock, but I must leave a poem. Sabina still believes I am a poet in her prime. When Hadrian calls me 'our own Sappho', he does so to amuse his friends. Sabina thinks poetry and plays are a more real version of life, that they stamp their approval on a moment and affirm that it is remarkable. If I incise my verse on the statue, then I shall be making this dawn her history.

Hadrian desires a Sappho in his gallery – well, he shall have one; I shall write as Sappho, and in her language, but I shall write of the nobility of Commagene and with the deepest cuts I shall write of Sabina, so that of her too there may be some permanent memorial. In death, remembrance of her will not be extinguished by the cities and honours of her great and unloving king.

It is our second visit. Sabina is much taken by the story of the constant hero. Against the pale sky the famous statues are just further dark slabs of rock, crouching on the plain, waiting not only for the sun to make them speak but for daylight to redraw their features. She, among all women, has seen and heard many wonderful things in this country, but the tombs of heroes and the libraries and temples with their sinister and fawning priests have not moved her, have not called her to return.

She says the effect upon her was all the more powerful because she had not believed the story of Memnon when it was spoken of in Rome; it was impossible, she thought, that the statue of the young king would sing to his grieving mother, would comfort her for her loss, faithful through all time. Now she knew the history and she had already heard its proof for herself; fidelity could be so strong, a mother could be so loved. When the statue sang, it sang to her too. It was a marvel, she declared. It was the first time that I had seen her with tears in her eyes.

It is true that Memnon had not at first sung to Hadrian. Unlike the philosophers of Athens, the statue could not be forced to speak, could not be commanded to complete a transformation from stone to something almost human. Here there were no threats which could be brought to bear, no service or sentiment which could be extracted. That power even Hadrian did not have. He was not a god. Not the sort of god, even in Egypt, who could make miracles happen. If he could, we would not all be afraid.

The statue did not respond to his loss, but it spoke to Sabina. It will sing for him eventually, I do not doubt it, but it was amusing to watch him come back trying to behave as if it were nothing to him whether it sounded or not. It was passingly pleasing to feel that it had yet again turned its song to women and that he had been excluded. First one desertion, then another.

So Sabina is waiting again. She is always attending on another's pleasure in the things that matter most. For once, she is waiting from choice; but although she is in good spirits, albeit not entirely impervious to the dramas unfolding about her, she does not feel well and the cold touches her more deeply than it does me. She is no longer young, and the illness and her nervousness of his medical attendants and the strain of the last weeks are telling; but to come here and not to see the statues sing would be to send a message to him, to the world. Not that he treats her badly; he ensures she receives the respect due to her. Due to *him*.

She is still not an easy woman. Life has taught her to be wary, restrained, cool. Among her friends she occasionally shows a flicker of the enthusiasms she had as a child. I did not know her then, but sometimes she talks of the great estate of her youth and the birds, all of whose names she knew. Even now she is curious about the unfamiliar, and in Egypt there is plenty of that. She asks the names of animals and draws them so that she may remember each variety. She has learned the names of medicinal herbs. Originally it was down to a lack of trust of Hadrian's doctors, but now she seeks out cures for this and that in every place we visit. Cobwebs, distillations of bark, goose-lard and crocodile dung – the perennial Egyptian crocodile dung cure; it is surprising the local people are not healthier.

Although her spoken voice is low and harsh when she is angered, she has a clear, rather girlish singing voice. I have heard her among her friends singing the folk songs of her childhood, and – with less charm – singing herself as a maiden abandoned by a rustic beside some Dorian brook. This is not music which Hadrian would think worthy. Not that he knows of any of his wife's accomplishments.

Mostly Sabina is a watcher, and not just by decree. She likes to see dancing; but for someone who is still so elegant in repose, she is clumsy if she takes a few steps herself, having little natural rhythm or delicacy. She enjoys plays and poetry, and although her own work is embarrassingly bad, an opinion which fortunately she shares, still she encourages young writers to recite their verse to her and is generous in her patronage. Yet she knows – and knows that he thinks – her life is pointless. Barren and lonely and first among women. There can no longer be any hope of children and perhaps that is good. She cared, once, that he treated her so coldly, but she was only a child herself then, and after so many years their indifference has long been mutual. Hers is not, as some whisper, the face of a disappointed woman, but a woman whose expectations have been fully met.

But his dislike of her is his alone, it cannot be echoed by court wits. There was a man once, his secretary, Suetonius, a clever, cruel man who made her laugh – she told me – but who, like so many, overstepped the mark, made some quip about the emperor, thought he was safe perhaps, thought he was being kind, did not understand that she *was* him. Hadrian sent him back to Rome at her request. Anyway the man, for all his charm, his *bons mots*, was a dangerous person to have at court; a writer, always scribbling, watching. *The Wit of the Mighty* was his next book, he said.

There are those now who look at her strangely, in fear compounded with excitement and curiosity. Some people draw back from her; she seems oblivious to them. Whoever comes, whoever goes, the rumours, promises, betrayals and now fear flourish independent of authorship; the court hisses with hope and malice. Is it possible that we shall all survive this disaster and that life will go on as before?

At their eastern edge the skies are now lightening from sullen grey to the palest blue, and great flocks of birds lift above the river.

In 130 two great battered statues stood on the plain of the west bank of the Nile by the road to Thebes. When Hadrian and his courtiers came to visit them in late November they were already more than fifteen hundred years old. They stand there today, in rather better condition, still carrying their disturbing message of the passing of all greatness. But even for second-century Roman visitors whose eyes were conditioned to monolithic statements of power and even within a landscape composed in vastness, the statues, enthroned on a plain of scree stretching from the river to the red-ochre sandstone cliffs, were remarkable.

It was not that they were particularly impressive as structures – they were nothing compared to the pyramids – but they were significant because in their isolation they were so obviously just a fragment of something conceived on a far huger scale. The shadow of the past hung over them, and they were perhaps most impressive as an indication of what might have been lost rather than as a remaining landmark between Thebes and the river. Blasted by sand, cracked by heat and movements of the earth's crust, they were slowly dissolving over the millennia from a man-made wonder back to organic matter. The torso of the right-hand statue lay broken on the sand close to its original base. In dilapidation they made conflicting statements about power: they were unmistakable evidence that individual power could create an enduring monument, but also that what might endure of that power could be arbitrary and its messages beyond the control of its creator.

When the imperial party arrived in 130 they were visiting what had already become an established attraction for travellers in Egypt. The ancient identification endures in the name of statues called, then as now, the Colossi of Memnon. When Hadrian and his courtiers stood at Memnon's feet on that second-century dawn the figures were already old enough for their history, like their substance, to be blurred by the passing centuries. Where sculpture was reverting to stone, where the original artistic intention was under attack merely from time's passing, the sharp edges of history had long slipped into myth. So the Romans journeyed to Thebes, and believed they were looking at a hero from the Battle of Troy.

Here was Memnon, brother of the king of the Ethiopians, slaughtered by Achilles when he led his army out of Egypt to fight for the Trojans. Memnon's mother Eos, goddess of the dawn, was notoriously attracted to beautiful young lovers – Tithonus, Cephalus, and Orion – whose lives, once entwined with hers, led invariably and through numerous reverses in fortune to calamity. Cephalus used his magical spear, a gift from the gods, inadvertently to kill his wife. Orion the hunter was turned into a star. Tithonus, father of Memnon, gained eternal life but with terrible oversight forgot to ask for eternal youth. Other legends, intricately plaited with history, attached themselves to the original tale of Memnon; one concerned the reported atrocities of the Persian king Cambyses, who, it was said, had gratuitously damaged Memnon's statues in the sixth-century BCE conquest of Egypt.

The mystical and heroic story of Memnon was widely known; it had been retold by Ovid more than a century earlier in his *Metamorphoses*. Ovid articulated a breadth of myth and pantheism in which organic things – human beings, trees, rivers, clouds and animals – all tangled with the gods and were saved from death by transformation. Nothing, in Ovid, was quite as it seemed, nothing could be relied upon; the gods were capricious and violent, the human form mutable and interchangeable with other life matter; but nothing was entirely without hope of salvation, even if human life or liberty were lost. His were all familiar myths which would have been well known to Hadrian; indeed, the emperor may have recognised the themes from them which seemed to suffuse his own story in 130.

The statues had long been one of the marvels of the east, a curiosity not just of inanimate, if instructive, beauty, but one of performance. It was as if the tragic but redemptive tale of Memnon was confirmed by the stones themselves. In the second century the truncated base of the more badly damaged statue was possessed of an extraordinary property: as the first light of day hit it, it hummed. As light broke, Memnon's mother, Eos (in Latin, Aurora), goddess of the dawn, could hear her son's voice again. The early travel writer Pausanias compared the resonance to a vibrating single string of a lyre. Although second-century travellers were not especially naïve, and there were a few sceptics who were less convinced of the phenomenal aspect of the stones and more inclined to see the sounds as man-made, possibly priest-induced, it was an attractive story. There was even a trick to be played on the pretentious, who might lay claim to have seen the great wonder yet be exposed in their ignorance that the statue 'spoke' not from its head but from its plinth.[1]

For most visitors in Egypt, a land of magic, of death and superstition, to hear Memnon's song was to be favoured. For Hadrian, Memnon's story, composed of elements of nobility, misunderstanding, bereavement, transfiguration and love, might have appeared particularly potent. But Memnon was fickle; he did not always sing – not even to emperors – and at dawn on his first visit Hadrian waited in vain to hear the statue call back through the centuries to his lamenting mother.

In fact Memnon seems to have attracted the emperor's wife, Sabina, more than the emperor himself. The statues were so well known, serving as a subject for the digressions of geographers, moralists, poets and historians, that Hadrian might well have preferred to take up a pose of aesthetic detachment.[2] Nevertheless, a show of respect at the memorials of dead heroes was usually central to Hadrian's agenda wherever he went. But there were other reasons why the emperor might have been reluctant to become part of the spectacle of so well-known a story at this time. Sabina had, it appears, been quick to make the Colossi part of her own narrative. (It is hard not to think of the late Princess of Wales visiting the Taj Mahal.) For her, they were evidently a compelling sight, and she visited more than once to hear the statues sing. The evidence for Sabina's visits for those demanding scrupulous verification of events to turn them into history, is found in the dense scar tissue of ancient graffiti – more than 100 inscriptions – which covers the surface of the base of the statue. More eminent Roman visitors were permitted to carve their names or a message on the statues. Many of these 'spontaneous' expressions, supposedly inspired by the Memnon experience, were carefully planned in advance and endure to this day: poetic, pompous, status-declaring or simply names carving themselves into a legend. To see Memnon's statues close at hand is to move from a distant observation of the grandeur of Egyptian achievement and history to reading about Romans – Romans able to annexe the Greek cities of Egypt, Romans who could confidently appropriate the past by adding their names to an extraordinary statue. But it was not, for illustrious visitors, enough just to scratch their initials or epithets with a piece of sharp stone or a stub of charcoal. It is likely the graffitists were charged for the privilege, and professional masons undertook the task of adding text to existing image. Priests had taken charge of the local tourist attraction and made it pay; the skill of the anonymous masons has allowed the inscriptions to endure. Among the clearly visible carvings are four poems by one of the Empress Sabina's companions, Julia Balbilla, which are dated November 130.[3]

Julia was for many reasons an appropriate person to accompany Sabina. She was sensibly middle-aged and herself of royal blood, descended from the old, if dispossessed, house of Commagene, and through it to most of the royal lineages of the New East. Indeed, she was arguably more aristocratic than her imperial patrons. Her brother, now dead, had once been a friend and patron of the emperor and she was a highly cultured woman. She had family connections with Egypt, which must have made her a desirable addition to Hadrian's peripatetic court, and a visit to Egypt must have held significant emotional and symbolic weight for her personally.

Julia's family was talented and famous in many fields. Her maternal grandfather, Balbillus, had been prefect of Egypt under Nero. Something of an early antiquarian, Balbillus had been responsible for the partial uncovering of the Sphinx from its bed of sand. Less creditably, he had – or so it was rumoured – encouraged Nero to surrender up the life of a man to ensure the emperor's prosperity. Balbillus had inherited his own ability in astrology following *his* father, Thrasyllus, astrologer to Tiberius, who also had charge of the Mouseion of Alexandria. Given Hadrian's fascination with astrology, and given the continuing dominance in the field of the Alexandrian circle, that connection cannot have passed unnoticed. Darker rumours persisted: it was claimed that Balbillus was an adept poisoner, while Julia's grandmother had demonstrated stereotypical regal behaviour in insisting on having Nile water brought to her wherever she travelled, in the belief that it had magical properties. This tale is one of many concerning the magical qualities of the river water. Presumably one of the qualities may have been fertility, as Egypt was utterly dependent on the Nile floods for its agriculture; many of its religious beliefs concerned the Nile. But as a demonstration of dissolute autocracy it also echoes the story of Nero, who had snow melted to provide the purest of water. As he faced death, hunted by his adversaries, Nero was to display his ironic sense of humour when he was forced to drink from a puddle and commented on the contrast in his fortunes. Nero was a man ahead of his times; today, of course, glacier water, though not that of the Nile, is freely available.

On her father's side, Julia Balbilla's grandfather had been Antiochus IV, the last king of Commagene. The family remained conscious of their status, even in defeat; her parents and siblings used the titles 'king' and 'queen' long after their kingdom had become a small segment of the Roman empire. Any modern reader of Julia's poetry might be puzzled by the apparent absence of sustained resentment on her part at her country's defeat, and her own consequent reduction to a subject of the Roman emperor. The troubled history of Commagene had not, indeed, impeded a flourishing friendship between her brother, Philopappus, and Hadrian. The balance was a subtle one; Philopappus had died about fifteen years earlier but had been in some ways a model for the emperor. Domiciled in Athens, compensated for loss of a kingdom by a consulship, he was a wealthy, urbane aesthete and he retained the glittering trappings of a Hellenistic king. Philopappus had returned the investment of Hadrian's friendship by obtaining prized Athenian citizenship for him. Through Philopappus, the Greekling could truly be a Greek.

Julia's poetry inscribed on the Colossus is not great literature; but when she handed the mason her verses, written in the Aeolic dialect of Greek and presumably, at least in part, in anticipation of her visit, there was more at stake than pretty composition. The dialect itself was a refined 'poetic' choice, associating her with the exemplary Sappho; it was also in keeping with the fashion for retrieving older forms of speech and versification, a popular literary conceit enjoyed and emulated by the emperor himself. To write in such a style was to align herself with the emperor and his aesthetic agenda; it was a wise decision for a courtier to make. But her range and treatment of her subject matter – the visit to the statues of Memnon – also less consciously represents the complicated assumptions, contradictions and resonances of Hadrian's relationship with Egypt, with history and with the recent past.

Julia Balbilla wrote a prayer to Memnon beseeching him to sing for the empress (on the first visit all had been silent). She carved a record of the statue's subsequent compliance. She asserted, albeit well couched in acceptable rhetoric, the nobility of her own lineage. She addressed the statue, wounded many centuries earlier, as she believed, by the vicious Cambyses (her source was probably Herodotus, who relates stories of the king's madness), in a statement of belief in its survival, but in a poetic convention which breached the boundaries between the human and the inanimate: 'I sense within you a soul immortal.'[4] Here in Egypt, stones were alive and statues sang. It was not surprising that mere human beings could disappear.

The combination of public setting and romantic history was poetically irresistible, even without the order of an emperor. At a first reading it seems that Julia tactfully displays no unease at the position of either the Greeks or the Romans in relation to the annexation of Egypt; Hadrian is, a modern reader might assume, not a second Cambyses, but a good, enlightened ruler, like Memnon, and like Balbilla's grandfather Antiochus. But in contemporary literature and myth such simplicity was rare. In over a century of sometimes capricious autocratic rule, the more adept of imperial subjects had learned how to express their discontents within the established frameworks of history and literature. It was rich soil for the genesis of satire. But it could be misjudged, and the freedom obliquely to laugh at or criticise the establishment was always a precarious one, as demonstrated by the sudden dismissal from the emperor's entourage of Hadrian's *ab epistulis* – his personal secretary – Suetonius, the biographer, after some unknown slight to the empress. (It has been suggested, among other theses, that it was Suetonius' book *The Lives of the Famous Whores*, a work sadly lost to posterity, which precipitated his departure.)

Julia Balbilla writes within a tradition of panegyric: elaborate praise of the emperor and his wife interspersed with self-promotion. It is a form that to a modern reader seems to overreach itself with adulation of those in power. But these were not private but public lines, lines written by a courtier to be read by her peers, and the very structure of formal conventions means that they may carry all kinds of information beyond the traditional expressions of awe at the site and loyalty to the emperor. The elite of the second century were by no means ingenuous, and Balbilla was probably in her forties – no longer under the protection of her brother but a survivor, experienced in both poetry and, at least passively, in politics. She had quite possibly been involved in the construction of the massive Athenian monument to her dead brother which, through its sculpture and inscriptions, made plain his claims to kingship. Certainly her poem makes her royal connections explicit; implicit, too, is the loss of sovereignty to a more powerful invader. It was seventy years since her grandfather had been deposed, but memories of lineage are pervasive, as proved in her recitation of the dynasty.

In the Memnon verse, the reference to Cambyses is followed by a reminder that the errant king did not go unpunished for his depredations upon Egypt and upon Memnon: Cambyses, in a moment's misfortune, cut himself fatally on his own sword. Conquerors could not, it seemed, behave with impunity. Educated Romans in the particularly sensitive circumstances of the November 130 visit would also remember that Cambyses had both secretly murdered his brother and been involved in some tricky dealing with a substitute, a magician, for the dead man. The linking of Cambyses and Hadrian in four short poems – an association even more marked in the context of Hadrian's journey to Egypt – was hardly felicitous. Balbilla's poetry is loud in its omissions.

There was a further irony in Balbilla's work, one unknown to her at the time. It was not, in fact, Memnon who sat and sang by the road to Thebes. The name Memnon, which had been given to the seated figures by the early Greek settlers in Egypt, may have lasted to the present day, but where Hadrian thought he was gazing on a war hero, travellers of the twenty-first century have a different identification. Today these monumental statues are confidently known – not least because Hadrian's name is carved on the statue several times – as depictions not of the Trojan warrior but of a far more pacific Egyptian: the great lover of beauty, opulence and sensuality, Amenophis III (also known as Amenhotep), fifteenth-century BCE pharaoh and god. Amenophis was a fortunate man; Egypt in his day was prosperous and the pharaoh could play with images of military valour while in reality his concerns were a unique programme of aesthetic renewal and personal commemoration in the Nile valley. He built temples, erected immense statues to the gods and to himself, and developed innovative techniques of painting and decoration. The Colossi were part of a huge mortuary temple of which no other fragment now remains; parts of his elaborate and prettily decorated palace, the evocatively named House of Joy, his pleasure gardens, his man-made lake where he once sailed on the royal barge *Aton Gleams*, with his beloved queen Tiy or one of his hundreds of concubines, do survive, although the disintegrating ruins have long lost their exquisite wall paintings.

Amenophis enjoyed a relatively stable political climate and could exalt in the trappings of power, calling himself Egypt's Dazzling Sun. The pharaoh, had Hadrian known it, was on many counts a ruler with whom he might reasonably have identified himself; although Hadrian deliberately associated himself with the lives of dead heroes and a life lived bravely in the face of political or military adversity, the sumptuous Amenophis was more Hadrianic in achievement and influence than the Homeric and untimely dead Memnon.

Hadrian was not favoured at first in his dealings with Memnon: the statues remained obdurately silent on the first imperial visit. Among all the heroes Hadrian pursued, Memnon was the least obliging; but then, Hadrian had already discovered that the gods were against him. Sightseeing and adulation was undoubtedly low in the emperor's priorities, because when Hadrian arrived at the Colossi it was only weeks after he had suffered a personal catastrophe. The sources are incomplete, but it is clear that just one month earlier, in the last week of October 130, Hadrian's favourite, the Bithynian,

Antinous, had drowned in the Nile somewhere near Hermopolis. The Greek historian Cassius Dio, born nearly thirty years after Hadrian's death, a senator who served under the decadent and bloody Emperor Commodus and who presumably had good access to the documents available in the late second century, describes the circumstances in some detail and with notable lack of sympathy.

In Egypt he also rebuilt the city named henceforth for Antinous. Antinous was from Bythynium, a city of Bithynia, which we also call Claudiopolis; he had been a favourite of the emperor and had died in Egypt, either by falling in the Nile, as Hadrian writes, or, as the truth is, by being offered in sacrifice. For Hadrian, as I have stated, was always very curious and employed divinations and incantations of all kinds. Accordingly, he honoured Antinous, either because of his love for him or because the youth had voluntarily undertaken to die (it being necessary that a life should be surrendered freely for the accomplishment of the ends Hadrian had in view), by building a city on the spot where he had suffered this fate and naming it after him; and he also set up statues, or rather sacred images of him, practically all over the world. Finally he declared that he had seen a star which he took to be that of Antinous, and gladly lent an ear to the fictitious tales woven by his associates to the effect that the star had really come into being from the spirit of Antinous and had then appeared for the first time. On this account, then, he became an object of some ridicule.[5]

The shape of this narrative is itself interesting. The paragraph opens with the accusation that the emperor was lying. The passage immediately preceding this one comments on the splendid tomb Hadrian prepared for his horse Borysthenes, and describes Hadrian's restoration of the tomb of the Roman general Pompey. Having placed Hadrian's lover in such a context, the writer leaves certain questions open: Was Hadrian, the properly virile admirer of horses and the military, not to be trusted? Was Antinous an indulged pet, an athletic hero, or, as we read on, something much more sinister? Whatever he was in life, it ended abruptly when Antinous was found dead in the Nile in October 130.

The strangely elusive *Scriptores Historiae Augustae*, whose authorship and motivation are matters of fierce academic debate, relates the episode equally critically if more succinctly.

During a journey on the Nile he lost Antinous, his favourite, and for this youth he wept like a woman. Concerning this incident there are varying rumours; for some claim that he had devoted himself to death for Hadrian and others – what both his beauty and Hadrian's sensuality suggest. But however this may be, the Greeks deified him at Hadrian's request, and declared that oracles were given through his agency, but these, it is commonly asserted, were composed by Hadrian himself.[6]

Although the historians were subsequently loud in their assertion of Hadrian's discomposure, stressing his undignified grief and defensiveness, the public poetry of Balbilla, a contemporary member of the inner circle of court, seems to say nothing concerning the recent tragedy to befall the emperor. But perhaps in her references to the nature and power of monuments, and especially in view of her own family's tradition for mammoth posthumous memorials, she was hinting at the programme of construction upon which Hadrian was already embarking in response to his bereavement. For there was nothing normal in the emperor's reaction.

History and speculation have placed Antinous at Hadrian's side as the one great attachment of the emperor's life, the loss of whom caused this mature, sophisticated and highly experienced ruler to allow himself to be subsumed by grief. Lonely and shocked, he continued his journey back up the Nile, through Asia to Greece, and returned for the last time to Rome. Although he functioned competently in his official role, which was by this time largely a matter of routine, he was, in this telling, never the same man again. What might have been considered an accident became a catastrophe. Hadrian's reign seemed blighted from then on, and the errors of judgement that marked its later years reduced his standing for ever. His military decisions inflamed a Jewish terrorist uprising, unleashing a full-scale war with unacceptably high Roman losses; on a personal level, these years were overshadowed by depression, irrationality and disloyalty to his friends.

Read in this light, Julia Balbilla's poetic allusion to Cambyses appears almost prophetic. The emperor seemed cursed from the time of his journey into Egypt to the end of his life.

Nearly all the ancient sights that Hadrian and his retinue saw in Egypt in 130 CE survive. It is the country's more modern history, the remains of the Romans, that has disappeared. Alexander's city was built on the coast, and the settlements that followed all shared the fertility and accessibility of the Nile delta; they also shared its unstable geography, and in time slipped into the sea or were proved all too accessible to other invaders. The ancient pharaohs had built upstream, and their constructions were, at least in part, impregnable to time and tide as well as to attack. Julia Balbilla's verses can be read where she carved them on the statue of Memnon; the one to Sabina, having been cut more deeply, has survived the best. Julia judged, rightly, that the statues would remain.

I do not think this statue of you would thereupon perish, and I sense within a soul hereafter immortal. For pious were my parents and grandparents, Balbillus the Wise and King Antiochus: Balbillus the father of my mother, a Queen; and King Antiochus, father of my father. From their stock I too have obtained noble blood, and these are my writings, Balbilla the Pious.[7]

The statue of Memnon has never sung since it was repaired a century and a half later, but it still stands on the plain outside Thebes, which is itself little changed in the intervening centuries. First repair put an end to the musical phenomenon, and then modern science made Memnon's magic disappear. Analysis revealed the petrological history of the statue. It was erected as one of a pair in about 1400 BCE. An earthquake in 26 BCE caused it to shatter, the top falling away, and from then on a resonance was set up as the first light of dawn hit the base. The vibrations may have been caused by expansion of moisture or air in the cracks of the base. Restoration of the statue, to the form we see today, was undertaken by either Septimius Severus, after 199, or Queen Zenobia, in the third century CE, and it silenced Memnon for ever. It is an interesting reflection on Memnon's supposed mystical, pagan properties, that the Christian author Jerome believed that the statue had fallen silent at the birth of Christ.[8] But Memnon had served his purpose, and around the ambiguous statues swirled stories and myths that tell us more about the Romans than the monuments explain of themselves: for over two centuries Memnon had not just sung but spoken.

5

Cities of gods and ghosts

I approached the very gates of death and set one foot on Prosperine's threshold, yet was permitted to return, rapt through all the elements. At midnight I saw the sun shining as if it were noon; I entered the presence of the gods of the underworld and the gods of the upper-world, stood near and worshipped them.

Well, now you have heard what happened but I fear you are none the wiser.

The solemn rites ended at dawn and I emerged from the sanctuary wearing twelve different stoles, certainly a most sacred costume but one there can be no harm in my mentioning. Many uninitiated people saw it when the High Priest ordered me to mount into the wooden pulpit which stood in the centre of the temple, immediately in front of the Goddess's image. I was wearing an outer garment of fine linen embroidered with flowers, and a precious scarf hung down from my shoulders to my ankles with sacred animals worked in colour on every part of it; for instance Indian serpents and Hyperborean griffins, which are winged lions generated in the more distant parts of the world. The priests call this an Olympian stole. I held a lighted torch in my hand and wore a white pal-tree chaplet with its leaves sticking out all round like rays of light.

The curtains were pulled aside and I was suddenly exposed to the gaze of the crowd, as when a statue is unveiled, dressed like the sun.

APULEIUS, THE GOLDEN ASS, (TRANS. ROBERT GRAVES)

From the memoirs of Julia Balbilla, spring 131

We are all actors, touring in this interminable play and weary of the script. The blood was spilt off stage, more hideous in the privacy of the audience's imagination than ever it could be performed in front of them. The calm pause of the voyage was a space in which we contemplated the future with unease.

We waited until the omens were good. These days we are back in the way of such things. Then we made a fair crossing from Alexandria, after the endless ceremonies of farewell in which they expressed their wish to receive the honour of a second visit and Hadrian sincerely expressed his wish to return when affairs of state permitted it. Lie upon lie. None of us would return to this uncomfortable, disease-ridden country except under penalty of death. Yet although we are all glad to be rid of Egypt, in Hadrian's demeanour there is something beyond grief and beyond relief at departing from this unsafe land. Is it possible he believed the slaves' rumour that there was a curse laid on him which would be made manifest while he sailed the Nile? Could he have been afraid even as his journeys led him inexorably to that blemished country? There was a terrible accident, to be sure, but not so terrible that he was not glad to have survived.

The last weeks creeping towards our departure were the worst. We passed on, we performed what was expected of us, we bowed our heads in temples, we nodded at interminable histories of ancient kings, we fed the crocodiles. Only at the little island of Philae could we pray to a god of speedy departures – a god Sabina decided was erroneously missing from the pantheon. All that Egypt demands of its visitors we supplied. Yet the people in the fields, outside their hovels, were dark and sullen. The land is barren this year and they blame the emperor, either as a bringer of misfortune or for not relieving them. It is not that they care nothing for his misfortunes, they simply misunderstand. What could it be for a man who holds the world and its gold in the palm of his hand, to lose one small nugget of pyrite?

The emperor was at first awake at all hours, demanding,

planning, dictating lists, calling in the priests, the engineers; and then, exhausted, finally accepting the help of doctors to bring him sleep. The sleep which came seemed to engulf him by day, so that while his eyes were yet open his gaze was fixed and his speech slowed down so that his interlocutors would bend forward as if to catch the last syllable as it dropped reluctantly from his lips. By day his words were indistinct and sometimes a sharp ear might hear the rustic tone of his youth, yet they say at night he called out clearly to unseen persons or sweated and turned in his bed like a sick man.

Meanwhile the court fell silent. I do not mean that it was quiet; there was little difference in the domestic round. Soldiers came and went purposefully, tethered horses snorted and fidgeted at flies, wagons still moved food about, the kitchen slaves called to each other, water was drawn and portered, there were the rituals of arrival and departure in one town or another – but there was no music, no joking about the gullible or dirty natives, no importuning artists, no hunting. If I have learned one thing on this journey it is that we are an empire held together by entertainment. From high to low we expect our diversions. So we have our circuses and our games, our public trials and ornamental punishments, our triumphs, our races and our priestly sacrifices. When we are neither watching nor providing the spectacle we are not sure who we are.

Despite their habitual good manners, the local Greeks were clearly disappointed when the long-awaited emperor appeared tired and preoccupied. The priests, less sensitive to the change of mood, still attempted to get his attention with one foolish sideshow after another: a badly stuffed ibis, a two-headed monkey, a woman dragged half-conscious from some unspeakable hovel with her litter of five live-born infants, a water-monster putrefying in a bottle – one abhorrence after another to amuse the emperor into remembering his generosity. The relics of long-dead kings, the altars of their vile gods and the stink of the river; we never escaped them until we left the country.

To be fair, even those who knew him were uncertain how to act. Within hours of the body being brought ashore he had demanded to see the place where the boy was found. It was not much of a place; a simple temple, a few huts, a few curious children. A dying village, typical of so many. A dying village enjoying its moment of notoriety. His secretary told me later that even this was a kind of deceit, although meant well. The body, sighted by fishermen, had been in the water some days by the time it was spotted. Those who drown sink to the bottom until, unrecognisable, they rise again transformed. Had they not known that an important man had disappeared the Egyptians might have left him; they were busy men with an urgent requirement for living fish, not rotting corpses, in their nets. Still, thinking there might be a reward for bringing this particular catch to the shore, or a punishment if they were subsequently known to have let him eddy and travel on, they dragged him in. Bloated and sodden, he was too heavy to pull into their shallow boat. So they roped him and dragged him by his head and an arm to the bank. There they lay him to bake in his muddy coat, covering him only with palm leaves to keep off the flies. Two men sat as far away from the corpse as was possible to ensure the valuable commodity was not appropriated by other covetous peasants while yet, as the day grew hotter, allowing them some redress from an increasingly less pleasant companion. The youngest and fittest of them went to find one of the emperor's search parties.

Hadrian was such a man for detail and personal inspection that it was probable that he would wish to see both the corpse and where the accident happened. 'The accident' is what we all call it; 'the accident', to make it clear that nobody considers the boy to have entered the water by any agency other than the hand of the most malign fate. Every time we repeat 'the accident' it emphasises how many doubts and rumours take flight each time the story is disturbed. The guard commander, finding that a local temple was not so very far away, demanded wisely that the body be taken there and placed under decent cover within the building until orders were given for its disposal. It had dignity. It was a place. It was somewhere with a name to it, not nowhere; the emperor who took such pains with accurate geography would want his friend to have died in a proper place. It had a little harbour where the emperor's boat might moor should imperial representatives wish to visit the spot.

Once the whole business had been officially reported it was obvious that cremation should be undertaken as soon as possible; so the commander, an ambitious man, used his initiative and got his men to drag together whatever wood and brush they could find to create a pyre. It was never lit. As darkness fell, a small party arrived and, covering their lower faces with cloth, lashed the corpse to a stretcher and carried it away. The body was never referred to again. Some said that Hadrian kept it with him all night, others that he demanded that the doctors open the body and search for signs of poison – but if there were any, the Nile had long washed them away. Some said the priests took him and with their rites made him perfect again, repaired him and restored him to a semblance of sleep. All that is certain is that from that moment he disappeared. For us, one minute he was dancing and singing with wine playing the part of his muse; the next, he was a god blazing in the firmament.

But for those of us still on the earth, now is a fine time to be a grateful citizen of the Roman empire. In Rome, I am told, the people are prosperous in the absence of war. Athens – and all Greece – celebrates a glittering and, they believe, deserved apogee of fortune under Hadrian; if a people cannot be self-determining, what more could they ask than that their very conqueror should wish to cast off the rough cloak of his own past and assume the fine mantle of their own more pleasing history? History is power, and its ownership much debated. It seems that every month a festival is rediscovered; each festival demands its acolytes, its temples, and the emperor, who has successfully achieved a lasting peace, is become a Pericles or an Alexander.

My brother's fine monument looks down upon his beloved

Bronze bust of Hadrian found at Tell Shalem, Israel (*Ancient Art and Architecture Collection*)

Late Victorian engraving of the construction of Hadrian's wall across the north of England in 121 CE (*Mary Evans*)

Empress Sabina (*theartarchive*)

Sabina *c.* 130 CE (*George Ortiz*)

Matidia, Hadrian's mother-in-law
(*Ancient Art and Architecture Collection*)

A nineteenth-century aquatint of the Colossi at Memnon, Egypt (*Bridgeman Art Library*)

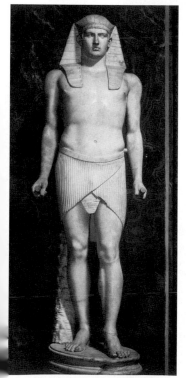

Antinous dressed as a pharaoh.
The statue is now in the Vatican Museum
(*Alinari*)

The lighthouse at Alexandria, erected 36 BCE
(*Bridgeman Art Library*)

The Damascus Gate in Jerusalem (*Sonia Halliday Photographs*)

Relief carving from the Arch of Titus, Rome, showing the spoils of captured Jerusalem, 79 CE (*Schwanke/Deutsches Archäologisches Institut, neg. no. 79.2494*)

Monument of Philopappos, brother of
Julia Balbilla, which stands in Athens
(*Bridgeman Art Library*)

The Acropolis seen from the
south east with Hadrian's Gate
in the foreground
(*AKG London*)

Hadrian's great
Pantheon in
Rome, still in
use after nearly
2000 years
Michael Bywater)

A statue of Atinous dressed as Bacchus, now in the Vatican Museum (*AKG London*)

A third-century hunting mosaic at Piazza Armerin in Sicily (*Mansell/TimePi*

The Canopus,
Hadrian's villa at
Tivoli, near Rome
(*Michael Bywater*)

Obelisk of Antinous,
the Pincio, Rome
(*Michael Bywater*)

Early eighteenth-
century watercolour
of Hadrian's
mausoleum
(Castel Sant Angelo)
in Rome
(*Bridgeman Art
Library*)

Entrance gate to Antinoopolis as seen by Jomard, 1798–1800 (*Bibliotheque Centrale M.N.H.N. Paris*

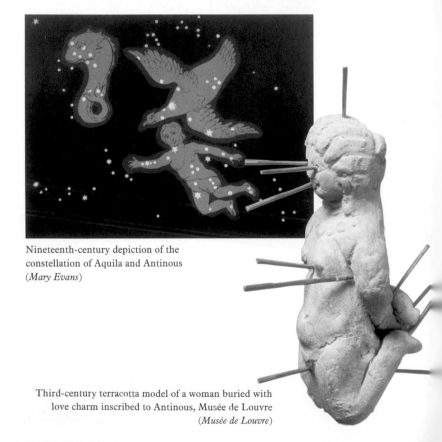

Nineteenth-century depiction of the
constellation of Aquila and Antinous
(*Mary Evans*)

Third-century terracotta model of a woman buried with
love charm inscribed to Antinous, Musée de Louvre
(*Musée de Louvre*)

city; how he would have adored all this. The back streets – the Athens Hadrian could never know or imagine – are still mean and decaying, unblessed by gods or gold; but the public face of Athens looks confidently on the world. By day billowing canopies cast vermilion and orange shadows on the marble beneath, and by night great flares illuminate the unbruised curves and the drilled curls of sharp new carving. We have games, dedications and festivals. Sabina looks well now that the crisis is past. The emperor is less brilliant but less challenging than is his habit. This is his moment of triumph, which he has earned, and darkness must not fall forward upon it.

Yesterday the Temple of Zeus was dedicated, all history measured in its stone courses. It was one of many formerly abandoned projects of great men. Until recently there were so many fine façades with only rubble and beggars behind, so many insulted gods in their single-storey shrines open to the skies. Julius thought they should be fined for erecting such monuments to the transience of all riches. Any would-be senator might have learned some lessons from our incomplete finery. What would those first builders have thought if they could have seen their work completed? By a Roman king? Even Julius, who wished he had the wealth to build such a place for the Athenians, how could he ever have equalled this work? There was for once no cavilling, no supercilious asides. Across the procession of the priests in their new robes, the children throwing flowers, the sacred priestesses, the censer carriers and the trumpeters, all Athens was amazed.

The high wall that has enclosed the precincts since the beginning of the restoration hid the emerging reality of Hadrian's plans for it. Of course there were rumours of jewelled gods and gold and silver treasuries – masons and carpenters and goldsmiths all have tongues in their heads – but it surpassed every whisper. It was magnificent. The perfection was painful; a moment of unsustainable beauty created by power. Who was worshipped in that great place, Zeus or his loyal friend and fellow god, the emperor?

The god was a colossus, creamy ivory tipped with gold

filigree. Like the statues of the myths, its limbs were waxy flesh that might yet wake. Yet the thought that such a being should be re-animated and breathe and move among us is a terrible one. As Hadrian walked across the courts of his temple, it was as if he paced down a corridor of mirrors, for everywhere, randomly placed, were statues in his image. Yet the living man with his sallow skin and the lines of grief was a more cheerful sight than the statues: the marble ones like corpses standing upright in the Egyptian manner, the painted the same after the attentions of the mortuary priests, and the porphyry figurines in their mottled purples and pinks glistening like flayed criminals.

The next day it was the perfect vaults of the new gate, the dressed stone roughened in the manner of the past. Then the library, the dizzy sight of a hundred columns, the tiers of steps; everywhere the stone was implacable in the sun, my eyes hurt, my head reeled. Even the architects, lined up to receive his thanks, looked oppressed by their achievements. I began to long for something flawed, something shabby and familiar. Sabina was the only one who seemed clear-headed. Despite the relative calm – we had known much worse – she had suffered with relentless sickness on the sea-crossing and kept to her quarters. The relief of being in Athens seemed to drive out every other consideration. Hadrian, though subdued, put on his usual performance and seemed genuinely delighted at his reception; Sabina played her part, dressed as a priestess at his side. The imperial couple triumphant. The worst was over.

This *is* a golden age. Here is the proof. So now I try to think of the gods and of the people of the city so blessed, their future ensured by the attractions set in place to lure visitors through all ages. The great Homer once called Greece the country of dreams, but the beauty of dreams is in their elusive quality. Hadrian has caught them, turned their amorphous charm into marble and precious metals, and in doing so put an end to their allure. We do not wonder, we know. It is too much all at once. Will Athens become a living city again? Not in my lifetime, I think.

Hadrian left Egypt for Greece several months after losing Antinous. It had always been intended that he would be in Athens for the winter of 131–2 – indeed, it was supposed to be the high point of the current tour – but the recent calamity could not accelerate the process. The size and requirements of the royal entourage inhibited spontaneous action, and both logistics and politics dictated that he must fulfil the itinerary which had been planned so far in advance. So Hadrian continued on down the Nile, following his expected agenda over the winter of 130 – dealing with the routine administration of his mobile government, meeting important officials, visiting what were supposed to be the long-established highlights of any sightseeing trip to Egypt. In his wake a subdued imperial court paused and waited for the disruption to die down, perhaps with some curiosity as to how Hadrian might respond. The man who erected a tomb and some verses on the death of his horse might be expected to come up with something more extravagant, something more Greek, for the loss of a lover. Hadrian did not disappoint his waiting courtiers; what he had in mind exceeded all precedent. The emperor's grief, fuelled by the emperor's power, was to find extraordinary expression across the empire.

The death of Antinous, however immense a private blow, cannot have affected the imperial schedule by more than a few days; nevertheless it was in this immediate aftermath of the drama that Hadrian began to draw up plans to institute not just a personal but a public recognition of his favourite. Even while he fulfilled his strategic obligations in Egypt, during the period between the death in autumn 130 and the departure in spring 131, and while he was receiving advance information of the fruition of projects in Greece, Hadrian's thoughts were elsewhere. He was in endless consultation with priests, astrologers, artists and architects, setting up the various projects to commemorate the dead Antinous. He did not, as far as we know, write a poem, although plenty of others did so, hoping for his approval. He may have erected a tomb; but if he did, it has long disappeared and its whereabouts are unknown. What he did do was more shocking and more permanent. At the end of 130, the Emperor Hadrian created the last great pagan god of ancient Rome. It was an extraordinary act which scandalised the emperor's patrician contemporaries and bemused biographers ever afterwards. In creating eternal life for Antinous, Hadrian crippled his own reputation.

Members of the imperial family were frequently deified, in consultation with the senate, but for the emperor unilaterally to honour a young man whose only claim to such advancement was that he had been the emperor's lover was unprecedented. Yet the beautiful Antinous became a god within weeks of his death, and the new cult was taken up swiftly by devotees throughout the empire. Although it was never to be as popular in the Roman west, worship of Antinous flourished in the east and reached its apogee, unsurprisingly, in Antinous' homeland of Bithynia. In some places it continued until it was finally displaced by the state adoption of Christianity.

Antinous was a compelling god; worshippers were inspired by the wonderful statues which were swiftly brought into circulation and upon which they could fix their devotions, and always eager to please an emperor who might visit their city. But it is easy to be over-cynical about the pragmatic nature of this worship. It is also quite possible that Antinous – a man with no official imperial or political status – could have seemed particularly accessible to those outside the powerful elites, and that his very ordinariness ensured the rise of a popular religion. Here, uniquely, was a god from and for the people. Analogies have been drawn with the creative catalyst of the death of the Prince Consort in 1861;[1] an equally tempting echo may be seen in the reaction to the death of Diana, Princess of Wales, in 1997.

As patron of what was already a powerful artistic and

literary revival, Hadrian was inevitably able to command first-class resources to commemorate his lost lover and celebrate the new divinity. The astonishingly prolific spread of images may have been directly under his control, but it is as likely to have been generated by the sculptors themselves, seeking imperial favour. Whatever the motivation, from the 130s onwards there was an obvious addition to the themes of ancient art. A new face appeared, and it was one of manly, though submissive, beauty. The surviving statues show a well-proportioned body, with downcast eyes and thick, curly hair nestling at the nape of the neck. It is a very classical and, unsurprisingly, a very Greek image. And it is one which remains very familiar as the archetype of perfect beauty. Antinous was not just the last pagan god; he was the inspiration of the last glorious florescence of classical art.

Three or four years later, Antinous' face was to appear in a more mundane but equally pervasive setting. In the eastern empire he started to appear on coins. Whether this signified local loyalty to his cult or merely reflected the widespread familiarity with his image, known from sculpture in the temples, or whether he was coming to be thought of as 'lucky', the emergence of coins and medals imprinted with his image was highly significant. For the vast proportion of imperial subjects, the only idea they had of their emperor was the face on a coin. In a largely illiterate society and an empire that covered vast geographical and cultural territory, visual images made powerful statements about Rome. Coinage was territory and propaganda.

Although neither the word nor the concept of propaganda emerged until 1622, when the Roman Catholic Church set up a congregation to disseminate the faith, many emperors were skilled proto-propagandists.[2] For over a century they had been manipulating their images on coins, associating themselves, or those important to them, with gods or honours or artefacts which would promote their policies and interests. Hadrian, for instance, had confronted the question of the legitimacy of his succession with official depictions of himself united with his predecessor, Trajan. He added a lyre to the iconography of his coinage to assert his artistic passions, an olive branch to indicate his wish for peace, and soldiers and warships to reassure the empire that he was prepared for that peace to fail. The design of the Antinous coins, however, was not officially released, or at least not controlled, by Rome; the coins were issued independently by Greek cities in the east, where the new cult was most successful. Antinous was never pictured with Hadrian, but nevertheless these coins circulated in Hadrian's world, where such images invariably transmitted public information; and as such they legitimised the status of the favourite. But most of those who saw and used them were unaware of and uninterested in the politics and logistics of circulation. The presence of Antinous' figure on coins from the time of his death onwards would have been noticed not least because it was so pretty.

Hadrian's acts of remembrance were wide-ranging and undiscriminating. While some debated the details of the new god's theological status, he went on commissioning commemorative works, permanent, ephemeral and didactic. At some point he was persuaded by his astrologers that a new star had come into being. He eagerly accepted the suggestion that a small red flower – a red lotus – had been fertilised by the blood of the lion that he and Antinous had killed in the desert and agreed it should be named after the dead boy.[3] He generously rewarded the composer of a long hymn to his departed friend. If what was emerging was not an affectation – the art of lament – then what we see is a man in despair.

An emperor's grief could be monumental. Among his extraordinary acts of tribute Hadrian was to create one startlingly ambitious and lasting memorial to the dead youth. Within days of the tragedy a new city was dedicated on the east bank of the Nile, near to where the young man disappeared. It was named Antinoopolis. Plans for the new city were developed at such speed that it seems likely that some such foundation had already been planned and would have been announced later on the trip, but that Antinous' death had defined the name and place. Antinoopolis was to be built almost opposite the existing city of Hermopolis. Now there was to be a traditional Egyptian city to one side of the Nile and a Greek one to the other. Hermopolis was another curious and inscrutable place: the Egyptian city of secrets, of the moon-god Thoth, the ibis-headed reckoner of time, god of scribes and learning, sometimes represented as a great baboon. Enigmatic Hermopolis was the last inhabited place Antinous saw.

The new city was magnificently laid out on the grid plan of a Greek polis and had its own constitution. The first settlers were given considerable financial incentives to move there. The city was completed in seven years, but inaugural games – The Great Antinoan – were celebrated there only a few months after Antinous' death, long before the first buildings were put up. Antinoopolis quickly became famous for its temples and its vast statues of both Hadrian and Antinous, and retained a reputation as a religious and magical location. Nothing was wanting in its development. A fine road, with its own inns for overnight stops and provisioning, led over the eastern desert, eventually connecting the new city with the Red Sea. Although Greek in inspiration, the city undoubtedly employed the skills of the greatest architects, builders and artists from all quarters of the empire in making it a huge work of art celebrating not just the life of Antinous but Hadrian's role in driving forward the cultural renaissance of the second century.

As Antinoopolis rose from the desert, the imperial entourage, its obligatory sightseeing completed, returned down the Nile. Winter passed with the court quartered back in Alexandria, and Hadrian forced to retrace steps he had taken with Antinous six months earlier. Initially he coped with his emotions, as he coped with most dilemmas, by an outpouring of energy, immersing himself in plans to advance the cause of the new divinity. Whether he, or others, mistook this almost manic response to loss as rejuvenation, rumours spread that Antinous' death had had a direct effect on the emperor's well-being. Cause and effect became muddled, and the darkest of speculations began to circulate.

If Hadrian was content with the progress of local arrangements to honour Antinous, a return to the comfort and gratifications of Greece must have seemed enormously attractive. Even without the recent death of his young lover, the trip to Egypt had not been an unqualified success. Whether there were less obvious ways in which Hadrian felt that his ends had been achieved in Egypt has been debated ever since, but in Greece, where the foundations of success had long been laid, there was certainty: loyal, grateful Greece, and the Greek cities of the east, were straightforward in delivering what they were supposed to. Their ways were comprehensible and he, Hadrian, comprehended them. To the projects he had already begun there, Hadrian now added a further one: wherever he went the cult of Antinous followed and was expanded.

Almost certainly Hadrian already intended to move straight from Egypt through Asia minor to Greece, where the court could spend the next winter – as it had done on earlier occasions – before the final leg of the journey took them onward to Rome. Greece held few surprises; ahead lay a period of consolidation and the fulfilment of the diplomacy and vision invested by Hadrian in previous visits. This visit to Athens was Hadrian's fourth (or possibly third: some commentators contest the first visit of 111–12, believing that Athenian honours bestowed on Hadrian then, before he became emperor, were conferred in his absence). It was intended to mark the fullest realisation of Hadrian's dream of a united Hellenistic world, a cultural renaissance and a golden age to compete with the spectacular reigns of the Greek kings and to exceed the more recent achievements of Augustus. Yet even as Hadrian prepared to celebrate the climax of his imperial dream, safe among the deserving and grateful, troubles were stirring further east.

Hadrian moved his court first to Syria, probably by sea convoy – an easterly sea voyage from Alexandria was relatively easy – and then, after a short pause for recuperation, moved on into the provinces of Asia minor which are now part of southern Turkey. It was a journey of memories through poignantly familiar landscapes. Hadrian spent time at Antioch, where he had once waited for the news that would make him emperor; passed on through Cilicia, where Trajan had been trapped by his last illness; and reached the delightful cities of Pamphylia and Lycia. The provinces of Asia minor were at their most beautiful: it was spring and the land was covered in wild flowers; there were swathes of crocus in between aromatic pine forests, small fields of grazing animals and ice-green water rushing downwards from mountain fissures to rivers in the valleys below. But Hadrian, like most Romans, was always moved more by architecture than any pastoral attractions. The emperor was a man of cities. Power could more easily be expressed in urban landscapes and the sort of 'wild nature' most powerful men preferred was that created by human artifice. This region had some of the most beautiful cities in the world. They were not dissimilar: numerous small classical settlements, carefully laid out to take advantage of the local geography and to provide every amenity the colonists could need, and constructed from the best of materials with immense craftsmanship. These Greek cities, deliberately planned to accommodate a community rather than just evolving in reaction to their immediate needs, defined the way cities were developed over centuries to come.

Cilicia and Pamphylia–Lycia are places woven into ancient history. The rural valleys, where today simple trans-human communities move with the seasons to grow tobacco and maize on gentle plateaux, were once a backdrop to the *Iliad*. These are lands caught up in the ambitions of Xerxes, Alexander the Great, the eponymous Mausolus, Ptolemy and Mark Antony, and written about by Herodotus, Strabo and the second-century travel writer Pausanias. In the early second century the coastal plains and hills of Lycia and Pamphylia were eagerly anticipating the visit from Hadrian which could change their fortunes. Whether or not the emperor would eventually honour individual communities with his presence, their consciousness of his supreme power and the advantages of cooperation were explicit. He might. He could. It was enough. Their relationship with him was sustained in rumours, hopes, negotiations, enticement and investment. Paradoxically, as Hadrian travelled among them finalising his great league of unified Greek communities, his presence itself acted to increase the endemic rivalry among them.

The summer of 131 saw the cities in intense competition with one another for imperial resources. The possible gains were immeasurable. It was not just a matter of acquiring or improving public buildings, but of gaining status. The greatest prize was the possibility of being allowed to join the Panhellion – the new league of states which could trace their descent from Greek beginnings and which had long relationships with Rome. Those ahead of the game were already busy proving or inventing their Greek origins. And there were other, more immediately tangible benefits. As well as the prospect of new buildings, there was the knowledge that when the emperor felt it appropriate he would found Hellenic games. Perhaps of all gifts this was the most valuable to a city of the second century, simultaneously conferring status and considerable economic opportunity. Games lay at the heart of Greek life; they made the lucky city the focus of attention every four years, bringing visitors and their money into town.

So the cities of the eastern empire resurrected their history, discovered ancient links with the homeland, excitedly re-named themselves: Hadriane, Hadriani, Hadriana, Hadrianoutherae, Hadrianeia, Hadrianoi, Hadrianopolis; and in the main, enthusiastically embraced the new cult of Antinous, just as they had always, unlike Rome, worshipped the living emperor. Individuals dedicated works in the emperor's honour and embarked on speculative building schemes that, when the money ran out, were left unfinished or unmaintained.[4] Gambling for imperial favour was a game of high stakes.

Tarsus, the greatest city of Cilicia, was already a thriving commercial centre with its own *stationes* – a local repre-sentative to assist Roman businessmen with their trading ventures – when Hadrian arrived in 131 and founded the hoped-for games. Long-distance trade was thriving in Tarsus, which produced felt and linen (Saul of Tarsus, later St Paul, had been engaged in the felt-making business), and whose surrounding fields of purple crocus produced the saffron which the ancient world treasured and for which it paid handsomely. Hadrian's visit was entirely expected by so important a city; his arrival affirmed its wealth and status.

Hadrian swept through the great Greek cities of Pamphylia and Lycia, distributing largesse, founding monuments. In his wake the cities set up monuments and inscriptions to record their gratitude; so pervasive was his influence in the area, so great the number of constructions that bear his name, that his exact route – and, indeed, the exact link of any of these memorials with the emperor – is hard to clarify. Arches were erected at Attalia (modern Antalya) and Perge. At Phaselis, whose historic Greek credentials were exemplary, optimistic locals set up a great gate to honour the potential bestower of favours; but their investment was in vain. No games were dedicated here. The emperor travelled on north – he needed to be in Athens by winter to prepare for the great celebrations of the following spring. He arrived at Ephesus on the west coast of Asia minor and celebrated at the new temple erected in his name. From there, Hadrian's entourage finally embarked for Greece itself.

What lay ahead was the culmination of his plans for a living re-creation of the Hellenic past. With his young Greek partner by his side, the excitement of this project had driven Hadrian on. Now Antinous had gone; but what he had stood for – the highest principles of Greek culture – lived on. Greece was where Hadrian had enjoyed the most profound experiences, where he felt most at home; after all he had worked to achieve, after all he had endured in recent months, this long-awaited visit could not now be allowed to fail. In Greece, Hadrian might still be a lonely, grief-stricken man; but he was also, unequivocally, an emperor coming in glory.

The emperor clung to the familiar, immersing himself in religious ceremonies. The dramas and elaboration of the rites had always appealed to him, and now, vulnerable and tired after the disaster of Egypt, he returned to the known and the comforting. At the rites of Dionysus he appeared in traditional Greek dress; at Eleusis he wore the saffron robes and myrtle wreath of a participant in the compelling mysteries. Greek religions had all the elements which appealed to Hadrian: they were high in dramatic content, they were ancient in origin – or claimed to be; and they were exclusive. Of them all, initiation into the mysteries at Eleusis held the greatest cachet. Yet for Hadrian the solemn rites were undoubtedly a time of acute awareness of loss. Those of the cult of Demeter at Eleusis included a procession from Athens which in the profundity culminated in a moment of revelation signified by a great light shining in the darkness. In the temple forecourts the women danced by torchlight. It was not just Hadrian who had been initiated into the cult, but also Antinous. Where they had once walked and worshipped together, Hadrian now returned alone to contemplate the cult's concerns of birth, death and transfiguration. To a degree Antinous the memory became an acceptable substitute for Antinous the lover.

While surveying the closing stages of the magnificent schemes he had instigated on earlier trips, Hadrian was still giving. Athens received money, buildings, dedications to Athenian boys, a corn dole for its poorest citizens and the gift of the island of Cephalonia. The best of Greek history and the hopes for a luminous future were represented in the combination of completion, restoration, new building and onward investment. It is not surprising that the provision of a massive library was a central element in the buildings Hadrian planned for Athens. We know much less about the library at Athens than about the one at Alexandria, but Hadrian's future library in his villa at Tivoli was to be extraordinarily comprehensive for a private collection, even that of an emperor, and no doubt Athens was comparable. It was a temple to Greek learning as much as an amenity for intellectuals.

Of all the festivities and ceremonies over which Hadrian presided in the winter of 131–2 – and they must at times have seemed endless – the one dearest to his heart was the grand inauguration of the Panhellion. A regular assembly of delegates from these city-states to decide on matters of religion and ceremony meant that the momentum of Greek cities throughout the empire would have a central focus. The cities which were to send delegates came from as far afield as the Black Sea and north Africa; what they shared was their Greek foundation. The Panhellion was never intended to have political power, but it gave a powerful sense of self-determination to the cities which were included in it. Though inclusion sounds a superficial honour, in this project Hadrian was reflecting the social structure of Greek life: ceremonies, games and festivals were central to Greek definition. Control of those was control of society; and although the emperor changed the cultural balance of power within the provinces, all

Hadrian's interests and donations were directly concerned with enforcing the social order. Libraries, games, festivals and temples were not about democracy and broadening the experience and access of the masses. Without exception Hadrian recognised and bolstered institutions where power, influence and rank were claimed and celebrated. The cities of the Panhellion were cities already possessed of a distinguished and prosperous past, and these were to be the major recipients of Hadrian's generosity.[5] An eminent past was to be rewarded with a clear future. In this spirit the Panhellion was of immeasurable social and symbolic importance. Hadrian, his political astuteness asserting itself as ever, had made entry difficult and protracted: delegates must prove their cities' lineage, their contribution, their determination. The cities clamoured to be admitted.

Around the solemnity and epoch-making alliances that engaged the elite, Athens was in the grip of genuine and unparalleled excitement. That the fortunes of Greece, so long neglected, were once more in the ascendant was declared in every new temple; now it was not just individual buildings which marked Hadrian's footsteps but a new quarter: streets, housing and theatres. A gateway marked the junction between old Athens and Hadrian's new city.

The supreme moment of theatre was the dedication of the temple of Olympian Zeus. The old Greek ruin – not in fact a ruin, but a shell that had languished, unfinished, for half a millennium – was an unmissable monument to the grandiosity of Greek aspirations and their subsequent failure to follow through. Hadrian's instinct for impact was magnificent. During the years of restoration the temple disappeared behind high hoardings while the work was undertaken, heightening anticipation. When it was displayed, complete, it was beyond belief. Elaborately finished, with no expense in material or craftsmanship spared, this was a transformation equal to any of the mystery rites of Greek religion. This time not just a god but the abode of a god – or gods: Zeus and Hadrian – was revealed. A magnificent ivory and gold statue of Zeus was unveiled. Hadrian, who was also worshipped there, donated a rare serpent to the priests. In an orgy of gratitude, statues of Hadrian donated by Greek communities were erected everywhere within the complex. Pausanias describes ones not just in local stone but in porphyry imported from Egypt – the contrast of the red and white figures rich and unforgettable. The relationship between Rome and Greece could not have been more clearly stated.[6]

There were parties, readings and music. At the theatre Hadrian, inevitably, excelled himself. Unlike Nero, Hadrian never appeared as a buffoon on the stage, but day after day he simply played himself, an extraordinary actor-manager of his own life on the stage of the city. The crowds entered theatres to find the seats had been sprayed with a mist of balsam and saffron, a fragrance which rose with the warmth of the audience. If the special effects of the building were breathtaking, the matter presented on stage was maybe less so: Hadrian put on the archaic Greek plays that his circle had learned to adore, but there were also pantomime and war-dances for those of less refined taste.[7] The private entertainments of the court were re-created in public spaces in front of crowds of ordinary Athenians; there were lotteries for small presents, and coins were given to the children. If some of the Athenians believed the middle-aged Roman with his weathered face and greying hair was a god, it was hardly surprising.

Hadrian knew when to leave, for departing was a necessary element of the effect; yet on this occasion it must have been hard to turn his back on the pleasures and spirit of Greece. His mood had been lifted by the overwhelming appreciation of his benefactions and the success of the worship of Antinous; at home there was a less entertaining reality to be faced. Returning to Rome meant facing a more demanding, more critical population. Returning to Rome meant placing Antinous back into an area of private, not public loss; the Romans did not need any more official gods, however decorative. When Hadrian left Greece in 132, he was doing so in the knowledge that the country he loved was as secure as it had ever been. But the current state of regeneration was by no means conceived as the final triumph; Hadrian was in his fifties and undoubtedly intended to return. As the pilots led the royal ship out of the harbour it was, in fact, the last time the emperor would see his beloved Greece.

Interspersed with modern holiday resorts and yachting marinas, and accessible, sometimes with difficulty, from modern coastal roads, the beautiful, rugged lands of southern Turkey are still littered with the ruined legacy of their great past. Unlike more densely populated parts of the classical world where later urban expansion has swallowed up much of the ancient cities or made their remains incomprehensible, this area of Turkey has become less broadly populated following the collapse of the Roman empire, and relics of the vigorous life of the Greek cities are everywhere. Some cities have been substantially excavated, but many others are almost forgotten or still gratifyingly undisturbed.

From the small villages which colonize some of the unexcavated sites the sounds of goat bells and children rise and fall with the breeze; hawks hover over deep gorges. Here and there a house has re-used a slab of Hellenistic carving as a lintel or doorstep. In south-west Turkey, craggy cliff-faces, under which ruined cities still sleep, are pitted with dark tombs, each the necropolis of its ancient city. The broad sweep of peaceful foothills is covered with scattered masonry, and the acoustics still work in almost perfect amphitheatres protected in the shallow bowls of valleys. The loose scree that makes the going hard is sometimes entirely composed of pottery shards and small pieces of roof tile: the crushed fragments of cities turning back into dust.

The fate of these loveliest of cities, which emerged in the eighth century BCE and which in the second century were competing for the imperial favour which might ensure their further embellishment, was sealed by the dissolution of the Roman empire. Without the protection of a single power, whether Greek or Roman, the provinces, not individually able to defend themselves against sustained aggression, were attacked by outside forces, including the Goths and the Sassanids. Earthquakes, too, took their toll, as did local quarrying to re-use stone or render it down to lime. (This was almost certainly the fate of one of the wonders of the ancient world, the tomb of King Mausolus at modern-day Bodrum in Turkey.) After the final assaults of the seventh century the urban glories of Asia minor were laid to waste and their sophisticated populations dispersed. For over a millennium their ruins simply disappeared from memory. The forgotten remains were substantial, and from the fifteenth century onwards they were rediscovered and in some cases restored; but survival has been a matter of chance.

Patara, which received Hadrian in 131, is one of many such lost cities. The biggest port in Lycia, it was sufficiently important for water to be brought to it by aqueduct. From the start the winds and the instability of the coast here must have been a problem; today Patara is most famous for its 22 kilometre beach and its relentless, shadeless heat. The ancient harbour now lies in an extensive area of marshland behind a huge sand dune; the remaining ruins are drowning in sand in this peaceful spot. To the far end of the harbour Hadrian's huge, vaulted granary, two storeys high, has survived, but the niches which once held his bust are empty. (An identical granary survives, with its busts, at Myra to the west.) Nearer the main road an arch, dedicated by a local citizen, Mettius Modestus, to his itinerant emperor, stands almost intact, the isolated grandeur of its three tiers a powerful gauge of Patara's slide into oblivion. Mettius made his mark elsewhere: he too had his private poet carve a few lines commemorating his visit to the Egyptian statues of Memnon, and stood with Hadrian watching the dawn rise in November 130 when the dead hero finally sang to him.

Ephesus, which had 300,000 inhabitants at its peak in the time of Hadrian and where the shrine of the goddess drew devotees in their thousands, is now one of the most complete and famous ancient sites in the world, as much for its biblical associations as for its stunning classical remains. The coach-loads of visitors scarcely detract from the effect of its broad paved streets, its amphitheatres, the incomparably beautiful restored library and the tiny details of sewers, water-pipes, latrines and graffiti which make it possible to imagine the past not just of a work of art but of a busy, functioning community. The small but intricate Corinthian temple dedicated to Hadrian is one of the city's glories.

Attalia stood in an incomparable position. Probably because of this, it has remained of strategic importance for two millennia and is still the principal port of the south coast, used by both warships and yachts. Between the mountains of the Lycian and Taurus ranges and the sandy beaches, the town sits on the huge gulf of Antalya whose name the modern town shares. In such surroundings it is hardly surprising that it has become one of Turkey's liveliest resorts, and it is expanding rapidly. Yet despite modern development some monuments survive amid the traffic and the hotels, and the best of these is the finely worked, three-arched gate celebrating Hadrian's visit. The substantial remains of disappointed Phaselis have also been excavated and restored. The theatre, baths, shops and aqueducts are still identifiable and are a fine example of a Hellenistic city, but the focal point on the south port is the great gateway with its long inscription describing its erection by a hopeful population to greet their emperor in 131.

Passed over by the arbitrary hand of fate, little remains of the historic fabric of Tarsus, the city steeped in history, where Cleopatra first met Mark Antony and which Hadrian visited and raised to pre-eminence in the region. Tarsus is a city only of ghosts.

6

War

Through the roar of the flames streaming far and wide, the groans of the falling victims were heard; such was the height of the hill and the magnitude of the blazing pile that the whole city seemed to be ablaze; and the noise, nothing more deafening and frightening could be imagined.

There were the cries of the Roman war legions as they swept onwards en masse, the yells of the rebels encircled by fire and sword, the panic of the enemy, and their shrieks as they met their fate.

The cries on the hill blended with those of the multitudes in the city below; and now many people who were exhausted and tongue-tied as a result of hunger, when they beheld the Temple on fire, found strength once more to lament and wail . . .

The Temple mount, everywhere enveloped in flames, seemed to be boiling over from its base; yet the blood seemed more abundant than the flames and the numbers of the slain greater than the slayers. The ground could not be seen anywhere between the corpses.

JOSEPHUS, JEWISH WARS, 6, 5.1

Meanwhile the Jews in the region of Cyrene had put a certain Andreas at their head and were destroying both the Romans and the Greeks. They would eat the flesh of their victims, make belts for themselves of their entrails, anoint themselves with their blood and wear their skins for clothing; many they sawed in two from the head downwards; others they gave to wild beasts, and still others they forced to fight as gladiators. In all two hundred and twenty thousand persons perished.

CASSIUS DIO, ROMAN HISTORY, BK 68, CH. 32

From the memoirs of Julia Balbilla, May 132

It seems that we must look to the heavens. First we have the god Antinous; now a Prince of the Jews is proclaimed by a star. There has been talk among the officers for some while, even in Egypt when sensible minds were elsewhere. They spoke of some problems in Judea, of a new Jewish general or some say magician, that the fanatics claimed – most dangerous of all – that Hadrian had slighted their god. It would have been easier to have ignored these rumours, but nothing was more convincing than the adamant denials at first, by all those who might know, that there was rebellion among the Jews. If it were true, as we were told in Athens, that the Jews too would see their cities endowed and, even as we worshipped Zeus, were preparing to accommodate our truths, if it were true it would have been the first time in history that they were not rebelling somewhere. That there was a star marking Antinous' transformation we are assured by the court astronomers. That there is none rising to illuminate the cause of the Jewish rebel we are also assured.

The Jews have long been a troublesome people, endlessly resisting the subjugation which might protect them; even among themselves they brawl and intrigue. They will foment trouble until they destroy themselves, not just their temple, my brother once said. Yet no one could ignore them – they were always clamouring for their space, irresistibly individual and uncompromising. My grandfather – a man of the cast of Hadrian – determined to lead the Jews away from their strange customs and he failed. My noble father sought an alliance in marriage with their most beautiful princess, Drusilla, and he too failed. Still, we who are monuments to expediency look across to them and wonder what it must be like to be so proud. There is something magnificent in the obduracy of the Judeans, their utter inability to learn from the past. Again and again they refuse to play their part in this secure, Roman world. Ours is an empire united by advantage. The Jews think otherwise.

Hadrian is a man of peace. The Jews may think this will go well for them, failing to observe that where one emperor falls another rises. In Judea and in cities where they have settled they think that they can plot and attack with impunity. But where one emperor may glorify the empire and his reputation with peace, aqueducts and good roads, another may make his mark in violent campaigns and the provision of weary barbarians to be torn apart in the arena. Hadrian is no Titus, no Trajan even. He is not the man he was a year ago, to be sure; but he is not young, he is not hardened to war, he picks no quarrels, he reads his histories and he counts the cost. Hadrian looks out over a broad landscape and now, when he reigns over it in glory, he will not descend to the provocations of a quarrelsome people; surely his heart is not in it.

And he has treated them as he has treated others. Their city too is being restored. Even as we passed through Judea, hopeful as we were then and oblivious to future catastrophe, his engineers were drawing up plans. The place – their citadel, Jerusalem – lay in ruins, and now it will rise as a fine city. But if they do not understand gratitude, well, the emperor is a sophisticated man, he will understand that that is how it always is with the Jews. They hate the Romans, they hate the Greeks. Their leaders love Hadrian, at least when he is close at hand, and counsel cooperation; so the Jews find other leaders, whose hatred of Rome is less diluted by the pursuit of advantage. Their god is an angry god who hates all other gods. It is not enough for their god that his followers should worship him; they must also refute the gods of all the rest of the world. Their god deceives them and leads them ineluctably to extinction. They have no armies, no discipline; the emperor could send in his legions to Judea and cut them down if he so chose; but he will wait, knowing that ultimately if they do not see sense they will be snuffed out and forgotten.

Still, Hadrian's prefect in Judea is a dangerous man, dangerous in his self-importance: a man who thinks he should be governing a more congenial people or a more prosperous province. Why should it be considered worthy, considered *effective* to send a Jew-hater to Judea? In our history men have hired poisoners, informants or thugs to do work too vile for them to accomplish with a sword. There is something in this that smacks of the same; that the task is one that some decent men fear. Tineius Rufus is well-qualified. He has put them down in Achaea; Jew-crushing is what he does. So he boasts. He is severe in the retribution that he metes out, yet lax in looking beyond the bruised child that he sends into some makeshift arena or the old man who is run through by a legionary. Rufus is concerned only that his actions should precipitate his speedy return to the civilised world. He has had enough of deterring the undeterrable. There are always more boys and more grandfathers to take their place, and always more swords and more mangy lions to meet them.

Rufus is an adequate soldier, I dare say, but little respected now by his men, who are as a consequence brutal and largely controlled by junior officers who are determined there will be no repeat of Cyrene laid to their charge. Rufus amuses himself with Jewish women – the same whose husbands and sons are writhing on their crosses; these matters, though supposedly a secret, are spoken of freely in certain quarters. Even in Hadrian's presence Rufus drank too much wine and presumed upon an alleged old friendship with the emperor to justify long-winded battle anecdotes which were terminated only by sleep. If the Jews see the values of Rome in Rufus, no wonder they revolt.

Hadrian was irritated and peremptory in his dealings with Rufus – not that the prefect seemed particularly inhibited by this – and demanding of the ranks, whom he had practising manoeuvres for three days in the desert heat. Apparently, as they wheeled out their machines and marched and reformed ranks, hordes of biting flies descended on them. All the while, on the heights, although it was miles from any settlement, a small group of dark peasants looked down. By the time Hadrian had addressed the exhausted troops from a makeshift platform, the observers had disappeared into the barren landscape. It was certainly the case that those soldiers who attended our departure showed their recent battle scars, swollen with bites and with sores from sand chafing under their leather bindings.

From Athens we shall soon leave for Brundisium on the coast of Italy. The passage home should not be long, but even for Hadrian it feels, I think, like a journey into exile. In the main, Athens has been the restorative we hoped. In the last few weeks the mood has lightened. As time has passed, fear has diminished, the whispers have subsided; there is no sign of the Bithynian, dead or alive. Commodus is constantly at the emperor's side trying to fulfil some of the duties of Hadrian's late friend; his poetry – pretty, clever verse – gets many hearings. He is a lazy man, Commodus, but not so lazy that he cannot stretch out to grasp an opportunity which is right under his nose.

Hadrian is genuinely moved by his own achievements. Those who shared his dream have been well rewarded and he has been drawing again, designs for small shrines through which worship of Antinous may be directed. The first statues were sent to him for approval from Italy, Greece and Egypt. To see them was disturbing – there is always that shock in seeing the stone reflection of a familiar face, something like first gazing on a body from which life has been recently extinguished. At first all statues look the same, of course, but the best keep something of the animated spirit in their cold contours. Not that Antinous was so familiar, and already the face of the statue – rather younger and plumper than the original – is how I think of him. *When* I think of him, which, away from the temples, is not often.

In 132 Hadrian, now in his late fifties, decided to leave Greece, the country he had placed at the centre of his empire, and turn for home. He had accomplished all that he had ever planned on the greatest stage set the world had ever seen. The council of the Panhellion had been inaugurated with games and religious ceremonies. Athens, basking in the generosity of an emperor who loved her, had never looked more splendid. Alabaster, gilding, bronzes and hundreds of marble columns and statues decorated the restored city, and festivals had been arranged in perpetuity. Great games – more to the Roman taste, of a kind rare in Greece – had been held, where 1,000 exotic animals from all over the empire were slaughtered. The celebrations went on for weeks on end. The cult of Antinous had been established in all the major centres of Greece and Asia minor. The dream of a Roman empire united by Hellenic nostalgia had reached its zenith.

Hadrian had been away from Rome for nearly four years, and there were domestic matters which required his presence. There was the succession to consider, and at Rome, too, there were great architectural projects to be inspected. In Hadrian's absence two magnificent temples had been completed, one the largest ever built by Romans; there was work in progress, too, on an extensive country palace for his personal use, and the beginnings of a grandiose mausoleum to dignify his posterity. Hadrian may or may not have felt the preliminary signs of the sickness whose symptoms were to become unmistakable only a few years later, but he was no Trajan turning in failing health to make a last desperate dash for Rome; indeed, he was perhaps already wondering where he might go next, once the exacting rituals of Rome were completed.

Embarking on the voyage to Ephesus, the first port of call on the long route home, Hadrian set out on a journey towards a more conventional imperial life; and in Rome, preparations began to receive the returning emperor in a manner due to a gloriously successful ruler at the peak of his powers. Yet even while Hadrian was celebrating in Athens, there had been worrying news from Judea, news perhaps suppressed in the hope that a minor intensification of apparently perennial Jewish problems would not interfere with the festivities. Soon, however, it was impossible to ignore the accelerating disruption, although the potential for serious damage to imperial interests was at first underestimated. Jewish troubles were rarely confined to Judea; indeed, they seemed to be ubiquitous. Nearly all the provinces of the Roman east had Jewish communities, and as suppression followed revolt, so the Jews driven out of one city would congregate in greater, and angrier, numbers in the next. Hadrian's policies towards the Jews may have been misjudged, but the Jewish unrest which he inherited had long roots stretching back nearly two centuries, to the time when Rome gained power over Judea. The glowing embers of hatred and discontent finally flared into a terrible conflagration in 132.

Rome had originally entered Judea on the pretext of intervening to restore order to the country's fractious internal affairs. Judea was an inevitable target for Roman expansionism. It was strategically invaluable, close to the power base of Persia, one of Rome's few serious contenders for eastern power, and with an extensive coastal border. The territory had long been unsettled; its possession was frequently disputed, and the lifestyle and beliefs of the Jews left them isolated and insufficiently protected against political predators. Crucially, it was also weakened by its festering internal dissent. So when one of the feuding factions asked Rome for assistance, it was guilty of extreme political naïvety. The standard Roman process of assimilation began, in which they would be called in by a would-be ruler to bolster a faltering regime, would provide military support, oversee the installation of a puppet king as a concession to the existing population, and in time eventually absorb the country into the empire.

For Judea, the beginning of the end came in 63 BCE. In the guise of arbitrating in an ongoing dispute between the Pharisees and the Hasmoneans, the ambitious and pitiless republican general Pompey – whose tomb Hadrian had hastened to honour when he entered Egypt – marched into the country. He besieged a starving and diseased Jerusalem for three months before his final assault, killing its inhabitants as they went about Sabbath observances. A Jewish king, Herod the Great, was put in place, but slowly the reality of the annexation became clear and from the first century Judea was a Roman province.

Unlike the inhabitants of more amenable provinces, Jews both within the country and throughout the cities of the east never totally accepted Roman domination, and clashes, varying in the degree of violence, became commonplace. Rome had annexed a highly politicised, nationalistic population who would never fully accede to the conventions of Roman rule, whose constraints struck at fundamental tenets of Jewish self-determination; for Jews with a proud tradition of independence, the Roman presence was and could only be intolerable. It was inconceivable that they would ever become integrated citizens of Rome; yet without greater cooperation they could not hope to see the rewards with which Rome blessed favoured provinces. In other annexed territories, however reluctantly they were enclosed within the empire, the protection and resources of Rome were sufficiently attractive to allow the process of incorporation to evolve without prolonged conflict. Although new members of the empire would be expected to honour the emperor in various formal rituals, they would otherwise be left to follow local customs. As Rome was broadly tolerant of other religions, the token act of submission and recognition of Rome and the emperor was usually performed. This degree of pragmatism was inconceivable to Judea. They had one god and he was not a Roman emperor. Almost every aspect of Roman civic life was at war with Jewish beliefs. Jewish worship of a single god brought them into immediate conflict with the tolerant paganism of Greeks and Romans. Jews could not join the Roman army because they were unable to perform military duties on the Sabbath; Romans recalled with contempt the ease with which Pompey had originally taken Jerusalem, citing the Jews' prioritising of religious observation over self-defence. The Romans were uneasy about Jewish circumcision, echoing the abhorrence of the practice felt by the Greeks, who disliked it largely on aesthetic grounds. It was not only a crucial defining physical distinction for the Jews, it was a distinction easily apparent were they to take part in the central Romano-Greek social activities of athletics and bathing. The Romans, who in the rest of their eastern empire were broadly sympathetic to indigenous characteristics, were unable to understand Jewish intransigence and were perplexed to the point of provocation by Jewish religious sensibilities.

The schisms which had allowed the Romans to enter Judea were not resolved with occupation by an apparently common enemy. The Jews remained split as to whether a degree of cooperation with the occupying force or rigorous separatism would do most to ensure the survival of their culture and beliefs. Jews who were strongly religious were adamantly opposed to interference in their ancient customs. The less devout were more pragmatic; in a volatile region of small monarchies and strategically important territory, life was one of constant or incipient power struggles and violence. For some, Roman rule at least provided strong government and the prospect of regional peace; for many, the Romans were – just – endurable; a minority kept the flame of resistance burning, and several were still tenacious in their belief that a messiah would come to free them from Rome. This hope, often held in the face of despair, obliterated any consideration of the resources first- and second-century Rome could muster to assert its will.

The relationship between Rome and this troubled province had repercussions throughout the eastern empire, with feuding, riots, proscriptions and unrest in any country which had a sizeable Jewish population. Local uprisings were put down, but they increased in ferocity and in the damage done to city infrastructure and urban life. Wider revolt was almost inevitable sooner or later, and in 66 CE, when riots in Caesarea turned into a full-scale revolt, spreading to Jerusalem, the relationship between the Romans and the Jews became irretrievable. The revolt escalated into war, in which the Jewish forces resisted the Romans for a while before the inevitable capitulation. In response the Romans inflicted a terrible blow on Judea, one which they hoped would finally cow the province into submission. In 70, Titus, the popular and bellicose son of the reigning emperor Vespasian, assembled a vast army. One-fifth of the total forces of the Roman empire entered Judea and made what was intended to be a final assault on Jerusalem. In August, after six months of siege, the city fell. It had been ill-prepared and the siege conditions were horrific; by the time the city itself capitulated, the population was already in extremis:

The famine strengthening its hold devoured the people, houses and families one after another. The roofs were full of women and infants in the last stages of exhaustion, the alleys with the corpses of the aged; children and young men, swollen with hunger haunted the market places and collapsed wherever faintness overcame them ... hunger stifled emotion and with dry eyes and grinning mouths those who were slow to die watched those whose end came sooner.[1]

Josephus was a Jew who has sometimes been accused of collaboration with the Romans – he was certainly a mediator – and he provides an eye-witness account of the final days of utter despair and degradation. He is one of the earliest war reporters, and his scenes are painfully acute in their observation, almost modern in tone as he recalls the desperate inhabitants of the city eating leather and old hay, one woman killing and consuming her baby. When the inevitable happened and the Roman forces overran Jerusalem, Titus' armies slaughtered everyone they encountered. When they reached the Temple, the Jews' holiest place, they tore it down. Soldiers entered the building as the flames spread and carried off any treasures they could find. Again Josephus wrote a powerful eye-witness account of the last moments of the sacred building and the Jews who had attempted to find refuge in it.

While the Temple was yet ablaze, the attackers plundered it, and countless people who were caught by them were slaughtered. There was no pity for age and no regard was accorded rank; children, and old men, lay men and priests, alike were butchered; every class was pursued and crushed in the grip of war, whether they cried out for mercy or offered resistance.[2]

Triumphant, Titus' forces moved on to butcher the remaining inhabitants of the city and fire the surrounding residential areas of Jerusalem. Recent excavations have revealed houses of this period which are blackened by fire. One contained a skeleton of a person burned standing upright. It seemed like the end. Of those who had survived famine and attack, hundreds were executed or taken as gladiators so that their more protracted deaths might entertain the Romans in the arena. As Judea lamented, the sacred texts and the *menorah* that had been looted from the Temple were taken to Rome to be displayed in triumph in a procession of Jewish slaves.

It was perhaps not surprising that at Masada, 50 miles south of Jerusalem, a community of perhaps 1,000 zealots who held on in the mountain-top fortress during a three-year siege by 10,000 Roman soldiers, committed mass suicide in 73 rather than fall into the hands of their oppressors. It was an act which horrified the Romans, while earning their respect; and it was the dramatic final act of that conflict, though only a precursor of what was to come. The destruction of the Temple and the tragedy of Masada were events which were seared deep into the Jewish consciousness; it is still so today, and it was certainly so in the early second century. Vespasian believed that the Jews would never recover, and indeed the Temple never rose again; but Jewish spirit and solidarity were invigorated by the depredations. Over the next sixty years or so disparate acts of anger and desperation became more focused, more organised and, although they did not at first realise it, much more dangerous to the Romans.

Since the war, the Greek cities of the empire had been flashpoints for many violent confrontations with the Jews. Atrocity stories were current on both sides. Nearly a quarter of a million had died at Alexandria, at Cyrene and on Cyprus. There were pogroms, there was retaliation; there were emissaries from both sides who made the long journey to Rome to plead their case before the emperor of the day; there was never resolution.

Given the continuing volatility of Judea and within Jewish communities throughout the east, it was almost inevitable that there would be further bloody disturbances during Hadrian's reign. They were not long in coming. Hadrian's political and military judgements, so shrewd and effective in other crises, are usually considered to have inflamed the situation in second-century Judea, and certainly his response to a delicate political situation seems out of character for an emperor whose policies were normally temperate and who usually had a good grasp of the broader implications of actions. How and why did things go so disastrously wrong in Judea under Hadrian? The answers to these questions have their roots not only in the long and often violent history of the relationship between the Romans and the Jews but also in the generally hostile Greek attitude to the Jews. Paradoxically, ancient antipathy to the Jews with their exclusive worship of a single god was fostered primarily by the culturally tolerant Greeks. Later, the Greeks were envious of the high-status appointments and wealth of some Jews in the eastern empire, and the separatism which grew from Roman attempts to permit the Jews to live under different laws within Greek cities.

As Rome extended its power eastwards, the acceptance of the Jews and the degree to which they might prosper under

Roman domination often depended on the degree to which individual Roman emperors identified with Greece. Hadrian, the arch-Hellenophile, was inevitably going to be sympathetic to the anti-Jewish sentiment of the Greeks, whom he counted as both friends and advisers. Yet Judea had some cause to hope for better things from Hadrian. As emperor, Hadrian had inherited the legacy of Jewish unrest from Trajan; but Hadrian's more inclusive policies were in marked contrast to those of his predecessor. Where Trajan had pushed out frontiers on which an uneasy peace was sustained only by military investment, Hadrian was a consolidator. Where Trajan had fought, Hadrian maintained peace wherever possible – indeed, his preference for construction and a pacific appreciation of the empire was criticised by some, including the writer Cornelius Fronto. The successful maintenance of a vast empire depended on pragmatic cooperation between conquerors and provinces; peace, often violently achieved, might be sustained by letting subjects experience Roman rule as acceptable, even beneficial. Religious and cultural tolerance was a factor in the *pax Augusta* or Roman peace. Under Hadrian there was a possibility of change away from an imperial power defined by militarism. His opportunity – and realistically, it may not have been a very hopeful one – came and was rejected in the early 130s.

Within Hadrian's agenda of urban regeneration throughout his empire, Jerusalem was an obvious candidate for restoration. It was, after all, many years since the last Jewish uprising, and Hadrian's policies had in the main been geared towards the maintenance of a mutually rewarding peace. This emperor was known as a man of moderation and poetical pragmatism. His early urban restoration programme had included rebuilding structures damaged or destroyed in earlier Jewish revolts in Cyrene and north Africa. Surely, some thought, he would rebuild the Jerusalem Temple and grant the Jews the same self-determination and religious freedom he had encouraged elsewhere. The more optimistic Jews hoped for such a gesture of reconciliation, one which would provide a focus for their culture and identity, would allow them a dignified role within a great empire. Their disappointments were to add fuel to the fire which eventually swept Judea.

Sometime in the early 130s the news of Hadrian's plans for Jerusalem became known. Exact chronologies are uncertain, but initial decisions were probably made as he passed through the country on his way to Egypt in 130. It was instantly obvious that, far from a benefaction, this was architecture as an act of war. Hadrian certainly planned to build, just as he had elsewhere, but in Judea he planned the construction of a wholly pagan city – a new foundation, to be called Aelia Capitolina. A new population, of Roman soldiers, would fill it. To erect what was to be essentially a military garrison on the site of the Jews' devastated citadel, their most holy place, was an act of immense provocation. The new gates of Jerusalem, the sacred city of the Jews, were constructed not to glorify its native inhabitants or to remind them of their emperor's generosity, as had been the case in towns throughout the rest of the Roman world, but explicitly to exclude Jews from Hadrian's new colony. Jews were now forbidden to enter their city except on one day a year, and a temple to Jupiter, appropriate to the needs of Jerusalem's new inhabitants but also an unmistakable symbol of Jewish humiliation, was erected on the foundations of the destroyed Temple. The crest of one of the occupying legions was a boar, and this was carved into the city gateway. Whether deliberately or in ignorance of local beliefs, the image of a pig, an unclean animal in the Jewish tradition, was deeply offensive. Hadrian's architectural statements, as always, bore out policy that was enacted in other ways: circumcision was banned, taxes were raised.

When Hadrian became emperor, there were still a few

alive in Judea who had lived through the horrors of the war of 70 CE and plenty who remembered the suppression of the riots in Egypt. Factionalism was still rife, and although there were periods of calm there was never submission. When the peace held it was uneasy; sporadic unrest was dealt with heavy-handedly by the local garrison. Although actions by Hadrian undoubtedly and catalytically inflamed local sensibilities, the Jews of Judea had been planning a more wholesale assault on the hated occupying power for some time, perhaps ever since their near-extinction by Titus in 70, certainly since the revolts of 115. They had had enough time to acquire the equipment which had been lacking in previous insurgencies. With what seems retrospectively singular ill-judgement, the Romans had forced the Jews to make weapons for them; some they had hidden, others they had made to such poor quality that they were rejected by the Roman ordnance, and these too found their way into the keeping of potential rebels. They had also prepared a network of subterranean passages and fortifications which were to provide cover for their forays and prove a major factor in their initial success when serious revolt broke out again.

While Hadrian was actually passing through the country in 130 there seems to have been a consensus among the Jews that, despite acute hostility to him, it was better to let the emperor pass on to another region before engaging the Roman forces. During the following months, as the low-level unrest became more focused, the apprehensive mood was exacerbated by strange portents, always powerful in a culture where unusual natural phenomena were closely observed for their political significance. Then the holy tomb of Solomon, the most venerable of Jewish sites since the Romans had destroyed the Temple, suddenly collapsed. This was quite possibly caused by the destabilising effects of the early stages of construction of the new pagan city nearby; some believed it was a deliberate dismantling of the last central site where Jews might congregate. Depending on one's individual disposition, it was either a powerful portent or a powerfully inflammatory act of destruction.

During this period, as the Jews faced the very real prospect of the obliteration of their religion and culture, a charismatic rebel called Shimon ben Kosiba began to change the face of resistance. In the hundred years since one compelling sect leader – Jesus of Nazareth – had been executed, there had been a succession of messianic claimants; when one failed to deliver, or was removed by the occupying powers or by schisms within the Jews themselves, another proclaimed himself in their stead. From 130 onwards, even before the establishment of Hadrian's new city, the previously unknown ben Kosiba began to draw together a more organised, measured opposition to the Romans. Slowly, sporadic acts of violence or sabotage became a more concerted campaign of attack. Hadrian's plans for Jerusalem were exactly what ben Kosiba had been waiting for.

When a new star was seen it was claimed by ben Kosiba as an endorsement that he was the new messiah, the Prince of Israel who would lead his desperate people away from slavery under the Romans. He changed his name to bar Kokhba – 'son of the star' – implying his fulfilment of an ancient prophecy. Rumours circulated that dramatic miracles had been associated with him: that he could uproot trees with his bare hands, that he could belch flames from his mouth. At the very least, bar Kokhba was a passionate demagogue, and although he had a local reputation for both ferocity and prodigious strength, he was compelling, intelligent and ruthless; it was a potent combination. His ever-increasing numbers of followers were, it was alleged, willing to cut off their little fingers as a demonstration of their loyalty and courage. Such stories drew more supporters to his side. Despite some continued opposition within Judea, bar Kokhba, unlike most other extremists, began to draw adherents not just among the fanatics and religious zealots but from previously less actively political communities across Judea.

There were still articulate intellectuals who scoffed at bar Kokhba's messianic claims, but his movement was supported by a number of Jewish scholars, including the elderly and respected Rabbi Akiba, and it grew in influence and effect. Against a background of escalating brutality in Roman retaliation for minor offences, his creed seemed more and more persuasive. Slowly the Jews, whose defence had so often been weakened by rifts, moved towards a semblance of unity under one leader. By late 130 bar Kokhba had 400,000 fighting men behind him. Around 132 the situation exploded into open conflict.

The Jews of Judea believed that their coreligionists across the east would surely support them against the Romans. With bar Kokhba at their head, many believed that the yoke of Rome might yet be overthrown. All experience suggested that this was a naïve hope; yet writers of the time report that, although there was not the simultaneous uprising the Judeans might have hoped for, trouble did soon spread, not just within the country, nor only into neighbouring communities in adjacent territories, but throughout the eastern empire. This was not yet sufficiently coherent to be a serious threat to Roman dominance in the region, but it was worrying for the Romans that support for the Jews was extending less into Jewish communities elsewhere than into other, non-Jewish but disaffected Roman possessions. The Greek historian Cassius Dio predictably attributed this to provincial opportunism:

Soon, however, all Judea had been stirred up, and the Jews everywhere were showing signs of disturbance, were gathering together, and giving evidence of great hostility to the Romans, partly by secret and partly by overt acts; many outside nations too, were joining them through eagerness for gain, and the whole earth, one might say, was being stirred up over the matter.[3]

Jewish commentators reported with bitterness that all over the empire, those hostile to the Jews saw the revolt as an excuse for further outbreaks of violent hostility against them.

To begin with, the experienced Romans on the spot considered the outbreaks to be containable; but the initial response by the prefect, Tineius Rufus, was soon revealed as inadequate. The attack on the Jews was prosecuted with the utmost savagery, yet the Romans failed to bring the campaign to a conclusion and Roman casualties began to reach unacceptable levels. It took the occupying forces too long to realise that the opposition was better organised, better supported and better provisioned than it ever had been before. It did not fight according to rules, nor did it wear a uniform, but it became obvious that there was, in effect, an army fighting for Judea. Slowly the numbers of Romans on the ground began to seem inadequate. For every rebel executed, another rose in his place. This intelligence was fed back to Hadrian; finally he acted, and when he did it was with drastic measures. Remembering the speed and extent with which the revolt of 115 had taken hold, it may have seemed essential to him that firm measures be taken speedily once the seriousness of the violence was exposed.

Hadrian's response to events in Judea was out of character. As the situation started to spin out of control, he appeared to have reacted too slowly to events as they were reported to him; and then, when he did act, he did so with atypical harshness and with little idea of the fighting conditions which would await his legions. Hadrian had taken part in difficult campaigns against the barbarian tribes of middle Europe under Trajan, so he understood military tactics. But Judea was a very different place from the thick forests of Dacia, and the Jews quite different in psychology and motivation from the barbarian forces. The Romans' opponents here were not so ill-prepared. They had learned the lessons of the first Jewish war and had never trusted the men who they regarded as their oppressors.

Judea was a land largely of villages, not cities; its communities were small and spread out, and it was hard to pinpoint where attacks were coming from and how they were being organised. Bar Kokhba made certain that opportunities for large-scale engagements were impossible, forcing the Romans to re-organise themselves into small fighting units. The terrain was rough; bands of rebels appeared, attacked and were spirited into the landscape. Individual fighters were captured, tortured and put to death but no inroads were made into the hidden Jewish strongholds. For every village laid to waste by the Romans, another would produce its own small band of fighters. The Romans learned what European armies were to discover hundreds of years later: that the best-trained and best-equipped fighting force in the world might come to grief against partisans fighting on their own territory and for a cause for which they would willingly sacrifice themselves and their families.

Tineius Rufus' local garrison of two legions, the VI Ferrata and the X Fretensis, was coming under such pressure that the nearest territories to the trouble spot despatched as many soldiers as could be spared. From Syria came the II Gallica; from Egypt, the XXII Deitoriana. It is possible that the III Cyrenaica, III Gallica and IV Scythia were also involved, and if so the fragile stability of the other eastern provinces would have been under threat with their diversion. The Jews liberated part of their country. It is possible that they moved on to take the ruins of Jerusalem, at least for a while; if so, this was in itself a victory. Successful actions against the Romans gave them control of strategically important coastal lands. The rebels confiscated imperial estates and redistributed them to Jewish peasant communities. They issued their own, Hebrew coinage, some of it created by overstamping existing Roman coins. It was an act of huge and inspiring significance. A century earlier Jesus Christ had been asked by fellow Jews whether they should continue to pay taxes to the Romans, in effect looking for his direction on civil disobedience; he looked at the image of Augustus on a coin and said, with great political astuteness, 'Render therefore unto Caesar the things that are Caesar's and unto God the things that are God's.'[4] Now the coinage was Hebrew, not Roman, and the question had become redundant.

Many emperors had been destroyed by movements which started within the army, and many good generals suffering heavy losses and uncertainties had faced mutiny in the ranks. A protracted campaign was always a hazardous prospect and it seems extraordinary that Hadrian, however provoked, should have become embroiled in such a war of attrition. As the world's mightiest army confronted freedom fighters and found themselves unable to bring the campaign to any kind of conclusion, military history was recorded and recalled. Varus' loss of the legions in the early first century had inflicted a devastating loss of confidence on the Romans, and it was a lesson they had learned well. Tacitus reports a Roman general years later having nightmares about Varus on the eve of a battle and records evidence of atrocities committed.[5] So much of Rome's pride and self-definition was sustained by the certainty of military pre-eminence; yet as war escalated in Judea, the whole empire watched and saw that mighty Rome could not prevail.

The Roman army had two great fighting strengths. It could fight efficiently on the plain, in set-piece formation battles, and it had also developed the manoeuvrability and the advanced weaponry for hand-to-hand fighting in woods and forests, where the more crude spears, slings and long, hacking swords of opponents could not so easily be brought into play.[6] The lethal short sword which the legionary was taught to use in a stabbing motion and the javelin thrown at a visible enemy were the standard weapons that made Roman soldiers so effective. Siege machines and the famous shield cover of the *testudo* had become the stuff of military legend, enabling legions to break down the defences of cities. But in Judea the Romans had to act within a military landscape very different from those in which they could invariably win the day. Skirmishes were fought in desert and hilly, inaccessible reaches with natural fortifications. Siege machines may have been used to gain access to groups established on hilly plateaux, but the insurgents also dug into a network of subterranean caves from which they could fight what was, in essence, a guerrilla war:

They did not dare try conclusions with the Romans in the open field, but they occupied the advantageous positions in the country and strengthened them with mines and walls, in order that they might have places of refuge whenever they should be hard pressed, and might meet together unobserved under ground; and they pierced these subterranean passages from above at intervals to let in air and light.[7]

It could be a description of strategies of many similar partisan actions, from the second century to the twenty-first. Men, their families, weapons and equipment were kept below ground. Much information about the times has been pieced together in surviving letters found by archaeologists surveying these passages.

Urgent recruitment campaigns were undertaken back in Italy, particularly aimed at the robust country boys who could endure the conditions of Judea. Senators toured the provinces, exacting a levy of young men to fight in the unpopular war. Emergency measures were set in place; sailors were transferred from their ships into military service. It was increasingly hard to hide the fact that Rome was embroiled in a military débâcle. It was not a disaster – yet – but there were already significant losses of men and esteem, and the financial price of a prolonged campaign was beginning to bite back home.

In 133 Hadrian decided, in some desperation, to replace Tineius Rufus, and sent for the experienced and resolute Julius Severus, governor of Britain, to take control of the legions in Judea. It was clear by now that every effort was necessary to restore power, and that the months of travel which would be necessary to move Severus to the east were not likely to see any resolution of the situation. Severus crossed Europe during the autumn and winter of 133 and arrived in the Judea sometime in midwinter, bringing his own troops with him to add to the forces now in place. His only brief was to annihilate the resistance, by whatever means were necessary. He quickly ruled out the possibility of conventional war, instigating forceful counter-insurgency measures; his aim, he said, was to 'crush, exhaust and exterminate' the Jews by starvation, enclosure and ambush.[8] Given that it was impossible to identify more than a few clear military bases, the vast Roman army set about destroying the entire population of Judea. Even then, weighed down by armour and with an enemy who could play the ground to their advantage, Roman losses were still far worse than anticipated. Among the casualties one whole legion – the 5,000 strong XXII Deitoriana – was almost certainly wiped out; a huge loss in terms of prestige as well as manpower. The customary salutation, 'If you and your children are in good health, it is well; I and the legions are in good health', was omitted in the emperor's formal despatch to the senate.[9]

What had been a matter of a few religious extremists under a ruthless but charismatic leader resisting the rule of a reasonably enlightened and non-belligerent Roman ruler became a movement which united the Jews and transformed Hadrian. The huntsman of the Libyan desert, the discerning art collector, the tolerant intellectual, disappeared, and in their place Hadrian emerged as a model of Roman power responding to perceived threat with absolute ruthlessness. Generosity became irresolution, tolerance turned into suppression, pragmatism into punitively enforced proscription. Some time around 134 Hadrian rode back into Judea, not at the centre of a brilliant travelling court but in the uniform of a general, with a pared-down retinue of legionaries and officers, to inspire and lead his army.

Atrocity stories hinted at the deteriorating conditions of war; psychological intimidation was a weapon fully employed by both sides. It was believed that the Roman troops had wrapped children in Torah rolls and burned them alive.[10] Bar Kokhba allegedly punished Christians who would not deny that Jesus was the Messiah. Burial of the dead was prohibited by the Romans and the stink of decay marked the scene of every engagement. It was obvious by late 134 that the tide was turning against Judea, and those Jews who now regretted their involvement in the uprising and knew they were looking upon the extinction of their race referred to bar Kokhba as bar Koziba, 'son of disappointment'. But there was no turning back. Bar Kokhba and his supporters could wait only for the now inevitable end.

The war finally turned with the capture of bar Kokhba's headquarters, a fortified settlement at Bethar, to the southwest of Jerusalem. According to Jewish tradition Bethar was taken in July 135, on the same date as the destruction of the Temple so many years earlier. A long siege preceded the fall of the fortress, which was not just a stronghold but housed the Sanhedrin – the Jewish high court – and was full of refugees as well as its rebel defenders. When it fell bar Kokhba, along with all the other inhabitants of Bethar, was killed. The bodies were left to rot, and bar Kokhba's head was paraded in front of the Roman commander and jubilant troops. Rumour had it that a great serpent was coiled around bar Kokhba's neck, and Hadrian is supposed to have looked on it with some awe, saying, 'If his god had not killed him, who could have overcome him?'

From the beginning it was likely that Roman might and resources would eventually subdue Judea, but it was three hard years before Hadrian gained the advantage and when he did, celebrations back home were muted. Victory, such as it was, did nothing to increase the emperor's popularity or augment his honours. Indeed, only thirty years later the author Cornelius Fronto, when discussing the recent loss of a legion in Parthia, compared it to the Jewish revolt of the 130s, implicitly conceding that Hadrian had been defeated in Judea. If they had not lost the war, the Romans had certainly lost face, esteem and confidence. They were determined that such a challenge to their power would never be repeated. This time Jewish unrest must be brought to an end, and they would ensure this by inflicting a mortal and permanent blow on their opponents.

Five hundred and eighty thousand Jewish men had died fighting and the number of non-combatants, women and children who died of attack, disease and famine could not be estimated. Judea itself was devastated. Fifty major outposts and 985 large villages were obliterated, and hundreds of thousands of Jews were slaughtered or sent into slavery. In the markets at Gaza and Hebron Jewish slaves were sold for the price of a horse. Roman perception was that Jewish religious observance had always made cooperation impossible. Hadrian gave orders intended to ensure its eradication. Teaching of the faith was forbidden, as was access to the site of the Temple.

When the Bar Kokhba revolt was finally over, the Jewish diaspora was complete. All resistance was obliterated and surviving members of the Jewish communities were widely scattered. It appeared not only that the potential for further disruption was removed but that the Jews could never again form a cohesive national and cultural group. The garrison town of Aelia Capitolina was completed on the foundations of Jerusalem and even the name of Judea was erased when the country became Syria Palaestina. It was a *damnatio memoriae* of an entire nation.

The Romans had always been capable of both dogged and implacable military action, and indeed instructive revenge, when faced with non-compliant enemies; Julius Caesar had slaughtered over one million people as he carved out his empire and probably captured and sold into slavery an equal number – but Judea was not a continent, only one small country. The Romans' campaigns of 60 CE against the British Iceni led by Boudicca, which also had as their objective the obliteration of a troublesome, unbiddable people, had left 80,000 dead: a hefty toll, but a small proportion of the deaths in Judea.[11] Hadrian's actions in Judea, set against the policies he pursued throughout the rest of the empire, seem almost unaccountable. In the context of the times it was not the harshness of his action against the Jews that was unacceptable but that he had inflicted a bruising and public blow on his own country and had exposed his army to the risk of ignominious defeat.

Yet there were some perceptible reasons, psychological, historical and strategic, for the emperor's response. They can be best understood as deriving from the emperor's vision of a Hellenized world. Hadrian's lack of sympathy for the Jews was possibly driven less by antisemitic prejudice than by his powerfully pro-Greek agenda. Antinous was Greek, Hadrian's greatest successes were in Greece, and it was to Greece that he had returned after the difficult period in Egypt. There Hadrian's welcome was, as always, unequivocal. There, as a Hellenistic king, he could bask in the respect, understanding and gratitude of the Greeks. Psychologically, the emperor was under great personal stress at this time. He was not young, he was not well, he had been travelling incessantly and he had suffered a major bereavement. The experiences of the early 130s can only have had a destabilising effect on a man already rendered vulnerable by intermittent depression and ill-health. In the wake of the disappointments of Egypt, he had let his passion for Greece become an obsession. When the death of his companion was so soon followed by the re-emergence of Jewish separatism, while Hadrian was still in the east, lapping up the adulation of the Greeks, the stage was set for disaster.

Whatever the nature of the personal connection between the man and the youth, Antinous represented the values and attractions of Hadrian's adopted culture. The circumstances of his death and the volatility of the emperor's emotions as he left Egypt appear to have exacerbated his exasperation with the hostility of the Jews to his wider plan and their unwillingness to submit to Roman domination. His lack of tolerance for opposition, which was to be so marked and so detrimental to his reputation in the last years of his life, was never more damaging.

Nevertheless, although at another time Hadrian might have attempted a compromise to settle the politically sensitive state of affairs in Judea, there were arguably sound historic reasons why he decided to take action that would crush the Jews once and for all, noting that even Titus' overwhelming victory over the Jews in 70 CE had not prevented recurrences of opposition. The cost of this constant insurrection was unacceptable. There had been outbreaks of violence, instability and civic destruction for decade after decade. Hadrian himself had undertaken extensive restoration of areas in Alexandria which had been destroyed by riots. But the Jews, he believed, could not be placated; they would regard all concessions as weakness. The numbers left dead as a result of these uprisings were always increasing and a serious Jewish revolt of 117 had spread with great speed and disruption east from Cyrene in north Africa, to Egypt and beyond. The Bar Kokhba revolt must have seemed to represent a grave threat to all Hadrian had achieved. Possibly, too, his absorption in the festivities in Athens had failed to alert him early enough to trouble further east; and by the time it became imperative to act, his options were restricted.

The sequence of provocation and response is impossible to prove, and in the absence of a clear chronology of the events which precipitated the crisis it is difficult to apportion blame. That Hadrian chose to erect a garrison city from which the

Jews were excluded on the ruins of Jerusalem is certain. Whether it was part of a campaign to repress the Jews, or a punitive reaction to violence already committed, or an unrealistic attempt, more in keeping with his broader policies in the empire, to avert further risings in the region is unknown, although most evidence suggests that Aelia Capitolina was begun before Hadrian went to Egypt. Whether the emperor prohibited circumcision is still more uncertain; and, if he did, whether he did so before or after bar Kokhba's rise is equally hard to establish. Sources are scanty and ambiguous. If he did ban the practice it is likely that his proclamation confused castration with circumcision; even so, the effect on the Jews was unlikely to be mitigated by a clumsy manifestation of Roman ignorance.

Whether Hadrian was ill-advised or miscalculated the mood of the Jews and their long history of resistance, he cannot have imagined that the foundation of Aelia Capitolina would proceed without igniting violence. Possibly his own passion for all things Greek and the unfolding success of his grand Panhellenic project blurred the reality of the impact of his policies on the Jews, who had been insensitively governed for so long. Possibly his pro-Greek advisers counselled that a subversive population must be prevented from spreading disaffection; possibly Hadrian's notorious anger overwhelmed him at a crucial time of decision. Athens brought a painful convergence of Hadrian's moment of glory and his grief at the loss of Antinous. His favourite's death had removed not only a lover but one of his few intimate companions; after 130 Hadrian was an isolated man. The disdain of some of his Roman court for his enthusiasms cannot have passed him by, and the increasingly intrusive news from Judea may have motivated his decision to impose his will once and for all over the natural enemy of the Greeks and the one nation who made no attempt to live constructively within the empire.

But there were other, more subtle considerations. There

were advantages to Hadrian in throwing the power of Rome into suppressing the Jews. Hadrian may have hoped that a vigorous campaign might deflect the hostility and speculation that were directed towards him in the aftermath of the mysterious death of his favourite. Roman criticisms of his Hellenic idealism would be silenced as the country united in war and Hadrian could demonstrate that, even in his fifties, he could turn aside from art and festivals and assume the martial characteristics that traditional Rome so admired. Those in Rome, as well as in the far reaches of the empire, would see that after twenty years he was still the unchallengeable holder of supreme power. A successful and conclusive operation against the Jews would unite Romans, pander to Greek prejudice and give Hadrian a military triumph to augment his aesthetic successes. The emperor who had re-animated the heroes of the distant past and cast himself as one of them was now challenged to compare himself with the Roman heroes of recent history, Titus and Trajan. He could reveal himself as young enough, strong enough, an implacable and courageous leader.

It was perhaps for this reason that Hadrian himself finally joined his armies in Judea. He had made himself so visible throughout his reign that to fail to take his place in the theatre of war would be remarkable. If he could not bring the explosive situation under control, if it appeared that, in a reign where international unity and the pursuit of the aesthetic ideal had been made a priority, the skills of Rome's proud military past had been neglected, much of what Hadrian had achieved would be diminished or mocked. The time of peace, the improvement in living conditions and the indulgences of the elite were all predicated on the perception that Rome's armies maintained the potential to seize or maintain power if necessary.

The Jewish war provided a clear if unlooked-for statement regarding the relationship of Rome and its provinces. There was an instructive contrast between the fate of Judea and the fortunes of more accommodating communities. Cooperation might bring all manner of benefits, from protection against attack to the amassing of individual fortune; nonconformity would be put down with brutal and uncompromising rigour. In the 130s the implicit was made explicit and the Jews became an object lesson in the price of disobedience.

In Rome, the dense ruin of the Forum has a few unmistakable landmarks. Turning up a cobbled slope towards the green peace of the Palatine, the visitor immediately confronts one of them: an uncompromising, fairly well-preserved ceremonial arch. The Arch of Titus was erected posthumously to celebrate the eponymous prince's triumphs in Judea during the reign of his father, Vespasian, and during the childhood of Hadrian. One of the relief carvings shows the removal of the sacred texts, trumpets and *menorah* of the Jewish Temple. They were not to return to Jerusalem for 500 years and the Temple itself was never rebuilt.

The remains of ancient Athens reflect Hadrian's benevolence in many fragments of the rustic, rough-cut masonry which Hadrian introduced to the city. The huge Temple of Olympian Zeus still stands, albeit denuded of the great numbers of statues of the emperor which once filled its forecourt. Just one remains, headless, in the confusing ruins of the Agora; its carving includes a beautifully ornate military breastplate. The Arch of Hadrian, which once led into the part of the city most restored by him, survives with its two inscriptions: on one side 'This is the City of Theseus' and on the other, triumphantly, 'This is the City of Hadrian not of Theseus.'

Bethar, in Israel, has not been completely excavated, but at En Gedi, on the shores of the Dead Sea, the discovery of caves revealed the desperate and long-sustained underground existence of the bar Kokhba rebels and their families. Letters, personal possessions and cooking utensils are all now on display in the Israel Museum in West Jerusalem. After 135 the Jews were forbidden entry to Jerusalem for nearly two centuries, but began returning to sacred sites within the city as laws were relaxed. The pagan city of Aelia Capitolina endured for 250 years, finally claiming back its old name in the fourth century. In the rabbinical literature Hadrian is still referred to with the prefix 'wicked' and the imprecation 'may his bones rot.'[12] The Jews have endured the depredations of many enemies, but this enduring curse was directed at the apparently tolerant ruler of a relatively peaceful empire who nevertheless became the most destructive enemy the Jews had yet known.

Perhaps surprisingly, Hadrian's presence is still discernible in the architecture of Jerusalem itself, as well as in the curses of religious texts. The old city follows the approximate shape of Aelia Capitolina, and two of Hadrian's great entrance arches survive. The Ecce Homo Arch was constructed in 135–6 to celebrate Hadrian's victory, incorporating the access ramp Titus used in the conflagration of 70, as its foundation. The northern Gate of Damascus has been covered with the accretions of many centuries and many cultures, but current excavations are exposing more of its original structure, as well as the Roman square and buildings beyond. Its Arabic name, Bab-el-Amud, 'gate of the column', still refers to the statue of Hadrian which once stood by the entrance, a visual proclamation of his dominion and Jewish exclusion. On the north-western edge of the Muslim quarter, near the ruins of Hadrian's building, a hologram of the hated Roman emperor is projected on to the site which now lies at the centre of the capital city of the Jewish State of Israel.

7

The captured world

Now the whole world was the Roman conqueror's. He held the sea, the land, and the coursing firmament, but this was not enough. His laden ships disturbed the foaming waters, and if there remained beyond some undiscovered bay, a country rich in yellow gold, here was an enemy, here destiny hatched the disasters of war as they searched for their wealth. Familiar joys grew stale and common pleasures dull. The sea borne sailor praised Corinthian bronze, and purple itself dimmed before lustres worked from underground; Africans cursed Rome, the Chinese bought new silks, and all Arabia ransacked its countryside.

PETRONIUS, THE SATYRICON

From the memoirs of Julia Balbilla, August 136

The seasons pass and he remains in the city. In winter on the Palatine, in summer in his beautiful pleasure house. This August, the heat has become unendurable, though endure it we must. In Rome the stench of the river, the rotting fish, the people crammed into the filthy alleys, is appalling. Athens could be noisy and dirty but it was never like this. He can transform cities with his marbles and sculpture but he can do nothing to control the stinking hordes, with their children and their animals and their passion for squalor. There are fires and floods – year in, year out, they seem almost to take them in their stride. Some minor disaster cut down a swathe of tenements last week – but still the inhabitants squeal and squabble and breed. From every point of the empire they crowd in, perched in their shoddy lodgings, six to a room. Sometimes they die on the floors, apparently, and go unnoticed until the smell has their neighbours round sniffing out a pretext for a fight.

Some senators' ladies hate to be carried through the streets; they shut their eyes, draw on some fragrant herbs and sink deep into the temporary oblivion of their litters. But there is a compelling fascination in peering out at the people; they are unfamiliar animals, bewildered and belligerent, pacing the arena; doomed but intriguing.

Hadrian has a menagerie, of course – fowl and beasts and serpents – but they live like feathered and scaly monarchs, his creatures. Only for animals is imprisonment a significant change for the better. They have the music of their silver chains, as they wander about, they eat from golden bowls, spend their leisure dipping into pools, some shaped to mimic the Nile or a craggy northern lake, they have trees to shade their day and aviaries and fine houses in which to pass the night safe from foxes or a hungry peasant.

Everything in Rome is of the best. In the provinces I have seen shows where the much-heralded 'fierce beasts from the forests and the deserts of the empire' turn out to be a few wild

211

cats, or a scabby, toothless, stinking bear and a half-blind ox covered in flies. At the circus here in Rome creatures are magnificent and unfamiliar specimens, their coats glossy, their rage untempered, enough meat on them to feed a village. The crowds are spoiled by variety and all this goes on for days on end.

The other routines are just hot and boring: identically muscled pairs of gladiators with their predictable routines and their melodrama are for boys and soldiers, although the action seems unreal, a bloody dance, almost scripted, so that they hardly seem to suffer, unlike the street Romans, who do so convincingly. As for the pathetic criminals, dressed in cloaks embroidered with gold, blinking in their last sun, losing control of their bodily functions; what civic triumph in that? You can find frightened, dying men in every squalid passage of the city.

I like to see the crowds – I wish I could pass through them invisibly but instead, once in a while, the slaves carry me through their markets, scattering huddled groups to let me through. I gaze out through a gap in the curtains and there is the whole empire in a microcosm. He has his statues, gods and goddesses from every part of his empire, but here, right here, are living exhibits. Tall ebony-skinned warriors reduced to skeletons in rags; men from the northern provinces with red hair and hot red faces; skinny fair women with unhealthy white skin from which all lustre has gone, their noses running, their children coughing. The dealers hustling for a bargain, the poor fighting to exist. Such survivors. Who would have thought it could be worth it to live in some rat-hole by the Tiber or to shelter under an arch of the Tiburtina Bridge?

This is one great market of humanity. Greeks everywhere, of course, as if they owned the place – which in a sense they do these days; people say you can't tell but I can, always. Then the locals cheating the incomers wherever they can. You don't have to be part of it to know. Everyone talks about it, some with a tinge of admiration: landlords prospering by charging foreigners three times the rate. Throwing their own countrymen out in the gutter to offer their place to a provincial who can't add up.

There are the still handsome veterans; scarred, one-armed soldiers. There have been many more of them since the trouble with the Jews, and there are just as many others hidden out of sight, no doubt, deformed and dishonoured. Better to be dead. But there are always a few enterprising merchants of the gutter who can sell their wounds, mutilating themselves – or their children – to get pity and money.

Outside the Thermae is where the beggars hold their convocations. You can tell when you are near the baths, even sitting back behind the hangings, sunk in the cushions. That smell; once you have encountered it you always recognise it again. Everywhere, every city, every land, baths smell the same. Rome sending its stink round the empire like a dog scenting out its patch. A wet, scented miasma which catches in the narrow lanes around the great building. A dirty smell, not a clean one. The beggars squat in the shade on the hottest days, and round their pathetic fires in winter. Some of them are hardly of an age to walk; others, ten- or eleven-year-old girls, will soon be moving on to more profitable ways of earning their food. The passing men already look at them, touch them, and their mothers – some of their mothers – look hopeful. Those women. Waiting to sell or be bought. Those who have flesh worth showing show it, the others share the shade and hope for drunks. Drunks can be importuned by any old hag and then it is a one-way bargain; round the corner the men lose their money and the women disappear.

We too are possessions, of course, though ours are the tinkling chains and contrived shade and the contrived courtesies. But Rome in the heat is very difficult and makes even the favoured querulous. He wants us to stay here, but Sabina much prefers the villa at Tibur to the city palaces. It is a great house, the new villa, a town in itself, but if he is there, though we never see him, we can sense him near at hand like a black mist. Sabina is tired and irritable and keeps saying, in a manner which would be irksome in a child but is particularly unappealing in a middle-aged woman, that it is not fair, and why should she stay in Rome? It had been her family's land, after all, she complains at nobody in particular, part of her dowry when as a girl she had been handed to her reticent and preoccupied husband as part of his longer-term ambitions. No doubt he thought her father's small villa much the best part of that bargain.

So why should she – who had as much right to be there as anyone – not pass the summer at the villa where the early mornings, at least, were comfortably cool? She was not well; she was tired and unable to keep her food down. The air was easier up in the hills and the water was wonderfully clear. Rome was a fine idea, but to live in, in summer, it was an ordeal. The central palace she hated: dark, menacing, an emperor's abode. The garden house in the city was better, at least in spring and summer, and she would happily spend her days there. The light and the pretty rooms and the terraces where you could almost believe you were in the community. But then Hadrian says that it is not an appropriate place for his wife to have her permanent residence and there's an end to it. All these grievances, and many others, Sabina rehearses endlessly, although not without justification.

It is true that Rome is less safe these days, and it is not just the yellow sickness. The slaves refuse to go the long way round now and Sabina jokes – or at least she smiles – that if the plague doesn't get you the plotters will. She believes that is what he hopes for: that she will fall ill and die, and he would go through the rituals – oh, how she would be honoured; more in death than in life – and he would never have to think about her again. If he did now, which was unlikely, as sometimes if he came into her presence you could see there was a moment when he strove to pick her out among the other bejewelled, ageing ladies.

He could turn her into a tidy image – just her face on a coin, perhaps, or some civic statue. Nowhere he had to pass it, you could be sure of that. He would turn her into a god, the senate would see to that, but would her temples be as beautiful and her worship as devoted as that boy's? No need to answer. He liked funerals. The emperor's wife would be a few handfuls of grit and grease and some shards of singed bone, and she would be placed in an urn and put away deep in the dark. Away with her secrets. But there would be no grief. Never again.

Sabina, the habit of years making her count her own infirmities, does not notice that Hadrian may rest in the mausoleum before she does. I do not think he will travel again. I have heard rumours that he hopes to return to Athens, where he believes his glory is still untarnished, but who would he go with? He calls for maps and officers of logistics, but his friends and suitable travelling companions are old or dead or on their estates, hoping to be overlooked. Nor can he leave the city so confident that all will go well in his absence. He has made enemies, that is for sure, and for every enemy he puts away another is created in the act.

He is an old man. He walks, rides, prides himself on keeping the body and health of a younger man – even I have heard him say it – but he lies. If he convinces himself, he is the only one. His feet are swollen; he may walk without faltering, but the leather straps of his shoes chafe his flesh. His skin is tight over his ankles and his veins are a map of rivers and frontiers. The weathered skin – he always braved the sun like a peasant – is no longer gold but the colour of withered leaves. He sweats; a slave runs forward to mop his brow and he angrily waves him away. His sweat may drip into his wine, but we must affect not to have seen it. He rises stiffly but holds himself upright; it is an effort and some days as he passes his breath labours to escape. But worst of all, what kills him from within is the black melancholy. His body and his spirit rot. Does he know in his heart that he will never leave again?

Noise of any sort he cannot tolerate. In the last weeks he has banished even his beloved musicians, who had comforted him through so much; he says their noise hurts his ears. His ears roar and pound like the seas in spring. He who has taken ship on so many oceans feels giddy and ill walking on dry land.

He has taken over the palace of Domitian. Brave or stupid or arrogant, he goes, as always, where others have not – would not. Would old Nerva, seeking ease, make use of its well-positioned amenities? He would not. Would fearless Trajan pass time in its dark corridors? He too turned aside at the gates. These days Domitian's palace is the court. Visitors are curious, of course, but they think it behoves them not to seem so; their glances around them are slight and made only when they think they are not observed. How labyrinthine their conversations, which attempt to exclude not just the name of Domitian but any thread which might lead to him. A foolish precaution, as the emperor is as obsessed with the last hours of the tyrant emperor as only he can be.

I have seen the very place where that other emperor was killed when we were children. A mean closet, scarcely any size; what a vile trap for a man to die in. And with all those great halls inside that vast hulk of a building. They talked of it everywhere, the powerful eagle turned rat, fighting pointlessly for its life. Gouging out eyes, scraping, screaming as the knife found its target. I sometimes think being in that palace makes Hadrian sick. Sick of fear like Domitian. In there he can smell blood. He passes the spot where it happens; though he has torn down the walls of the room, it is there.

Underneath the proud armour of an emperor is an apprehensive man. His blood flows from his gums and his nose and they catch it in fine basins. Then his doctor comes and opens a vein; no wonder he is weak and faints for air. Yet he lets it go on. When we came here, before he became tainted by the infections of the palace, he once asked me if I knew the words of the dead Domitian who, having all revealed by the chieromancers, dug at a festering sore in his own flesh, asking, 'Will this be enough blood to satisfy the oracle?' Then at first when Hadrian heated the rooms of the palace he joked and played at Nero, saying to the engineers as they lit the fires beneath, 'Ah, now I can live like a man,' rubbing his hands together. That was back when Hadrian knew no man could paint him in the colours of a tyrant and the comparison would be a matter of wit not threat. Then he covered with hangings the hall of mirrors in which Domitian hoped to catch the

reflection of approaching assassins. Now the mirrors shine again
when he is here. He feels his enemies out there, as yet unknown.

He is right to feel oppressed. There were angry murmurs
when he put the old man and his grandson to death, but old age
does not dim treachery. They are all at it, speculating and intriguing. Servianus was never his friend and senility had caused him
to lose, if not his wits, then whatever caution he had. Fuscus was
worse and more vigorous. They all sense the failing organism,
those ambitious young men. They watch, they note, they trade in
information. The emperor must guess at the length of their
patience. Although his rages are less focused now, he is still a man
to be wary of. Sabina has known his cold anger, but now he
bellows with fury as the pains in his head grip hold of him. It is not
her, or us; it is suffocation, the palace, the city, his body.

Up at Tibur he can breathe. The air is light and surely every
beautiful thing is in that place. When I leave, when Sabina no
longer has need of me, it is the only place here I shall not wish to
forget. He has given great buildings to many people and cities, but
this marvel he has constructed for himself must be the greatest
palace in the world, with every part of that world laid out like a
map built in stone. Birds of the field and caged beauties sing in the
courtyards and everywhere there is water; we walk always within
the sound of streams and fountains, which throw a fine mist into
the heat of the day. As some drops are blown by the breeze to fall
on the rim of the shallow basins they are dried in an instant on the
heat of the stone. Marbles in every colour from honey to livid
purple to blue-white, some like whey, or clouds. Gilded metal and
carving; fruit so real you cannot but reach out and touch it, feeling
that it must soften and moisten in your fingers; already they are
buffed by the touch of every passing hand, these pomegranates
and grapes hanging from stone vines.

No man ever loved Greece more who was not a Greek. Here
at Tibur, it is Greece. Here are their gods, their sculptures, their
greatest of buildings. Conquered but supreme, he has relit the
flame that burned once so strongly. The statues, the books, the

217

paintings. There is a monstrous water organ and a fine hall where the musicians play when it is too cool for the terraces. Do they bring him pleasure any more? If they do, he hides it. The pipes and strings are stacked by the walls and the magic of the early days, when a faint sound of music drifted across Tibur on an evening breeze, is gone.

It is not the boy who killed him, or the foolish rumours; it is the disappointments, it is being back in Rome. He judged badly, but the boy was just an amusement, no more; who would have thought he would be so much trouble? But we cannot judge kings by the habits of men.

As Sabina grows weaker, she believes herself poisoned, or she wishes it were so; some last dark deed to follow him into posterity. But she is just old and sick, like so many are sick this season. Bitterness lays her low; it is not the bitterness of venom but of being overlooked. Would he wish to kill her? I think it unlikely. He could not, I think, be bothered. He does not hate her, so she is not at risk like Servianus or the wily Fuscus; he is indifferent. She is consigned to oblivion, part of a plan for his life when that life still lay ahead and was in need of planning. Hadrian hates those whom he has loved; those who, offering so much, are revealed as flawed as if they deliberately deceived him as to what they could be for him. He came to hate Commodus, who had been the most favoured of his intimates, when his ill-health made the emperor look a fool. He was always a jealous man. If it seemed impossible that he who had everything this world offers could envy his own subjects, yet as he grew older no man dared show greater skill than him or be his equal in any matter. To choose an heir he must find a choice who reflected his glory but did not surpass it. And the collector in him could not resist the beautiful object; in this case Commodus, no longer the flawless youth of his prime but still the most elegant and accomplished of men, though every prediction, not least simple observation, showed that Commodus' days were short. The handsome heir, the sensualist and poet who promised so much, slipped away from him into death almost as soon as the emperor's choice was made. The young man wasted away, lost his looks and died, it was said, of the doctors.

Others say that Hadrian is cursed. Some believe from the days of his journey to Egypt, some say by the priests, others by the river. Yet others that Servianus, facing death, condemned him and that now everything he treasures is blighted. Everything he touches rots. Where he touches his skin it darkens. He rots and he longs for death.

About twenty miles to the east of Rome the land rises from the flat plain of the Campagna to several ranges of hills. The ancient roads which led from the capital to the desirable estates in the Alban, Sabine and Tiburtina hills are now modern highways through the industrial estates, hypermarkets and ribbon development of the suburbs. It is a monotonous and unremarkable route, typical of any outskirts of any European city. Yet between the cheerless blocks of flats are the works of the engineers and stonemasons whose much earlier incarnations can occasionally be glimpsed in the form of a single arch of an aqueduct or a hefty slab of unidentifiable masonry now abandoned in the twenty-first century.

Even in the first century BCE the roads were busy. The cooler and fertile hills were always a popular location for the rich wanting to build large houses within the 25 mile radius of Rome demanded for senatorial duty. The list of known residents is a roll-call of antiquity and includes the poets Horace and Catullus; Caesar's assassins, Brutus and the 'lean and hungry' Cassius; Cicero and the Emperor Trajan. Outside the city they believed they could live a simple existence embracing wholesome rural values. It was a popular fantasy, one fed by pastoral poetry and the decoration of wall-paintings and a belief that all true Romans were farmers at heart. To the extent that those who lived here were removed from the disease of the city, the ideal of the healthy life may have had some basis in reality; but given that most rich Romans went backwards and forwards to Rome and that the large households' great villas were provisioned not just from home farms but also from the city, the benefits of distance were largely those of perception. Moreover, providing the streams, birds, vines and hives that produced the idealised setting for the country life was an expensive business. The search for statues and the competitive installation of landscaping features was only for those with considerable time and resources at their disposal. Martial was among many who extolled the healthy life in the country, but he, at least, retained his sense of irony.

> *My orchard isn't the Hesperides*
> *There's no Massylian dragon at the gate,*
> *Nor is it King Alcinous' estate;*
> *It's in Nomentum, where the apple-trees,*
> *Perfectly unmolested, bear a crop*
> *So tasteless that no guard needs be kept.*[1]

Soon after his succession, Hadrian left Rome on the same road to confirm the setting for his own country palace and begin building. He was to return there between journeys to examine progress and adapt his plans for it, and in the last three years of his life, after his return from Judea, it was his principal residence. It had taken many more years to build than he had left to enjoy it; but perhaps his chief pleasure was always in potential and creation rather than a completed project.

Hadrian undoubtedly knew the area well through his family connections and visits to Trajan's villa. Hadrian's long involvement in architectural projects – he was already in his forties when he began to build at Tibur – and his discerning eye make it unlikely that he chose his site with anything other than careful deliberation, but it is not at first an obvious one. The villa sprawls over a large area of the plain outside Tibur (modern Tivoli), just where the Campagna

meets the hills. Most aristocrats who had built in the countryside around Rome preferred a hilly site, both for the slightly
cooler weather it offered and for the contours that could be
used to create some of the views and effects they enjoyed.
Hadrian's choice was a predominantly flat plot which was prey
to hot, dry winds in summer. However, even in the early days
of his reign Hadrian had the means and vision to see an
inviting challenge in creating an artificial topology out of a
bland existing landscape.

For wealthy Romans, building was always a political act.
Whether dedicating a public institution or creating an ostensibly private house, to build was inevitably to elicit a critical
response. Throughout history ambitious building schemes
have been a manifestation of power and wealth, but in ancient
Rome construction was not a simple act of self-promotion.
Building was profoundly connected with two crucial elements
in the dynamic of Roman society: the manipulation of popular
support, and the ability to entertain lavishly. Erecting public
buildings and subsidising public leisure were considered so
potentially politically seductive that at various times legisla-
tion was enacted to curtail involvement in such schemes by
anyone outside the imperial family. The creation of magnificent private homes could not easily be legislated against, but a
complicated code of behaviour evolved. If the erection of a
fine villa was an easy way to demonstrate riches, taste and
sophistication, it was also an easy way to make oneself vulnerable to criticism or contempt. Meanness and poor hospitality
were derided, but excess and spectacle came in for critical, if
rather envious, scorn. Those who would prosper in elite
society had to be adept at manipulating outward symbols of
power and wealth.

To a degree the emperor operated within a broader range
of acceptability than other patricians; he was, after all, no
longer negotiating for position but affirming it. Yet contemporary literary assessment of private imperial houses nearly

always mirrors the perceived personalities of their occupants. In the first century the cruel and reclusive Tiberius was criticised for removing himself to the isolation of Capri, the gluttonous and profligate Nero for swallowing up public space within Rome to create his glittering palace. The paranoid Domitian's palace was disorienting and fortress-like; the benevolent Vespasian lived quietly in a garden palace which he opened to the public. The palace was a stage upon which the emperors put on a performance intended to convince or compel. If the performances got out of hand it could become a place of execution; Caligula, Domitian, Vitellius and later Commodus were all murdered within their own palaces. For an emperor all life was public, and there was no place of safety if the show went wrong.

That emperors were unaware of the messages that their houses could convey is unlikely. What is assumed to be Augustus' palace was discovered recently on the Palatine and has been excavated. The domestic simplicity which was part of Augustus' self-promotion was certainly reflected in the unostentatious public rooms. However, in his private apartments it was a different story. Here, out of sight of the general population and beyond the reach of public criticism, were the coloured marbles, the statuary and the fashionable wall-paintings. Augustus was an astute man and a gifted politician, and he set an example in moving beyond mere visual display to contriving a conscious landscape of metaphor and allusion. Building was a medium that Augustus found irresistible. When overseas he initiated expensive projects wherever he went, but it was in Rome that his most ambitious construction was undertaken throughout his reign. Having proved he was the right man to be the first emperor of Rome, he set about making Rome the right place for him to rule from.

Apart from his time at Tivoli some miles from the city itself, it appears that Hadrian was rarely happy in Rome. It was not that Hadrian's love for all things Hellenic could not be indulged here – there were more Greeks, particularly intellectuals, in Rome than in any other city in the world, including those in Greece; but for an emperor who must typify Roman-ness, Hadrian could observe but not really immerse himself in Greek values and pleasures at home. Yet his schemes in Rome were, as everywhere, the works of a perfectionist, and much of the Hadrianic building in Rome was structurally and aesthetically immensely successful, even if raised in a spirit of civic duty. Augustus changed the face of Rome, but no emperor after Hadrian so improved and ornamented the fabric of the city.

Hadrian, from choice, worked on a broader canvas. Although the three superlative achievements of the Temple of Venus and Rome, the Pantheon and his own mausoleum were his major contributions to the city and almost certainly he was directly involved in their design, he invested little time or energy in improvements to the palace of Domitian, which he had designated his principal residence. Augustus had made his mark on his home city to a degree that Hadrian would struggle to equal, let alone exceed, and Hadrian acted best where he could excel and astonish. Building in Rome was simply what was expected. In Rome the old unease he felt among his peers expressed itself in driven competitiveness; in all three of his major Roman conceptions the salient feature was that they were bigger than anything directly comparable. The biggest temple, the biggest vaulted ceiling and the biggest tomb were his bequest to the city. Immediately outside Rome these were joined by the biggest palace, the villa at Tivoli.

When he started to build at Tivoli Hadrian may have been motivated by the idea of extending the much simpler villa which was already owned by Sabina's family in a manner he considered appropriate to his new status. No doubt the design evolved over time and was very different in its final state from what had been intended at its inception. Certainly its collections were enriched by the emperor's travels; by the time the villa's 900 rooms were completed, it was one of the most extraordinary contributions to art and architecture that the Roman world had ever seen. Hadrian was to enjoy it for very few years, but it seems to have been the one place where he could let his purse, his imagination and his aspirations run untrammelled by the constraints of life within Rome or the more inhibiting aspects of imperial duty. Because we know that he was closely involved with the specifics of the design – indeed, there is evidence that his returns from forays abroad coincided with amendments to half-erected buildings – it is not so fanciful to view it as the place where the modern visitor can feel closest to a more private Hadrian.

Yet the villa at Tivoli also lays bare the extraordinarily alien economics, excesses and inequalities of ancient Rome. Political life was defined by money. Having it, taking it and giving it were the principal concerns of the powerful. It was not just a matter of lavish expenditure on public shows or comfortable living in the innumerable houses that one man might possess; set amounts of capital were required for a man to become an equestrian – a knight – or a senator. A man with 400,000 sesterces could become a knight, whereas for admission to the highest rank, that of senator, a fortune of 1 million was required. One modern historian, Colin Wells, believes 8 million was more frequently the case. It was not wealth in itself which was desirable, but the dignified and productive life it enabled its possessor to lead. In a social construction which has echoed down the centuries, the Romans believed that a gentleman should not work. A gentleman should be a man of leisure and influence, beyond the constraints of money-making. Ideally, he should be in a position where he could be called upon visibly to make good the financial losses in a state disaster.

Rome's early expansionism had scoured the resources of the empire; merchants and ship-owners made fortunes finding and delivering to an expanding Rome the materials and novelties it sought. Safer seas, policed by Rome, increased the rate of trade and new colonies were markets for Roman exports. Trading was not *quite* for gentlemen, but investing in trade was acceptable and lending money for ventures commonplace. Investment in property was widespread. Agriculture was generated from great rural estates, and booty (including slaves) from endless wars filled Rome's coffers. Everything was taxed, and the taxes went into Rome's, and ultimately the emperor's, treasury. War generated enormous sums; under Augustus so much money came into circulation – largely from Egypt – that the interest rate dropped from 12 per cent to 4 per cent. The extensive building schemes of the first century onwards set up a demand for materials, so the owners of quarries prospered, as did those who owned bronze and gypsum mines, the brickworks of aristocratic estates, and the ship-owners who could procure exotic marbles or fell timber and carry it to the city.

As extraordinary displays of apparently relaxed wealth became a political tool, in reality more and more gambles were taken in finding it. Not every wealthy man might choose a public life, but anyone who chose public life must be a wealthy man. Corruption, coercion and predation ensured the determined could acquire fortunes. Augustus, while still a teenager, had amassed enough money to support a private army. Ambitious men gathered the support of peers and bestowed patronage on numerous clients. Patronage, indeed, was at the heart of the whole system. The emperor sat at the top of the pyramid and whatever others had, he had, or took, fourfold. Taxes were raised for him; a portion of legacies went to him. Those on the make gave willingly and generously; those less well inclined towards the emperor stood to lose their fortunes or their lives.

Confiscations of estates from rich men who had fallen out of favour enriched the emperor's personal holdings. There were rumours that less high-minded emperors than Hadrian had killed just to possess a pretty garden. By the reign of Claudius, the imperial treasury was synonymous with the treasury of Rome. Even so, there were emperors sufficiently profligate to eat into the reserves and to conceive desperate ways of refilling them; Caligula anticipated inheritances from wealthy knights by executing them.

But as with so much in Roman politics, the line between success and disaster was so narrow as to be nearly invisible. New men with new fortunes were grudgingly accepted, but their pretensions were the butt of snobbery. Profligate spending, even by emperors, was mocked and criticised. Nero's iced water and Caligula's baroque parties were seen as self-indulgent in a way that Augustus' mausoleum or Domitian's stadium, now the Piazza Navona, were not. Thrifty emperors had their day; Vespasian imposed petty taxes, including, notoriously, one on public lavatories, to buffer Rome's wealth, and when Tiberius died, a semi-recluse, he left 270,000 million sesterces. The most successful freedman – Narcissus, adviser to Claudius – left about 400 million; but then, freedmen had entrepreneurial opportunities which were unhindered by ideas of social status. Nevertheless, the wealth of an emperor was immense, and his power to extract more meant that he was, in effect, limitlessly rich. And when wealthy freedmen died, their fortunes reverted in part to their previous master or emperor; one of the resources an emperor could capitalise upon was the energy and acumen of those he patronised.

It is impossible to give a meaningful modern worth for ancient wealth. The whole way of life was so different from ours that there are just no points of direct comparison. The gulf between the few rich and the hordes of poor was huge. The very fact that Hadrian could build a palace such as the one at Tivoli places him and his times far outside any modern framework of comprehension. A loaf of bread cost a quarter of a sesterce. So did a glass of wine.[2] We know from graffiti at

Pompeii that a prostitute, perhaps not a very elegant one, charged half a sesterce for her services. Entrance to the public baths was just twice that. Roman soldiers earned 1,200 sesterces a year and although there were some perks, they had to buy their own equipment. A casual labourer earned perhaps 2–3 sesterces a day – when he got work. A charity scheme to support poor children, presumably at a fairly basic level, paid between 10 and 12 sesterces a month. A lecturer in rhetoric under Vespasian received 100,000 sesterces a year and this was considered remarkable. It was a similar amount to the purchase price of a first-rate, intelligent slave in the second century, when lessening warfare had reduced the market. One foot of road cost 22 sesterces to lay and a large and elaborate tomb anything from 100,000 to half a million sesterces.[3]

The cost of Hadrian's villa, with its forty formal main rooms and many hundred supporting and administrative complexes, is beyond calculation. The building bears no comparison to anything else, and so the price of other known great houses of the period is almost irrelevant. The most recent estimate for the cost of construction of the villa – very much a guess, and a conservative one at that – is 60 million sesterces, and that is before the luxury items and possessions of the final fitting-out are considered.[4] The cost of maintaining it and the staff of hundreds who ran it is, similarly, inestimable.

It was not just a question of scale and elaboration, but in every sense the villa amplified and transformed things that had gone before. There had been other magnificent imperial residences, both the monolithic buildings on the Palatine, from which the word palace was derived, and Nero's Golden House – the *Domus Aurea* – built sixty years previously in the heart of the city. Nero's house had several themes in common with the new villa: it was expansive, Greek-inspired and a showcase for architectural, structural and functional novelty; it is quite possible that it was literally golden and sparkled provocatively at the centre of the city. It also – in Nero's choice of an urban site – represented a fatal misjudgement of Roman tolerance. *'Now I can live like a human-being,'* Nero is supposed to have reflected upon seeing the new establishment which was, in effect, to be the death of him.[5] Hadrian was more ambitious; at Tivoli he could pass his days as *'a super-human monarch among the most select of men'*.[6]

At Hadrian's villa all the themes that the rich had incorporated in their out-of-city villas – the water features, ornate gardens, elements of foreign design, libraries and art collections – were taken to the limit. The extraordinary dimensions of the country palace, safely removed from any threat on the territory of the city of Rome itself, were spoken of with uncompromised awe by the ancient biographers: *'His villa at Tibur was marvellously constructed and he actually gave to its parts the names of provinces and places of the greatest renown, calling them, for instance, Lyceum, Academia, Prytaneum, Canopus, Poecile and Tempe. And in order not to omit anything, he even made a Hades.'*[7] The conceit of naming parts of the villa after noted places and buildings of the empire was not entirely new – it seems likely that Nero had aimed at a similar effect – but Hadrian had, as always, expanded the theme. Among the elements of his fantasy cosmos, Canopus, named after the notorious Egyptian resort, had strong emotional associations for the emperor. And Hades was just possibly a witty play on the whole tradition. It is no longer thought that the many buildings were replicas of famous wonders of the empire; Hadrian was subtler than that, and the names were probably either commemorative or clever allusions. It is not difficult to think of contemporary variants of this approach which summon up a mood or a set of values or simply a significant event. Modern conference centres with a Versailles Room or Windsor Suite, Gatwick airport with its shopping 'village', pubs named after Waterloo or the Royal Oak all create effects, and occasionally unintentional ironies, with evocative names.

With its public and private rooms, service tunnels, kitchens, stables, observatory, swimming pools, library and shrines, the completed villa was more like a small town than a single residence. There seems no doubt that from time to time Hadrian undertook some imperial administration from here, but it was primarily a place for him to entertain. The villa was a place to live, and it had private areas and studios, but it was above all a place to be seen. One of its unique features is that the 900 rooms were arranged in groups. Rather than being linked into a coherent whole, each set of buildings, from reception room to maritime baths, from pavilion to water court, seems to have been remarkably self-contained; and each is of differing, unique design. The result was that every complex was a staggeringly impressive stage on which to meet the emperor. The architectural techniques were innovative and extraordinary in creating the historical fantasies; intricate vaulting, hydraulic engineering and light-wells permitted the emperor to be revealed to maximum effect; in the emperor's absence, his possessions – statues, fine metal treasures, *trompe-l'oeil* effects – spoke for him. For Hadrian it was a powerfully triumphant declaration to his contemporaries and to posterity.

The Canopus, its vaulted apse once lined with blue and green marble, opens on an ornamental canal edged with statues, and is probably the most familiar and most discussed feature at the villa. If the villa as a whole reflected the breadth of Hadrian's travels and his interest in the wider world, then the Canopus had direct connections with his time in Egypt. Although it was part of a phase of building which began after 123, it was possibly not completed for a further five years, and the final arrangement of statuary which gave it its particular mood may well not have been in place until after the disturbing events of 130. As with so much of the evidence for Hadrian's life, interpretations range from the simple to the esoteric. The Canopus has been interpreted as a formal garden, a banqueting hall, an extended visual metaphor for the world, and the tomb or cenotaph of Antinous. But whatever other more complicated role it played in Hadrian's life and imagination, it was almost certainly used as an enchanting summer dining room.

In the 1950s serious excavations began of this area of the villa. These were far more exciting than anyone had hoped, exposing not just the strange shape of the Canopus but, interred in the long basin, some of the original statues. There were graceful caryatids, which seemed to be copies of ones known in Athens, the Egyptian lion demon Bes, and Silenus, a comic Dionysian figure. Around the pool further statues had once stood – Athena, Hermes, possibly Scylla dragging her victims under water, other gods and heroes, representations of the Nile and the Tiber, and a crocodile. It was a sculptural wonderland; all the strands of early second-century myth and religion re-created in stone. How they had originally stood in relation to each other was never going to be clear, but it was evident that the Canopus complex was a brilliant showcase of art and fantasy. Under a waterside colonnade, the statues had once been reflected in the green waters of the pool and its fine fountain. For those in perhaps uneasy receipt of the emperor's hospitality, sitting in the shelter of the open-domed dining room, where miniature waterfalls cooled the air and light reflected off the glistening marble and mosaic interior, the view down the clear water to the furthest arches and statues can only have been extraordinary.

Perhaps because they were so eclectic in style and so ambiguous in their message, the finds have continued to grip the imagination, not least in generating numerous theories about how the whole complex worked. What had Hadrian meant to convey when he placed his assembly of statues in this perplexing context? Did they represent anything beyond the cultured tastes of their collector? For half a century debate has raged over whether this was simply a fashionable collection of, in effect, souvenirs, or whether the avenue of statues was specifically as well as artistically chosen. And was it here that Antinous' body was laid to rest? To stand on a hazy evening at one end of the now opaque green pool, gazing through the colonnades to the debris of the collapsed apse, anything seems possible. To academics it is an inevitable but contentious question. The mood and arrangement of this unique structure suggest that the waters and the sculptures could mark the last resting-place of Antinous. The villa as a whole contained numerous images of the young man; some experts believed that the Egyptian obelisk which now stands on the Pincio in Rome had originally stood on the west bank of the Canopus and that this was, in effect, Antinous' original tombstone.[8] Test diggings into the bank to that side of the canal at Tivoli seemed to show that there were indeed further Hadrianic structures underneath, but this was not in itself conclusive; almost anywhere in the area would probably have shown the same results. But the possibility remains a compelling idea and can never quite be discarded. Perhaps it is more realistic to conclude that Hadrian added some mementoes of Antinous to a pre-existing and favoured part of his villa so that it became, rather than a shrine, simply a place where Hadrian could remember his favourite.

Then there is the further proposition that the complex within a complex is a delightfully creative reconstruction of the world of Hadrian's travels.[9] In this appealing interpretation the pool at the centre becomes the Mediterranean, with the surrounding artefacts representing the major areas of his journey, each placed carefully in a relationship to the water which would create a symbolic and beautiful geography of allusion. Hadrian travelled to almost every country of his empire, as far north as Britain and as far south as Libya, but the main themes of the Canopus are the three areas of major cultural influence and strategic importance in the first century: Rome itself, Greece and Egypt, which together form the basis of the Hellenistic world. The historic, religious and mythical foundations of Rome emerged from these civilisations and drew on them. The Canopus could have been a schematic map of territory as well as of Roman ideas and sensibilities. If Hadrian had succeeded in making the empire a more integrated, stable unity, and by so doing had made Rome wealthier and the position of emperor more impregnable, then it made sense that the villa and the Canopus in particular might celebrate his achievements and the strategies by which they were made possible. Only later in his life could the relative success of his policies be judged, and it was during this period that the ultimate refinement of his villa took place. It would have taken a second Hadrian to understand it all – a man who had all the literary and visual references, who had travelled widely; but that is to assume it was *meant* to be understood rather than to impress in its opacity.

Throughout his reign Hadrian was constantly commissioning new structures and although he drew on ideas from the past, many of his additions to Rome experimented – almost always successfully – with entirely new techniques and forms. If at Tivoli Hadrian was enthused by the relative freedom to satisfy his own passions and preoccupations, then within Rome his schemes flourished in response to the disciplines of urban tradition.

He built public buildings in all places and without number, but he inscribed his own name on none of them except the temple of his father Trajan. At Rome he restored the Pantheon, the voting enclosure, the Basilica of Neptune, very many Temples, the forum of Augustus, the baths of Agrippa ... Also he constructed the bridge named after himself, a tomb on the bank of the Tiber and the temple of the Bona Dea.[10]

Inevitably some of his known works have disappeared under subsequent city building; of others, such as the once huge temple of Roma and Venus, the largest temple ever built in Rome, only fragments survive within later building. Archaeological research increases the range of other works which can be attributed to him, such as the discoveries at the Baths of Titus. (Attribution is assisted by the date stamps on bricks; it is hindered by the fact that Hadrian's name is rarely inscribed on his buildings.) But some architectural master-pieces remain on view; and they retain features which may indicate the abilities and aspirations of Hadrian's architects and engineers who worked at Tivoli.

The greatest of these Hadrianic survivals is undoubtedly the Pantheon. A former temple, inscribed to Marcus Agrippa (the original dedicatee of the first Pantheon to be erected on this spot, which was one of two destroyed by fire), the Pantheon probably survived the demolition which was the lot of many pagan buildings at the hands of the popes because of its early re-use as a church. Built between 118 and 125 CE, it became the Church of St Mary and the Martyrs in the seventh century and is still a Christian basilica today. Inside are two great glories of ancient architecture. The vaulted roof, made of concrete poured into wooden moulds, was the greatest span of such roof ever known and retained this record until the 1950s.[11] The coffered concrete ceiling may once have been covered in sheet metal, and even rendered as it is today it is strikingly elegant. Like so much of Hadrianic design its appearance derives from its function – in this case, a need to lessen the weight of the ceiling. But on stepping into the dark, circular, unencumbered space from the bright light outside, the eye is taken immediately beyond the vault of the ceiling to the oculus at the summit of the domed roof. The impact of a single shaft of light pouring through the 8-metre, circular opening is unsurpassable theatre. Each season creates its own beauty; in summer, rays of sun seem to descend directly to the floor, when rain falls it lies briefly on the marbled floor before it evaporates, and in winter fine columns of snow spiral downwards. The oculus provides the only natural light and much of the ventilation for this unique church. The temple of the Pantheon is marvellous in its own right, but invaluable too in suggesting the sort of effects Hadrian sought and achieved in architecture and what may once have existed at Tivoli.

By the mid-130s Hadrian's villa had reached a state of perfection. The spray of numerous fountains provided a form of air-conditioning; deep-shaded walks and plunge pools offered relief from the intense heat of summer. It was the oasis of peace and beauty that Hadrian had sought. Yet the ill-health which had dogged Hadrian since the fateful trip to Egypt was getting steadily worse. His ankles and belly were swollen with fluid, his frequent heavy nosebleeds debilitating, his breathing laboured and painful. In the summer's heat he suffered terrible headaches. The personality of a man who had never been easy was deteriorating. Anger, irrationality and distrust seemed to drive his actions. Hadrian, the man who had kept the empire in balance even during long sojourns abroad and who had, after the initial years of his reign, no real challenges to his power, had become, like so many of his predecessors, a petty, even paranoid, domestic persecutor. He appointed an heir – Lucius Commodus – ever though his choice was already showing signs of illness, possibly tuberculosis, himself. Rumours circulated that the decision had been swayed by the emperor's sexual attraction to the still handsome young senator. In the climate of uncertainty – the emperor ailing, the succession secured but the successor appearing unlikely to outlive the present incumbent – political tensions increased. The emperor insisted that Lucius Commodus go through the motions and tour the armies of the provinces; it was a death blow for the sick man. He did as bidden and returned, but died shortly afterwards, leaving the question of succession still dangerously open and Hadrian's own judgement in question. The emperor muttered about the wasted cost of the now pointless adoption. Speculation around him gathered pace, intrigue encouraged by the weakness of Hadrian's choice, and eventually there came a denunciation of Hadrian's ninety-year-old colleague, Servianus, and his grandson, the young Pedanius Fuscus. Both were charged with having plotted against the emperor in respect of his choice of heir. Both were peremptorily executed, as were others tainted by involvement in their affairs. Before dying the old man sacrificed to the gods and cursed the emperor: *'That I am guilty of no wrong, ye, O Gods, are well aware; as for Hadrian, this is my only prayer, that he may long for death but be unable to die.'*[12] The imprecation echoed the one Hadrian had felt himself under for some years, a threat which his actions in Egypt had allegedly sought to avert.

There was anger at the despatch of such an old man and such a young and promising youth on what was thought to be a slender pretext. Men of judgement retired to their estates or went abroad, fearing a reign of terror to compare with that of Tiberius or Domitian. Hadrian's most loyal servant, the guard prefect Marcius Turbo, was removed from office. The emperor became increasingly vulnerable and isolated, and his personality deteriorated further. He did, however, act wisely in his second adoption, made from his sickbed, this time choosing the apparently impregnable combination of an heir and an heir-apparent. He chose two men whose virtues were evident and uncontentious: the stolid Antoninus Pius, who became, in the words of one modern historian, 'one of the dullest figures in Roman political history';[13] and, to follow him, the worthy and bookish young Marcus Aurelius, whose *Meditations* are the one great surviving work of literature and philosophy by a Roman emperor. Through this act Hadrian finally set in place two successive emperors who would assure the Roman world of stability for nearly half a century. Antoninus stayed in Rome throughout his life; but by the time Marcus Aurelius became emperor, there were some serious problems developing in the wider empire and he was forced to travel continuously to quell the many uprisings at its fringes.

For Hadrian life had become as intolerable as the condemned Servianus had wished. A man of action and would-be hero, his illness exhausted and immobilised him; a man obsessed with control, he found circumstances slipping away from him; a lover of beauty, he was forced into the constant contemplation of his failing, bloated body. His wife died, and he had alienated such friends as he had. Towards the end there were stories circulating of vague augurs of death. It did not need supernatural powers to observe the inevitability of Hadrian's final decline, but for a man who had been susceptible to fortune-tellers and portents since he was a youth, the observation of minutiae had long been a fixation. Now he returned to magic and charms in a desperate effort to relieve his physical condition. He no doubt endured being purged and bled by his doctors. He wrote letters bitterly expressing his longing to die. His attendants removed poisons and sharp weapons from him. He was not the first emperor to beg a slave to kill him. It was an impossible situation. Hadrian's choice, his former huntsman, Mastor, was first threatened, then cajoled; whether he obeyed or conceded he was doomed. Hadrian drew a line above his nipple where his doctor had told him would be a fatal spot for a blade to penetrate. Mastor refused to assist.

In the end, the historians record rather vaguely, he pursued a course of slow suicide, embarking on a bout of massive over-indulgence which brought about first oblivion and then the death he sought – a death whose timing he had himself predicted years before. Yet in the middle of all this there were episodes in which his old personality asserted itself and he considered his position with some dignity. At some period in the last part of his reign he dictated his memoirs, memoirs in which he tried to explain the episodes in his life which had reflected badly on him and which now weighed heavily on his mind. He set down his version of the killing of the four consuls at the start of his reign; he denied, yet again, that the death of Antinous was anything other than an accident. Finally, he wrote to his heir, Antoninus, in calm acceptance of his imminent death; and this letter, too, was apologetic.

I am being released from life neither prematurely nor unreasonably; I am not full of self-pity nor am I surprised and my faculties are unimpaired – even though I may almost appear, as I have realised, to do injury to you when you are at my side, whenever I am in need of attendance, consoling me and encouraging me to rest. This is why I am impelled to write to you, not – by Zeus – as one who subtly devises a tedious account contrary to the truth, but rather making a simple and accurate record of the facts themselves. [14]

Hundreds of years after his end, there have been various diagnoses of Hadrian's symptoms. The most persuasive evaluation deduces congestive heart failure and the very modern affliction of depression. The indications were certainly consistent with heart disease, but this is not the only plausible explanation of his illness. Liver disease is perhaps more likely and fits in with what we know of the timing of the symptoms and Hadrian's movements and reactions. Liver disease causes the fluid retention, the haemorrhages, the headaches and, crucially, the volatility of temperament that was so marked in Hadrian's last years. Hadrian might have understood his mood as melancholic rather than as depressed, but that too, along with a degree of paranoia, is a notable concomitant of liver failure. The final bout of excessive eating and drinking which is supposed to have acted as a medical *coup de grâce* would certainly have killed a man with liver disease, protein and alcohol being notorious in exacerbating the condition.

One of the commonest causes of liver failure is hepatitis, and it is entirely possible that Hadrian could have picked that up while travelling overseas. Sabina, too, was unwell from the

Egyptian visit onwards, dying in her fifties just months before her husband. All we know of her last illness was that its symptoms could be accounted for by poisoning – or by viral hepatitis. The yellow skin of jaundice is not invariably seen in all forms of the illness, and when it does appear is not always permanent until the illness becomes overwhelming. If it existed at all, it could well have been hidden by the tan that we can assume was habitual for Hadrian, who had always been known for walking in the sun with his head uncovered.

Liver disease can be associated with malaria, with a variety of bacteria and viruses, and with several parasites. All were rife in the second century. It is unprovable, but tempting, to see Hadrian's first symptoms, and possibly even his wife's, as coinciding with his journey from Alexandria to Thebes. Before he visited Egypt he seems to have been well, with the onset of symptoms following the time he spent there. Then as now, poor hygiene was a contributing factor. It is not unlikely that contact with contaminated water might have produced the initial infection – and some transient neurological symptoms, of which the poor judgement which the emperor displayed could be an obvious manifestation. The portents, indicating personal misfortune and local disaster, that Hadrian seemed to believe from the start were waiting for him in Egypt may in reality have lingered unseen in the magical waters of the river Nile.

Hadrian did not die in the cool peace of his beloved Tivoli. In his final illness he was moved to fashionable Baiae, south of Rome, perhaps because its coastal climate was considered more bearable in summer for a very sick man. The resort was much frequented by the rich and was renowned for its scenery, its amusements and its seafood. Although it had a reputation for cloudless skies it stood in the centre of a volcanic region and was popular with convalescents who believed the sulphur baths were restorative. Hadrian was not, of course, convalescent. He died there, at *blandissima baiae* –

pleasantest of places – in July 138, by the sea which he had crossed so many times and in a place supposedly founded long ago by one of Odysseus' voyaging sailors, Baius, who was diverted here on his way home.

The Temple of Hadrian was commissioned as a memorial by Antoninus Pius, Hadrian's successor, and was completed in 145. It reflected very Roman virtues. Most of it has vanished or been incorporated into later buildings, but a remaining run of eleven Corinthian columns, made of marble from the Alban hills, can be seen on the exterior wall of Rome's stock exchange, La Borsa. Relief carvings that were probably once part of the fabric, and which depict Hadrian's achievements in the provinces, are displayed in the courtyard of the Conservatori museum and in Naples.

Hadrian's more enduring memorial survives little altered since the second century. Outside the Pantheon today, the untidily shaped Piazza della Rotonda is a bright muddle of café tables, umbrellas, *gelateria*, scooters easing their way down tiny congested side streets, and tired tourists sprawled in shade under the rim of the large sixteenth-century fountain. On one corner La Tazza d'Oro dispenses refreshing granita – frozen coffee crystals – and locally famous bitter black coffee. The composer Mascagni lived in lodgings overlooking the piazza and behind its fading ochre stucco the Hotel Sole al Pantheon has welcomed those wishing to stay in view of one of Rome's great marvels since the fifteenth century. Guests have ranged from the Renaissance writer Ariosto to Simone de Beauvoir and Jean-Paul Sartre. For many visitors this is the heart of Rome.

If there is a disappointment in this busy, very Roman scene, it is that the square seems too small to contain the Pantheon. There is no room in the confined space to step back and get any sense of exterior perspective; it is as if ancient Rome were built for a bigger people than the later city which largely survives around it. But the Pantheon remains a hugely dramatic statement, almost a stage set in front of which crowd scenes are played out that are not much changed in two millennia: flower sellers, state funerals, private rendezvous, tourists from all over the world, hawkers and sleeping shapes under the portico. It was a powerful choice of Peter Greenaway to use the location as an early mood-setting shot in the sinister film *Belly of an Architect*.

The Pantheon was designed to make an impact, but it was not always so compressed on its site. Its original surroundings included a great colonnade which, it has been recently suggested, stretched back far beyond the confines of the present piazza with open views to the mausoleum of Augustus on the Field of Mars. On the other hand, the Hadrianic rotunda itself was less exposed than its predecessors; Hadrian had caused it to be buttressed on either side by two other buildings, the Saepta Julia and the Basilica of Neptune.[15]

A fantasy of obliterating the sixteenth-century surroundings to reveal a broad vista of the Pantheon unencumbered by history was conceived by Mussolini in 1925. Among other ambitious plans to reshape the city, he promised to create a visual corridor from the Pantheon to the Piazza Colonna.[16] To do so would have cut a swathe through the largely medieval streets, including, it appears, three palaces and possibly a church. It did not happen, although elsewhere in Rome similar projects destroyed much that was not grand or ceremonially useful, in pursuit of self-aggrandising antiquarianism.

Despite being hemmed in by later construction, despite standing disproportionate to its surroundings and despite external depredations, the Pantheon still has remarkable dignity and presence. When it was completed in around 125, it must have been a breathtaking sight, an appropriate house for the gods, with its marble facings glaringly white in the bright light of Italy and the gilded bronze decoration dazzling in the sun. In the seventeenth century the church was stripped of its bronze, which was used to cast cannons for the Castel sant'Angelo on the west bank of the Tiber. In one of the coincidences which Rome's complicated, amorphous past so often throws up, the apparent transfer of bronze from one bastion of the establishment to another, from church to fortress, was in fact a transfer from Hadrian's Pantheon to Hadrian's Mausoleum. In 1888 some of the same cannons were melted down once again to construct the tomb of Vittorio Emanuelle, King of Italy, in the Pantheon – and so the metal was finally returned to its home.

Yet although the marble and the bronze and the ornamentation of the façade have long gone, some of the original columns of pink Aswan granite are still in place. Today, without its exotic carapace, the exterior is a reddish brick within which the arches and buttresses that made such a feat of engineering possible are clearly visible. They have their own beauty; through such structural expertise the Pantheon has been in constant use for 1,875 years.

Hadrian's villa at Tivoli fared less well, and with the fourth-century fall of Rome it too fell into dilapidation. Many hundreds of years later, another wealthy and powerful Roman – the sixteenth-century Renaissance cardinal Ippolito d'Este, son of Lucrezia Borgia – began to build himself a villa in the same range of hills that had first attracted Hadrian. The design, art collection and, in particular, fine terraced gardens of the Villa d'Este were to draw visitors first of all from out of the city and today from all over the world. The site was still a fine one and not least because it had a readily available quarry at the edge of the Campagna – a rich source not just of stone but of marbles and classical art dug out from the buried remains of Hadrian's long-vanished country palace.

Since its heyday in the 130s Hadrian's villa at Tivoli had disappeared under the undergrowth, the soil and the effects of time. However, to one side of the 300 acres over which the great palace had once been spread, sufficient ruins remained to suggest a remarkable former grandeur. Memory and rumours were fed by the occasional discovery of intricate carving or coloured mosaic, and land subsidence into subterranean potholes. In the sixteenth century excavators started a more systematic unearthing of the buildings but also began the process of removal of much that was portable from the site; the villa survived these depredations simply because much of the complex remained underground.

Little was done to explore beyond the immediate remains, although the site itself became better known, and by the 1700s, for the romantically inclined Grand Tourist, the villa was evocative, melancholy and overgrown in just the right proportions. Further excavations were largely still motivated by the appropriation of statues into private collections, but slowly, as more and more masonry was exposed and archaeology evolved as a discipline, there was a growing fascination with understanding exactly what extraordinary buildings had been in this place and what they meant to the emperor who built them and the people who entered them. So large is the site that even today it is not fully accessible or understood; still new artefacts regularly turn up and further bits of puzzling construction are discovered which engagingly overturn existing theories.

A visit to the luminous ruins of Hadrian's villa is one of the most delightful ways of spending time in or around Rome. Shady avenues between cypresses, olive groves and pools of silent water are interrupted by empty fountain bowls and vacant plinths, haunting and potent architectural echoes of magnificence. It is easy to scramble freely through empty doorways and over fallen stone to enter one small, roofless space after another. Inner courtyards contain broken brick and wild flowers, while broad steps and colonnades now lead into ploughed fields and wide views of the Campagna. Arches of long-dismantled public rooms provide shade at midday, and here and there a mosaic pavement or a still attached fragment of porphyry provides a visual echo of what once glittered on this spot. In some more restored parts of the complex, replica statues recreate the second-century environs, but mostly the remains are tantalising in what they hint at. That they are still so substantial after so long is testament to Hadrian's demands for excellence in structure as well as style.

In June 1944 Allied troops approached Rome in the final exchanges of the war for Italy. In briefing the troops, much had been made of the ancient heritage to which the British and Americans assumed they were naturally heir. A year earlier Dwight Eisenhower, supreme commander of the Allied invasion forces, had exhorted his officers to give special consideration in battle to the antiquities of Italy, *'which by their creation helped and now in their old age illustrate the growth of the civilisation which is ours'*.[17] Long before cruise missiles introduced the illusive idea of precision bombing, the incoming forces had the welfare of ancient monuments in Rome as a central tenet of the offensive. In the propaganda war antiquity was another weapon. Much had been made of the allegedly deliberate firing of ancient Roman galleys by the Germans at Nemi and the destruction of tombs at Tarquinia, and the Allies were determined there should be no repeat of the destruction at Monte Cassino, where a medieval monastery had been obliterated. Officers from the Sub-Commission for Monuments, Fine Arts and Archives were among the front-line troops entering Rome, and each soldier was equipped with a handbook in which the ancient and medieval architectural treasures were clearly marked; in the manner of a tourist guide book, the most valuable were given one to three stars, according to historic or aesthetic worth. Nearly all the works which had been commissioned or restored by Hadrian were classified as part of the essential fabric of twentieth-century culture. Hadrian's Mausoleum, hard by the Tiber, had two stars, as did the ruins of the imperial palaces high on the Palatine. The Pantheon was accorded three stars and so was the whole

Forum area, which included the Temple of Rome and Venus. The obelisk to Antinous on the edge of the city, hidden in the trees of the Pincian gardens, was nevertheless protected, appropriately, with just one star.

The city of Rome itself was placed in category 'A', denoting cities (also including Venice, Florence and Torcello) which were *under no circumstances to be bombed without authority* from the headquarters of the MFAA. Tivoli, however, was placed in category 'B': *'if it is considered essential that objectives in any of them should be bombed, there should be no hesitation in doing so, and full responsibility will be accepted by this headquarters.'* In the event the Germans left the Italian capital without any serious fighting, and damage was not as great as had been feared. In summer 1944 Allied aircraft dropped high explosive first on Palestrina, just outside Rome to the south-west. Here the damage exposed a section of the Temple of Fortuna, once the site of one of the greatest oracles of antiquity, but leaving untouched the intricate beauty of the Nile mosaic. The bombers went on to Tivoli, destroying medieval churches and houses and causing some damage to the Villa d'Este. At Hadrian's villa a direct hit was sustained by the large building known as the Praetorium, only 500 metres to the north of the then unexcavated Canopus and its hidden treasures. The building – a general service block – was substantially damaged but not destroyed.

The casualties of that war were buried in the city they had come to liberate. At the foot of the second-century man-made hill of broken amphorae known as Monte Testaccio lie the 500 or so war dead of the British Military Cemetery. They come from all parts of the British empire; from Madras, Mauritius, Ireland, South Africa and the United Kingdom. A central inscription records the gift of land for this purpose by the people of Rome. Within the wall is set a fragment of stonework under which a dedication reads:

This stone from Hadrian's Wall, the northernmost boundary of the Roman Empire, was placed here at the wish of the citizens of Carlisle, England, to commemorate those servicemen from Cumbria who died in the Second World War.

Meanwhile, in the postwar report on the aerial bomb damage at Tivoli and the extent of necessary repairs at Hadrian's villa, the officers of the Sub-Commission for Monuments, Fine Arts and Archives commented admiringly on the superb robustness of Hadrianic masonry. The quality of second-century design and workmanship had enabled the idea and reality of Hadrian's ambitions to survive for nearly two thousand years.

8

Writing in stone

Consider how the great architect of Cnidos acted. After constructing the tower on Pharos, the mightiest and most beautiful building ever, so that he could send a beacon-signal from it to sailors far and wide on the seas, to stop them being carried on to Paraetonia, a cruel spot they say, with no escape for anyone running on the reefs – well, after completing the building, he inscribed it with his own name inside on the stones, plastered it over with gypsum till it was hidden, and inscribed over that the name of the king of the day, knowing that, as actually happened, the letters would very soon fall away with the plaster to reveal 'Sostratus of Cnidus, son of Dexiphanes, in dedication to the Saviour Gods on behalf of seafarers'. So too he kept his eyes not on those times or his own brief life, but on today and eternity, as long as the tower stands and his craftsmanship survives.

Well, history too should be written in the same way, with truthfulness and hopes for the future rather than flattery to please today's recipients of praise.

LUCIAN, HOW TO WRITE HISTORY, 63

From the memoirs of Julia Balbilla, 137

Now she is gone. It is winter here – a cold, hard winter – and the movement and light of the summer gardens are just a memory. Even her face, whose individual features I came to know so well, is hard to recall. Of course, her face changed a great deal in the last days, and the curious impassivity with which she always gazed upon the world disappeared as little spasms crossed her face and her tongue darted out to moisten cracked lips. But when I think of her – try to call her up – I see only her face in stone. Her carved image, with its smooth cold cheeks and drilled eyes, looking out over Rome, is more powerful than the once living Sabina.

We both said we wished that she could see another spring, but it was not true. She was frightened of suffering as her mother had – she had already endured enough – and although it was desolate to leave in winter, it would have been worse to quit the gardens when they were smelling of jasmine and honeysuckle and when the birds wheeled high, catching invisible insects before swooping to the pools to drink. From the warmth and light of a Roman summer, the journey to the underworld would have been too long. Now the beautiful roses which she loved are reduced by the gardeners to sharp-edged sticks, the vines are long twists of lead, where there were berries there are mildewed briars and the fountains are silent and icy. Dead leaves float in the pools and Sabina is left by the grey Tiber for ever.

The next morning, I walked to the terrace and looked out across the city that she had, in her way, loved. The sky was overcast, but to the south blue sky was seeping in over the distant plateau where the tyrant's palace stands gloomy as ever under the trees. Was he inside, returning again and again to his auguries and seeing nothing? Was he dining or reading, asleep or awake, as her spirit fled with the day?

In the end she died as she lived – with a few complaints, but causing little trouble. The owls called to each other; she moaned in her half-sleep. Night fell over Rome. Then she was frightened, begging me not to put out the lights. I shall not see dawn again, she said, and I fear the darkness. This was true; she once told me that even as a child she had been scared of the night, even with a slave sleeping by her bed. She was hot, pushing down the cover, and then, when they had bled her, first fainting then shaken by chills so insistent that even with my arms round her, she juddered. Her bones seemed to shake within her and the little piece of amber she liked to carry dropped to the floor. When I next looked it had gone; a bauble to delight the child of a light-fingered slave, no doubt.

She had been ill for many weeks by then and her maid – a good servant – was pained by the skin tearing away to let the bone through, like the tooth of an infant pushing through the tender gum. And Sabina did not like strangers to look on her wasted flesh. So it was I who moved her a little and rubbed salves on her rotting skin which, although they could not heal her, could take away the pain. She ate nothing now, and to move her head to drink caused the nausea to return. So I wrung out a fine cloth in wine and water and let drops trickle into her mouth. Sometimes she sucked like a kid at the corner. The Greek doctors had given her draughts to stop the cramps and the vomiting which made her dream and see things. She saw creatures and demons; she spoke of her mother, her voice small and young again. She seemed to think Hadrian was already dead. 'He's safe over there,' she said, 'in his little house,' pointing towards the great mausoleum in its swamp across the river. 'No, there,' I said, smiling, 'in his big house,' pointing in the other direction, east to Tivoli. Some of the more foolish attendants looked anxious, because foreseeing an emperor's death was perilous, even hearing it was treason, and these were dangerous times, but I made them leave. She said to me that he had never really taken her as a wife. That she had no chance of providing him with an heir because he thought her repulsive. He had relations with many married women but not with her. He was always reaching for what he had not already got, she said. She bought charms to attract him at first when she wanted him to like her and to give him children. All failed. She said, only right at the end, that she had once taken a lover and then that there had been, could have been, a child – a child of Hadrian's – and that she had distilled herbs and when that failed used a woman to take the unborn infant from her belly. He was a monster, she said, and as he wanted nothing from her, she had nothing to withhold to punish him. Except that time when she bore his son inside her.

Was it true? Had he known? Who could tell? She said the three-headed dog was slavering in her bedroom, she said she could smell things – burning flesh, the blood of sacrifice, filthy water – she heard wings heavy and waiting. All these were true to her. We burned oils to clear the room of any miasma of decay. We could not change the linens because every movement hurt her, and so we all came to wish it would be soon. I held her hand where her skin fell in small blemished folds; it scarcely moved between my fingers. Her lips moved and no sound came.

She never asked where he was. What was strange to others – that the emperor should not be there – was not of consequence to her. He hated sickness or weakness, and her own condition too closely mirrored his own for him to look on her with equanimity. He was, some said, too sick himself to travel from Tibur. When she first fell ill he had travelled to the house before going to the senate; although he did not go in to see his wife, he was there; the people knew it. That was what mattered. He tried to insist she should be moved to the palace, saying that a summer-house was no fit place for an empress to depart this life, but the doctors, loyal to Sabina, persuaded him that it was most likely, if he insisted on this course, that she would die in the streets like the poorest native before ever reaching the Palatine.

The last clear thing she spoke of was remembering, as a child of the house – one of a brood of loosely related children – seeing Hadrian, tall and handsome, laughing with her uncle. He paid her no attention but she watched him at table, she noticed the hairs on his arms, reddish gold against skin browned by days on campaign. Once she heard him sing – at a private gathering; he was seldom angry in those days. He was not at all interested in small girls, she said, but would play briefly with the boys and their wooden swords or heft one of them into the saddle of his favourite horse. Once, just once, he saw her looking at the horse – a white one with a dark grey muzzle, she still recalled – beautiful but terrifying, pawing the ground and tossing its mane. He smiled at her and gave her some fruit to put out on her hand for the great horse to bend his neck and suck from her shaking palm. He steadied her little hand, with his brave one holding her fingers out stiffly like a starfish so the great horse would not gobble her up with the fruit. A few years later, when she was told she was to marry him, she thought it was a joke; how could he have remembered the serious girl of ten amid all the noise and spectacle of the household? But she was glad to be taken away and to be protected. Later, someone told her that when the arrangements were being made he had to be reminded which one she was. 'Oh, the plain one,' he had said. She did not think he ever smiled at her again.

The Pyramid of Cestius is a visible marker for all confused pedestrians as they wander south through Rome down the dusty roads beyond Caracalla's Baths. It was already in place when St Paul was taken out to his execution in the first century, nine years before the birth of Hadrian, and it was little changed seventeen hundred years later, when Keats' wretched cortege passed through the winter night on its way to the Protestant cemetery. Today, seen emerging from the trees, it is an unmistakable shape at the far end of the Via della Marmorata, conveniently marking both the mainline station of Ostiense and the famous exiles interred at Testaccio. The pyramid marks the edge of the city, and for some the end of the journey.

At the time of Hadrian's birth the pyramid was just seventy years old, whereas Caracalla's luxurious baths, which were themselves to become a landmark, and now lie in ruins, were still a century from being built. Long before he set out to view the 'real' Pyramids, Hadrian would have been familiar with the pyramid standing here and at least one other, now long vanished, near which he was one day to site his own imposing tomb. Both in antiquity and through the ensuing centuries some critics have seen the pyramid only as a glaring anachronism, but in reality a city like Rome overwhelms such a concept. Against the uneven rooflines, the distortion and the chaos that have always characterised the city landscape, the pyramid's uncompromising geometry and whiteness are both stark and dramatic.

For Hadrian, important journeys were made as the principal representative of Rome and Rome's power. They ensured a permanent place for himself within the landscape of the empire and within history. But from the incessant nature of his travelling it can be assumed that his was probably also a personal search for an exemplary, inspiring past, a hope of revelation and a prospect of transformation. He collected *things*, particularly beautiful things; but he was also an almost compulsive collector of ideas and experiences. Any journey is a set within the greater journey from birth to the grave, and Hadrian was not the first to use travel as an illusion of evaded mortality.

When Cestius commissioned the great blocks of tufa, the fine marble tiles and the internal wall-paintings, he was setting out to erect a monument both to the allure of the exotic and to his personal resources, material and intellectual. Whether he had actually been to Egypt is uncertain, though it is quite possible; in any event, for him, as for many others of his class, Egyptianising style celebrated Rome's earlier victories – not just over territory but over desirable cultures. In building it was possible for a wealthy Roman to make a powerful declaration of his own attachment to other lands, ideas and times. The use of the specially made hangings for the tomb was pre-empted by new sumptuary laws and gives an indication of the perceived need to control such public statements of self-worth. As others, notably Augustus, had demonstrated, in death it was possible to create a permanent memorial to aspiration. Tombs could jostle for a place within an existing mythology, becoming landmarks in history as well as along the main roads leading from the city. About Cestius himself, the successful Roman praetor whose visual impact on the city has endured for two thousand years, we know virtually nothing; but he embraced death like an ancient pharaoh, achieving an immortality he could never have conceived with a memorial which outlived even his own language.

On the same bank of the Tiber, but on the city's northern edge, is another, much larger, green space which has been cultivated as a place of beauty and peace since antiquity and is now known as the Borghese Gardens. From the wide and noisy road on its perimeter, the promise of a broad expanse of dark greenery at their summit still tempts the passer-by to climb what seem like interminable white steps blasted with the day's heat. At the top of the flight stands a dead fountain into which stone tortoises forever clamber into unmoving water; from this natural pause in the landscape, paths heavily over-hung with foliage lead away in every direction. To follow one of these in late summer sunlight is like walking into a cool house whose corridors, defined by heavy-leafed orange and walnut trees, give on to courtyards of gravel, edged with damp flowerbeds and shallow depressions of grass. Numerous benches are set into niches in the shrubbery and small cafés ply a desultory trade. The trails across the gardens are lined with statuary: Italian heroes, patriots, legends, in a display of magnificent moustaches, stern expressions and significance. There are soldiers with capes or the quaint hats of Alpine troops, men in evening dress, aviators with goggles and names both well-known and forgotten – but I have only ever found one woman and she, inevitably, is in the garb of a nun. Like emperors, women in the city's history are made invisible by virtue or grotesque by notoriety. Here children play, lovers lie closed and entangled on grass banks and elderly women take precarious turns on the Viale Madama Letizia. Little painted stalls sell sugared sweets, cold drinks and balloons, and skaters skim and leap in the broader spaces of the avenues; the prevailing mood is timeless.

The park conceals all manner of whimsical delights: there is an almost derelict rustic hunting lodge, a grotto, a formal villa serving tea, a strange water-clock. Everything is slightly neglected, slightly forgotten, ruins of ruins; it is hard to know what is 'real' antiquity and what a nineteenth-century illusion. Rowers move up and down a large lake, their laughter rippling across the water, and on one island a perfect classical temple, its steps covered in a mess of ducks, emerges out of the foliage. The temple is a pastiche of one dedicated to Asclepius; a smaller, circular one is named for the goddess Diana, and close at hand is a centuries-old copy of the sturdy arch of the African emperor Septimius Severus, the military victories of its roundels and inscriptions flaking into time and the dried leaves at its foot.

At the end of an avenue of magnolia trees the Borghese Gardens imperceptibly become the Pincio, at the centre of which stands yet another decorative curiosity: this time no reproduction but a nineteen-hundred-year-old Egyptian obelisk long believed to be associated with the dead Antinous and, it was thought, holding the key to his final resting place concealed within some hieroglyphics on one side. The Pincian Gardens obelisk had, it is assumed, found its way to western Europe like so many other Egyptian antiquities of better provenance; in 1822, at the behest of Pope Pius VII, it was erected in the quiet Roman shade. Where it was before it was resurrected by papal decree is a further mystery; found in fragments outside a city gate in the sixteenth century, its earlier journey to Rome – if there was such a journey – is unrecorded.

It is not surprising that, despite prevailing cultural

prohibitions, Antinous rose again to become an object of desire for first the Grand Tourists and then the more bohemian circles of the nineteenth century. The Europeans who lived in Rome and were directly exposed to the images of antiquity, were, anyway, often exiles from convention as much from the cold of the north. As archaeology became more organised, images were being excavated that were readily, if not securely, identifiable as Antinous, and many of them were objects of great beauty and craftsmanship. A popular fascination with Egyptology and Hellenism blended with the homoerotics of the aesthetic movement to invigorate interest in the mysterious end of the imperial favourite. But this emphasis had in its way brought the legend full circle, not in finally arriving at a solution but in echoing Hadrian's own obsessions with Greece, with Egypt, with travel, beauty and Antinous. One of the posthumous statues of Antinous which Hadrian commissioned for his villa at Tivoli is now in the Vatican Museum; the proud, flawlessly athletic youth dressed as pharaoh is an artefact which might plausibly be a product of the more kitsch extreme of Victorian symbolism. Just as a bereft Hadrian had once caused the dead youth's images to be disseminated throughout the empire, so, as they were unveiled a second time, plaster casts were being reproduced and bought by collectors all over Europe.

It was very unlikely that the Pope knew the identity of the obelisk, as when it was erected the hieroglyphs could not be read, but in the later part of the century the code was broken. The romance of the mystery might perhaps have been diluted by the partial translation of the inscriptions, but it was not to be: in fact their ambiguity raised more questions than the translation answered. We now know that the obelisk hieroglyphics neither account for Antinous' death nor reveal the location of his tomb. There are no details of a traditional Roman cremation or, as is more likely given his place of death, an embalming. There is no specific implication that his body was brought from the Nile and buried at Tivoli, but neither is there any confirmation that he was buried near the site of the tragedy at the city of Antinoopolis. Ancient Egyptians were traditionally buried on the west bank of the Nile; the new city was on the eastern side of the river. The material remains of Antinous seem to have vanished once his body had slipped beneath the water, to be resurrected as a thousand statues.

The stone is possibly not even a single memorial; it might have been part of a mortuary temple complex in Egypt. It is increasingly believed that the obelisk did not even arrive in Rome until the third century. But the obelisk and its carvings *are* Hadrianic, and the inscriptions do point to its having indeed been part of a memorial to his favourite, and they do include some magical incantations among the more conventional dedications and prayers.

Unintentionally, Pope Pius VII had chosen a delightfully appropriate spot in placing the obelisk on the Pincio. The gardens take their name from the ancient family and the long vanished sixth-century Pincian Palace. The present public gardens were landscaped in the early nineteenth century by Valadier, and no doubt the obelisk was set in place shortly afterwards to ornament an ambitious project and to impose the Pope's tacit presence upon it. But the choice of the Pincio brought Antinous back into a tradition of beauty, intrigue and lavishness. The Pincian Hill was never counted within the seven hills of Rome, as it lay outside the ancient city, but it was always, even in antiquity, an area of beautiful cultivation. Long before the reign of Hadrian it had been known as the Hill of Gardens. These gardens – *horti* – on the edge of the city were not just a place of quiet reflection for the Roman aristocracy who developed them, nor were they *just* gardens; most had a small villa or summer-house at their centre. They became synonymous with intrigue, with excess and with transgression. Their very position, neither urban nor truly rural, not constrained by the normal laws of civilisation, made the gardens synonymous with stories of patrician misconduct. As a backdrop they appear and reappear throughout Roman history; in the *horti* Caligula watched opponents put to death, Messalina made her assignations and was eventually killed by Claudius' soldiers, Vespasian expired; and numerous sexual and political plotters spun out their webs between the walks and fountains of these ancient Roman pleasure gardens. The most beautiful gardens were even plotted *for*, coveted as objects of desire in themselves. Nero's elaborate gardens, with rivers and woods, vineyards and a zoo, built around his Golden House on the ashes of the notorious fire, engulfed the heart of the city and were, at least partly, responsible for his fall from favour.

But while it is easy to embark on an academic deconstruction of the gardens as a metaphor for disarray in a highly controlled urban society, there are, as any first-time visitor soon discovers, less complicated ways of understanding them. You only have to be in Rome for a few hours of summer to realise that a place of shade and greenness and water must have been irresistible, especially on a hillside above the dust and noise of the city. Part of present-day Rome's great charm is its proliferation of parks and groves, and it is not surprising that so many of the great green spaces of ancient Rome have remained open, even as, from the middle ages onwards, space was increasingly at a premium and the city sprawled beyond its walls.

The first known gardens on the Pincian Hill were owned by general and senator Lucius Licinius Lucullus, who served under the dictator Sulla in the first century BC. After campaigning against Mithridates and pursuing a successful political career, he threw his considerable wealth and energy into luxurious living and his name became synonymous with hedonistic extreme. Dictionaries still include 'Lucullan' as an epithet for sumptuousness. Centuries later, semi-rural

Renaissance villas, the properties of cardinals and popes, re-created their own formal gardens, and notoriety, in the same area, and some have survived; the Villa Medici (now the Accademia di Francia) is only occasionally accessible, but the pretty Villa Guilia, built in the mid-sixteenth century, and the elegant Villa Borghese, completed some sixty years later, are open to the public. It is quite possible to trace a dynasty of delightful but disreputable gardens, with their artifice and classical conceits, from Lucullus' conspicuous horticultural consumption to Hadrian's villa, and from ancient Rome to the present day.

Only a few yards from the obelisk the Viale della Obelisco comes almost at right angles into the Viale Gabriele d'Annunzio, and in front of you unfolds arguably the most glorious and heart-lurching panorama of Rome. It has become a cliché to look across Rome from the Pincio to the Janiculum, from one great green hill to another, and it is a tradition that has not been diminished by being much recorded in diaries, letters and novels. When the English were flocking to Rome in the eighteenth and nineteenth centuries, this was the place for the carriage rides, the self-display and the outdoor life of polite society. In the many lodgings at the foot of the hill they created an expatriate community where those exiled by choice, political compulsion or illness lived a life of salons, collecting, drawing and letter-writing while the less fortunate grubbed out a living from the whims of the rich or waited hopefully for the Roman climate to effect a cure.

To step on to the Pincio in early evening is still the most potent introduction to the city. Looking out over the haze and the browns, terracottas and golds of a city that seems surprisingly small to bear the weight of so much history, it is not necessary to identify specific landmarks, although some, like the huge Victor Emmanuel monument, are dominant. There are cupolas, baroque, gleaming with gold leaf, or dull and leaden, and inevitably dominated by the great dome of

St Peter's. Medieval campanili, roof gardens and the formal architecture of decaying palazzi stand seemingly without regard to proportion or perspective; and across the city the plateau of the Janiculum, with its famous pines dark against the sky, looks like a stage set.

From the broad terrace near to the obelisk, there is one conspicuous monument that can be seen relatively close at hand, on the other side of the Tiber, between the Pincio and the Vatican. The medieval fortress of Castel sant'Angelo is readily identified by the great bronze Archangel Michael at its summit; partially clad in martial costume, his solid wings low on his back, he is frozen in the act of unsheathing his sword above the city. From the outside the origins of the bulky building are not immediately obvious. As citadel, as papal residence, and as a prison immortalised in the final moments of the opera *Tosca* when the heroine flings herself off its heights rather than fall into the hands of a corrupt regime, this imposing edifice has had a very long life.

It is in fact almost exactly the same age as the obelisk, because it was first built as the mausoleum of the man who ordered both works – Hadrian. Even in the matter of tombs, Hadrian was competitive. His mausoleum, capped with trees and decorated with relief carving, bronze ornament and marble, stood across the river from the great mausoleum of Augustus and was reached by the Pons Aelius, a bridge completed in 134 and named after Hadrian's family. Unquestionably it set itself up to equal or rival the resting place of the first emperor. For centuries the two monuments to dynastic pretensions, erected by men who had no living descendants, stood 800 metres apart on either side of the Tiber.

Augustus' tomb, once a landmark of the city, had many subsequent incarnations as a fortress, a walled garden, a bear-baiting arena and an opera hall. Today it is derelict, inaccessible; a crumbling tumulus, inhabited by cats, at the centre of a square of Fascist architecture erected in the 1930s. Augustus' posthumous statement of his achievements – his *res gestae* – which once greeted visitors to his tomb, has been re-created on bronze and placed on the outside of the Ara Pacis, a short distance away. The Ara Pacis – the altar to Augustan peace – is a triumph of first-century Roman relief carving. It was discovered in many fragments under a house on the Via Flaminia and re-assembled as part of Mussolini's Augustan renaissance on its present site. But the glory of Augustus' tomb is gone for ever.

At the core of the Castel sant'Angelo, Hadrian's tomb, where his ashes and those of his successors, including the notorious Caracalla, were once interred, has survived under its belligerent medieval accretions. The bridge which once led to it, the Pons Aelius, has long been known as the Ponte sant'Angelo after the fortress. Much of its fabric has been replaced or ornamented since the second century, but the arches that bear the weight of the bridge over the Tiber are still those that Hadrian's engineers constructed.

Hadrian, for whom it was rumoured the beautiful Antinous had sacrificed himself in the hope that his lover might find health and an extended life, died on 10 July 138 CE, less than eight years after his companion. On the Pincian obelisk he had inscribed a prayer for his own longevity: '*He that is beloved of Hapi and of all the gods, the lord of the diadems – may he live safe and sound, may he live forever like Re, in a fresh and rejuvenated old age.*' Just one year later the mythical phoenix, which some claimed to have seen at the time of Hadrian's accession, was due to rise again in Egypt. Hadrian's mausoleum was not finished at his death and was rushed to completion by his nominated successor Antoninus Pius, who also pushed through the customary posthumous divination – against some opposition from those who had long memories and those who had more recent cause to hate the late emperor.

Reports differ as to whether Hadrian was initially buried

at Puteoli, near Baiae, or in the Gardens of Domitia near his unfinished mausoleum. Given that he died in the middle of summer, it was obviously necessary that some intermediate disposal of his body be undertaken fairly swiftly. In any event, after the usual cremation, Hadrian's ashes, and those of his wife Sabina, were buried in a chamber at the heart of the sumptuously decorated tomb by the side of the Tiber. The urns inside are long gone, and it is not even certain which space is the original funerary chamber; but the interior of Hadrian's tomb has been well restored. On a dark internal corridor at the heart of the mausoleum the words of his famous valediction have been carved.

> *Animula vagula blandula*
> *Hospes comesque corporis*
> *Quae nunc abibis in loca*
> *Pallidula, rigida, nudula,*
> *Nec, et ut soles, dabis iocos.*

> *Little wandering soul,*
> *Guest and companion of my body,*
> *Where are you going to now?*
> *Away, into bare, bleak places,*
> *Never again to share a joke.*

Antinous has no known memorial. The waters have long closed over the truth of how he came to his premature end, and any contemplation of his life fixes disproportionately on its uncertainties and the effects of his death on his protector. There is a Roman saying which seems entirely appropriate as his epitaph: *sit tibi terra levis* (let the earth lie lightly upon him).

From the memoirs of Julia Balbilla, 138

By summer they were both dead, united in death and in the tomb. The mausoleum is a splendid place to face eternity, and it has an eastern cast which carries Hadrian's message to Rome forward into all time. The turf has not quite taken on the rising slope of the summit – hanging gardens were perhaps a little ambitious – but the statues are very fine and the bronzes flicker like flames in the evening sun.

It was in the main a dull summer; the first of many. Antoninus did the decent thing by all the decaying relics of Hadrian's court, and life in this airy villa is pleasant enough to dissuade me thus far from return to an Athens which I may hardly know. I have my books, a dog and a little slave girl, the granddaughter of the Commagenian maid who first set out with me, and I am teaching her to read.

Did I perform a service for Sabina? Did I make her last years easier, if only in that I too was growing old and had been not much loved? Sometimes I find myself missing those very aspects of her character that I found most grating in life: her girlish laugh, or the interminable self-regard in her fascination with Hadrian's antipathy towards her. But she was not an over-demanding companion; she was strong, she could be kind, and she listened so gravely to my new verse that I continued to compose long after the muse left me. She did not notice.

So, Sabina, goddess, friend, for the last time, here are my words for you.

Animula vagula blandula
Hospes comesque corporis
Quae nunc abibis in loca
Pallidula, rigida, nudula,
Nec, et ut soles, dabis iocos.

9

Retrospective

The River God circled around me as I stood shrouded in darkness and, not knowing what had happened, searched all around the hollow cloud. Twice, unwittingly, he walked around the place where the goddess had hidden me and twice he called: 'Ho there, Arethusa! Hallo, Arethusa!' Alas what feelings did I have then! Assuredly I was like a lamb when it hears the wolves howling around the high sheepfold, or like a hare, hiding in the branches, watching the jaws of hostile hounds, and not daring to move. Still Achelous did not depart; for he did not see any footsteps leading further on. He kept watch on the spot where the mist was. A cold sweat broke out on my limbs, when I was just trapped, and dark drops fell from my whole body. Wherever I moved my foot, a pool flowed out, moisture dripped from my hair. More quickly than I can tell of, I was changed into a stream.

OVID, METAMORPHOSES, BOOK 5 (TRANS. MARY INNES)

From the memoirs of Julia Balbilla, 143

With the passage of time I have had time to think, to apportion blame and to retrieve it. At the time it was easy not to feel sorry for him, and not just because we were all apprehensive as to the parts we were destined to play. As always when trouble pressed, Hadrian took refuge in self-pity and ill-temper. Almost immediately the death took on the cast of a personal injury to the emperor. There was the boy and then, like a spirit summoned up by an Egyptian spell, there he was not, without so much as farewell, much less leave of absence. Hadrian, who so craved new experiences, found humiliation might be one of the most novel.

Yet there was a moment when he seemed almost human. Not in the endless recitations of metric sorrow, public laments which he encouraged; hymns celebrating the new god by shameless opportunists with tears in their eyes and gold in their palms and a sturdy way with the old dialects. It was scarcely tolerable, but such was the emperor's need to have the gravity of his loss recognised that his usual discernment seemed to have been set aside. He was for a short while almost greedy for valedictory drivel. Then there were the commissioned works of prose and music being readied for the games which Hadrian was already planning to inaugurate in the dead boy's honour. There were clumsy narrations, pose-striking, ash-smeared poetasters with execrable rhymes. All was endured with equanimity. I considered my position – we all did: would a poem be appropriate, would it be expected or would it only draw attention where it was least wanted? Safer perhaps to frame a response in another's words. Within three days Adonis had been done to death, as had Hylas and, less convincingly, Narcissus. The pretty boys of legend were languid corpses in our artistic landscape.

I did nothing. But a few days later in the evening I saw him by the river, near the place they call Hir-Wer, where, by consent, it happened. He was surrounded by a handful of his closest associates; the self-regarding, and thus unperturbed, Commodus, and young Fuscus, looking out of his depth in a situation which called for more than beautiful manners. There was a boy standing almost on the water's edge, singing with a simple accompaniment on the double pipe. It was supposedly a piece written to mark the death of the Bithynian, but although its beauty and skill suggested that it had been composed earlier and pressed into service, it was remarkable in its simplicity. Amid all the cloying over-elaboration of this unimportant death it was painfully poignant. Of course, music can create grief and melancholy and as such is the falsest measure of emotion; but perhaps just because of its plain expression of regret, the short lament conjured up an immense sorrow at the loss of any young, hopeful life. Hadrian who loved music so much, was not immune to its effects and just for a moment, sitting under a canopy in the setting sun, he looked stricken and bewildered.

He never spoke to us directly and of that I am glad. After all, what could the disappearance of a boy, no longer even a very beautiful one, be but a relief to everyone who had to watch his antics? Even to Hadrian perhaps? The Greek – they all called him the Bithynian boy – had kept his youthful laughter, his youthful ways, but when I was near him – oh, perhaps twice – I saw that he was no longer a boy at all. Once as they came back from hunting I smelled his man's smell; the smell of fear, a smell you could sometimes detect on slaves. They say he moistened his skin with milk and bread so that his beard would not grow, and in that way he tried to believe he would always be pleasing to the emperor. Some know 'for a fact' that Hadrian asked the surgeons to ensure the boy never reached manhood. Towards the end the Greek boy had taken to lining his eyes so that they might smoulder at his lord.

Sabina, at least, whose lot was to be unexceptional, did not have to dance, nor pretend to courage in the hunt. She did not have to amuse. Her friends – there were not many – remained friends, loyal to the last. Her enemies were checked by the emperor's authority, not because he cared for her discomfort but because he was conscious of injuries to his dignity. A slight to her was a slight to him; and yet the greatest slight to her, beside which all others were insignificant, was his continued existence. Let the philosophers expound on that one.

She had, she said repeatedly, no feelings for the boy, who was, anyway, over; but she recognised the desperate failure of dignity; recognised one who existed in a world without choices. He was not the first, nor would he be the last, and when they had to go, when they disappointed, or he wearied of them, or they lost their fresh beauty, how he grieved even as they disappointed and he turned his favour from them. She observed how his love grew as the distance between his passions and the present lengthened. Memory, for him, was where love was located. Memory and desire for what he had not already possessed: people, objects, places. The ultimate impossibility. As for his wife, possessed, unloved, undesired ever, permanence made her hateful. The same permanence made her resentful at first, then desperate; then these emotions passed into a more or less suppressed antipathy. Only in the last weeks, in Egypt, had she shown a little spark. The ruins and the enigmas of that ancient land intrigued her. She too had commerce with the priests and the magicians and the masons and the silversmiths.

As for their speculations, Sabina said to the end that she was indifferent. Let them talk, she said, her voice inflected with excitement, let them write their poems of consolation, name a flower after him, name a city after him and buy some citizens to live in it, let those filthy priests chant, let the astronomers scour the skies – a boy with rouge and charcoal-smudged eyes become a star, a god? It seemed unlikely, unless the gods too were susceptible to a mediocre singing voice and easily commanded smile.

And let him suffer for his lost youth. She was beyond caring.

The weeks and months afterwards were hard. Whispers, alternate frenzy and inertia. We did not expect to understand but waited for the emperor to smile upon us again, and we remained in the dark. An accident. No more. Surely no more?

Ours is a society of opportunity and calamity, hopes and

sudden reverses, and the wise traveller is ever vigilant. There were always many deaths while we travelled. Epidemics, disappearances, accidents; slaves sickened and were replaced; the children and the elderly were taken off by fevers. For some we grieved, some we missed for their wit or ability to tell stories, others passed unnoticed from our lives. Hadrian's friends were not inviolate, and those that did not fall ill sometimes fell out of favour and were sent back to Rome or to Athens or to some chilly province in the north.

All I do know for certain is there was no star. I know the stars, have known them from a child. There was nothing new in the heavens; everything was as you would expect. And yet now that boy's likeness looks down on us from every street in the empire. That silly boy had a city raised to his glory. A boy of the humblest birth, a trophy the emperor brought with him from Mantinea or some such place, made immortal in bricks and stone. What greatness will travellers read who walk in the streets of the boy's city?

At first we did not even notice he had gone. There were many such as him about. Hadrian had many like him before and had some since; there was nothing particularly remarkable about this one. I do not even think we would have recognised him should he have reappeared. But he did not of course reappear, not in the flesh.

Later, we thought he had run away. Something had made the emperor angry, though there was something else there too, Sabina said. Despite her habitual coolness she seemed apprehensive for the boy – when the horsemen went off – he was obviously going to be caught. His fair hair, his light eyes – they all have fair hair and light eyes, these boys – trying to conceal himself among these dark, dark people. Where could he go? What skills did he have? He was, as we all are, the emperor's property. Those who know this prosper. But the hunters returned without their prey and the emperor's rage had an edge of despair about it. He looked tired and old and bruised. And then they found the body. I never saw it.

They said it was the boy's, but I heard the face was damaged, an arm was splintered. Perhaps the beasts of the water attacked him, perhaps the prow of a boat crushed those pretty features. Perhaps in a fit young body the heart was not strong. Perhaps there was a mistake? For their different reasons, everybody was eager for the problem to be resolved.

And the rumours went on and on and on. Some saying the death was not so much an accident as convenience. Others that it was convenience shaded with animosity. Some that it was an unimpeded act of hate. Some whispered as we passed. It was not hard to imagine what they said. My position was for a time dangerous; they might easily forget my royal blood, but they have never failed to remember my descent from those who look into the future and who make salves and potions to ease the ills of man. Sabina was his wife, Sabina was a well-connected Roman; if they looked for a murderer they would be relieved to find the creature in a foreigner, not the emperor's wife.

A few doctors and priests were taken to view this body – if it was him. Some say that like Nero before him, who anatomised his mother that he might see that place from which he drew life, Hadrian offered the physicians money to cut into the already mutilated body so that he could look for the essence of his obsession. Others believed that with the shell so damaged Hadrian searched for an answer to the mystery of desire thwarted in the preserved internal flesh. Some said he sought for signs that the boy had surrendered his life deliberately so that the emperor might gain immortal life. Had he lived he would have seen such a fancy as folly. The emperor aged more rapidly afterwards than he had with the boy alive to encourage his delusions.

And then what? Like a magician's bird in a twitch of cloth, the body disappeared. Entombed in the new city? Taken to the vaults of the ancient kings on the west bank of the river? Reduced to ashes in some distant spot and sent to his homeland in the north or parcelled back to Rome? Fed to the crocodiles? Any of these could have been true, but I told Sabina then that in that land where death's craftsmen may confront the demands of a stinking corpse not by turning it into cinders but creating a fragrant statue with salts and cedar dust, Hadrian may have found an attempt to keep his boy with him, even after life, irresistible. Could the embalmers' skill extend to repairing the torn limbs, the battered face? Would that youth still travel with us, quieter but as irksome?

We did not do it. We laughed to think of the power we could have to cast him down, to halt for one moment the smooth running of his days. We talked about it, although even to dream about incommoding the emperor was unsafe. We conjectured how much gold would be necessary to send the boy discreetly on his way. If he could be prised from the emperor's side, of course. Still, obscene lampoons and jokes about Hadrian's susceptibilities were the daily amusement of the court back then. We did not do it. At least, I did not and Sabina, for all her resentment, would surely never have acted alone, would never have *been* alone long enough to prepare and administer a fatal dose. Nor did the empress ever trust another soul, certainly not enough to expose herself to potential disaster. Sabina's response to the affronts she perceived was always a terrible, impregnable endurance, not action. Did she see anything? Know anything? It is possible. She wanted us to think she had a secret. Whether she did, or whether she wished to infuriate the man who had injured her for so long, who can tell? Sabina was always mistress of the look, not speech. Whatever she may have seen or known, she was never quite the same woman after Egypt. She was, just a little, happier.

It would have been easy, of course; though important to Hadrian, the boy was of so little importance to anyone else that he was not guarded. His only value was in what he gave to the emperor, and dignity forbore that the emperor of the world should set guards to ensure the fidelity of a youth. A concoction in his wine; I have seen the herbs for sale openly in the city markets here. Gentler, if less certain, than a blow to the head or a knife in the belly. Nothing crude, no fits, no violent spasms of agony and vomiting, no pallor, sweats and shaking but a gradual slipping away, first into drunken slumber then into unrouseable sleep – and then let the Nile have him and finish the task. As indeed it did, one way or another.

But no, not an act of hate, I think, but an act of love turned, for one moment, to hate. Had the emperor wished to discard Sabina he could have done so many years before. Hadrian's feelings as far as she was concerned were constant. It is in the sudden alterations of passion that violent and irrevocable deeds are done. Fear and anger snatched the boy from Hadrian's side. Hadrian's love for him raised him up and Hadrian's love dashed him down.

In the Museum of the Louvre in Paris a crude terracotta figurine is on display. Disturbing to modern eyes, the female statuette has her hands tied behind her back and her genitals, chest, eyes, ears and mouth have been pierced through with large nails. The figurine dates from the third century and was found buried in a clay pot in Egypt. Inside her body she may contain a parchment scroll directing her power; outside an attached lead tablet is inscribed with a charm calling on Thoth, Anubis, Antinous and the spirits of the dead to potentiate the spell.

Whatever one can squeeze out of the sources concerning Hadrian's personal grief, whatever the true circumstances of Antinous' death, one hundred years later the idea of him had evidently acquired magical significance. The exact purpose of the charm is unknown, but the general treatment of the figurine is similar to the procedures for making a love spell, versions of which have been discovered in numerous ancient papyri. Among the most popular charms were those for making the object of desire become compulsively attracted to the person who enacted the ritual. It was an appropriate use of Antinous' memory, for the dead Antinous had become infinitely more potent than the living man. Both in Hadrian's reactions to his death and in the accretions of myth, the easy and ordered view of Roman civilisation and sophistication begin to be infused with older forces of superstition and vulnerability.

During the days immediately following the death, the night skies over Egypt were particularly spectacular. In the still warm early November nights, Hadrian stood outside in the dark and contemplated the movements of the heavens. However bright the lights of his retinue and the small fires of the Nile-side settlements, the clarity of the stars was undiminished. From Hermopolis, the small city on the riverbank where Antinous had last been seen, the sky was a vault of visible stars and within a week this was dominated by a full moon. Shortly after Antinous' death Hadrian observed, or had drawn to his attention, a bright new star over Egypt. By the lingering convention of the time this could be taken to indicate the death of a significant figure. One hundred years later the historian Dio Cassius wrote, '[Hadrian] *declared that he had seen a star which he took to be that of Antinous, and gladly lent an ear to the fictitious tales woven by his associates to the effect that the star had really come into being from the spirit of Antinous and had then appeared for the first time.*'

There are two possible responses to this. One is that Hadrian, destabilised by recent events, simply saw what he wanted to see in the star-filled night skies over the Nile. However, for both the Egyptians and the Romans, the now separate disciplines of astrology and astronomy were not distinct from one another, and the movements of the stars were both a potent force for interpreting the world and a crucial tool in locating the place of humankind on the earth. In the lives of emperors sudden and dramatic celestial events were invariably part of the narrative. When Hadrian's illustrious predecessor Augustus had returned to Rome after the assassination of Julius Caesar, a combination of a rainbow-like aura around the sun and lightning striking from a clear sky encouraged him to expect success. Presumably the same omens were less favourably interpreted for the newly dead imperial victim Julius Caesar; thunder rumbling in a clear sky had certainly presaged the death of the virtuous Titus, and almost identical omens predicted the violent death of Caligula.[1] The reading of such signs was a delicate matter.

For the ancient Romans the stars were always significant to the lives of men. In his *Natural History*, written late in the first century, Pliny inveighs against the prevailing belief that stars were attached to the fortunes of individuals, but this was still a popular convention. Then as now it was not impossible for people to believe aspects of two apparently conflicting systems of understanding. Pliny was not alone in arguing for an understanding of cosmology as separate from the fortunes of the great but, broadly, it was still attractive to see the movement of the stars in a relationship with human existence. The city of Alexandria was a centre for the study of the stars as it was for many disciplines, and Hadrian was himself adept in what was one of the intellectual preoccupations of his age, but his interest was not merely intellectual; he was, again typically for his time, superstitious as well as learned, and in his sumptuous villa complex at Tivoli he was already building an observatory. His knowledge of the subject and his access to experts in the field make it extremely unlikely that he would claim to see a new star that did not exist, or that he would have accepted a fictitious one. It was, equally, highly probable that he would look to the heavens to suggest some significance in Antinous' demise.

Looking down the Nile towards the unknown spot where his favourite must have died, he would have seen the sky dominated by a star known then as now as Canopus, one of the constellation called Argo Navis (the ship Argo). The star Canopus had been named for the pilot of the Trojan war hero who died on that spot in Egypt; and the geographical Canopus was, as we have seen, synonymous with amusement and sensual pleasure. Hadrian may also have hoped for a favourable prediction at the famous Temple of Serapis which lay within the confines of Canopus. That Canopus was or became significant to Hadrian seems beyond question because on his return to Tivoli a model of it became a centrepiece of the marvellous villa, its vaulted end being a schematically developed copy of the Serapeum, the Temple of Serapis. Like so much that was associated with Egypt, Canopus also had a darker meaning, and was given to the human-headed vase in which the entrails of the dead were embalmed.

Shocked, grieving and impressionable, an able astronomer staying in a country whose culture drew heavily on stars to order its life – it would have been surprising if Hadrian had not seen something in the heavens that made sense of what had happened. But what Hadrian saw was evidently something out of the ordinary. Fifteen hundred years later, the French astronomer A. G. Pingré identified the convenient star as a probable nova – a new star which burns with unusual brightness for a short time before fading.[2] It was a charming and familiar metaphor for the fortunes of the young Greek. But auguries are notoriously flexible in their message, and this radiant new star might possibly have been the same astronomical portent which the Jews took as affirmation of their own intention to rise up against the Romans in Judea under the leadership of the rebel Shimon bar Kokhba, whom his followers called 'the star'. If this was indeed the same phenomenon that inspired the emperor to honour his dead lover, there was an irony in its appearance. For it was Hadrian's strategies for the suppression of bar Kokhba, beginning not long after his bereavement, which aggravated the harsh guerrilla war in which the Jews were virtually eradicated and the Roman legions sustained severe losses; and it was this military action which was further to confirm the contemporary view that Antinous' death had permanently destabilised the emperor's character.

Modern astronomers cannot detect any extraordinary phenomenon in the years around 130 which matches the historical accounts but concede the possibility of a new star.

More likely is that an existing star was named around this time. Certainly Hadrian's approximate contemporary, the astronomer Ptolemy, mentions 'stars around Aquila, to which the name Antinous is given', and this constellation would have been clearly visible over Egypt in 130.[3]

Although Dio Cassius, himself from Antinous' home province of Bithynia, introduces an element of ridicule into his version of Hadrian's reaction to the tragedy, the individual elements of the aftermath are not as irregular as the historian makes out. If, as seems likely, there was a star, then it was not surprising that an association was made with the recent dramas. The link between star movements and significant deaths was long established – the Emperor Claudius' death eighty years earlier, for example, had coincided with the appearance of a comet. Despite the cynical note in Dio Cassius' retelling, that imperial astrologers should confirm anomalous indications of the spirit of a new god ascending to heaven was nothing new – at least, it was not new in circumstances surrounding the deaths of emperors: Suetonius records it for Augustus. Emperors' favourites did not, however, usually leave this world for such lofty destinations.

A belief in Antinous' posthumous power seems to have exceeded even the formal declaration of his new status. Although there was greater resistance to the acceptance of an emperor's sexual partner as a god in the more urbane society of Rome, in the Greek east Hadrian's own philhellenism assured the new god's absorption into the Greek pantheon from the moment the emperor decided on his deification. However, the large number of gods worshipped in Greece and Rome were often identified with one another, so that a god might be worshipped in the guise – and visually, the costume – of another immortal with whom they had some characteristics in common. So Antinous was worshipped as Dionysus (the Roman Bacchus), a god associated with wine and the casting off of inhibition. He was also worshipped as Pan, the god of pastoral pleasures, and Pan's father, Hermes (the Roman Mercury), the youthful patron of travellers and guide to the underworld. The connections were all obvious. But it was inevitable, given the place and means of Antinous' death, that he would also be assimilated into the Egyptian underworld.

The dark tale of Osiris is one of many shadows that fall over this story, and it is one of the aspects of the death which raised questions as to its circumstances. Antinous died only a few miles downstream from the cult centre of Osiris at Abydos. More provocatively, he died on or about the festival of the Nile and the celebration of the birth of Osiris, which fell on 24 October; and he speedily became part of the Osiris legend, worshipped and represented in Egyptian costume as the god Antinous-Osiris.

The flourishing cult of Osiris already had its own magnificent temples and its loyal devotees. Osiris,

dead god and god of the dead, brother and husband of Isis . . . did not truly begin to exist until he was assassinated by Seth. Almost nothing is known about him before his death. When it is said that Osiris lives, the reference is always to his resurrection, which takes place in the hereafter, not in this world, definitely closed to him. The rites that make possible his resurrection ensure that the king, and later, all the dead, will have a fate identical to his after death.[4]

The tale of the bereaved Isis searching the Nile for her murdered lover and brother and reassembling his body parts in order that he might possess power after death came to have resonances in Hadrian's own drive to create immortality for his lost favourite. Its essentials – violent death, resurrection and redemption – were all present in the story of Hadrian and Antinous. They were compelling elements in many other early religions too, including Christianity, the troublesome new sect which was already infiltrating the empire, and they were probably central to the secret proceedings of the Eleusian Mysteries.

The connections to the legend of Osiris – and indeed to Christianity – were curious, with the echo of the creation of a new god, and the circumstances of Antinous' death also echoed the superficial but alluring themes of popular Greek myths. There was Hylas, companion of Heracles and the Argonauts, who was drowned by adoring water nymphs who drew him into the spring where he had been sent to fetch water. There was Narcissus, who under Aphrodite's curse was fatally entranced by his own reflection in the surface of a pool. Antinous the god joined the company of beautiful boys with powerful, if capricious, protectors, who met strange, watery deaths. Antinous was a perfect divinity for the second-century world of the imagination.

If Antinous' death is a mystery, his life, and any reason for such posthumous recognition beyond Hadrian's affection for him, is almost imperceptible. His home town of Bithynium, also called Claudiopolis, a Greek city in what is now western Anatolia in Turkey, has become modern Bolu: a large, charmless town on the lethal Ankara–Istanbul highway. Far from being a place to visit, it is a place to leave as quickly as possible, if only among the coarse-running engines and diesel fumes of the heavy lorries on which Turkish industry depends. It was not always so. In the second century the province of Bithynia, lying between the uncompromisingly dry Anatolian plateau and the Black Sea coast, was a land of hills, rivers, lakes and orchards. Antinous seems to have spent his childhood in a village to the north-west of the city, in forested hills near the border. It is tempting to construct a tale of a wild and beautiful boy elevated from pastoral simplicity to a life of unimaginable sophistication – but this would be overstating the case. Bithynia was an influential province with which several powerful and cultured men, both in the second century and earlier, had connections through birth, residence or profession, including Hannibal, who died there, Dio of Prusa, and Catilius Severus; the writer of witty love poetry, Catullus;

the stolid historian, Arrian; Pliny the younger – and Cassius Dio, who was born at the end of Hadrian's life and became one of his principal biographers. Bithynia was no generic rural backwater, no erotic Arcadia.

Hadrian visited the province in 124 and it is possible that he saw and was captivated by the beautiful boy then; but if he did, the moment passed unnoticed by the writers of the time. It is just as likely that Antinous came to court in the retinue of a patrician Bithynian or that he was selected to take part in an athletic display and caught Hadrian's eye that way. (Roman emperors are frequently related as finding lovers in this fashion.) That he was the emperor's sexual partner is widely accepted today. Early Christian writers railed at the sexual decadence of imperial Rome, and Hadrian's sexual and theological tastes in particular; even Gibbon takes the relationship as Hadrian's ultimate disgrace. Later theories owed more to the constraints and preoccupations of nineteenth- and twentieth-century European scholarship. Some suggested that Antinous was a straightforward companion, a proxy for the son Hadrian never had or an unacknowledged blood relation; educated *fin-de-siècle* pornographers put hand-tinted, and highly explicit, engravings into private circulation.

Yet the issue of Hadrian's homosexuality, which was to dominate his later reputation, assumed importance only in the last decade of his reign, when the effects of a private relationship were to be publicly imposed across the empire. His choices were entirely consistent with his adoption of archaic Greek mores. In ancient Greek society women were so little regarded beyond the necessity of their involvement in the procreation of children that a relationship with a man was considered a much more desirable, erotic and elegant matter. Beautiful boys were celebrated and idealised in art; and, though such relationships were argued for in intellectual terms, they were also undoubtedly sexual.

Relationships between upper-class men flourished, but only within a very strict social structure. To step outside this was to invite opprobrium. For the Greeks, the relationship must always be between unequals. A boy younger than eighteen would have a mentor and lover of between eighteen and forty. When the boy began to show the unmistakable signs of later adolescence – facial hair, deepening voice and increased musculature – the relationship was concluded and the young man could, if he chose, proceed to being the older partner in a new relationship. A man who persisted in having love affairs over the age of forty was thought to look ridiculous; a man who continued to be the passive partner once out of boyhood was derided. In a highly structured society such containment was the key to same-sex relationships, and same-sex relationships were a key to social organization.

Homosexuality was not viewed in the same way in Rome, not least because it was firmly identified with Greekness in the Roman mind, but also because what to the Greeks was the pursuit of the ideal in the form of physically perfect boys was in the eyes of Romans simply a matter of urgent sexual gratification. Romans perceived homosexuality as more morally precarious and more threatening to public order; and so it had the potential to sweep away reputations. Anxiety and contempt centred on any hint of passivity or bestial lust; moreover, any kind of perceived deviance, not least because it tended to be pursued in secret, was synonymous with political corruption. For Romans, any otherwise incomprehensible route to power was invariably a homosexual one. For Greeks, particularly the Greeks of history, nothing was purer or more beautiful than the love between men. For Romans, the civic virtues were pre-eminent and sexual passions a diversion from duty which left a man exposed to ridicule.

Hadrian did not parade his favourite in Rome, but in the Greek east he may have persuaded himself that nothing could be more in keeping with the spirit of the times. But even in Greece times had changed, and if he was intending to brandish a lover as a testament to his aesthetic and cultural agenda, Hadrian broke the rules. By the time he arrived in Egypt Hadrian was by ancient standards too old to be openly conducting a love affair; and yet as his most famous lover, Antinous, reached manhood, Hadrian was unwilling or unable to surrender him to the conventions even of tolerant Greek society. Both men were diminished in the eyes of the empire by their continuing association. One way or another, the relationship had little future in 130.

Hadrian was not perceived as effete. Unlike Caligula and Nero, he had come to rule in maturity. He had seen serious military service, he was fit and well-built. The sources speak admiringly of his endurance – he could walk 20 miles carrying a military pack, he stood in all weathers with his head uncovered, he was scrupulous in his review and management of his imperial forces. There was no suggestion that his opinions were influenced by improper connections. Yet it is his place at the centre of a great homosexual love affair, not his undeniable achievements as the patron of an artistic renaissance or consolidator of an empire, that has ensured lasting public interest in Hadrian.

So it is curious that the nature of the affair is intangible. Antinous is virtually invisible until he surfaces in the histories of Hadrian as the emperor is about to set out on a day's hunting. He appears, it seems, just in time to make his dramatic exit, just in time to become a work of art. Again as in a detective novel or film, when Antinous first steps on to the imperial stage the spectator is presented with the drama of a young man whose fate is already sealed. *Iacta alea est* – the die is cast. Antinous is already on the river's edge.

It has become a given that Hadrian was profoundly in love with Antinous, in a very modern Romantic/erotic sense. Yet there is no existing account of their relationship together except for that briefest, though well-recorded, hunting scene just weeks before the tragedy. Everything – the mourning, the obsession – is extrapolated backwards after Antinous' death, more after the construction of a modern novel than of a history. The narrative would be easier to penetrate if contemporary writers had provided details of their first meeting or indeed any reflections on the two together in the intervening years.

Hadrian wrote letters and poetry, but there is no hint that he wrote either to young Antinous; the one piece which seems on first reading to have the rudiments of an elegy to his dead lover turns out to be a movingly worded but fairly conventional farewell to the world by an emperor who knew that he was dying. Fragments of surviving poetry written by contemporaries, and art which appears to show the two together, are rare, equivocal and created in the aftermath of the tragedy when to indulge the emperor was to the advantage of artists within the court circle. Hadrian's memoirs, lost, but used extensively as source material in the surviving works of ancient historians, stated that Antinous' death was an accident. It was an extraordinary intervention by an emperor even given the doubts and speculation repeated in the histories; imperial memoirs did not usually mention any informal or potentially discreditable relationships, and self-justification was a subtle business, conducted on the solid ground of public events. That there would have been some rumours was inevitable, given the taste of ancient writers for conspiracy theories and the lurid embellishment of events. Also, at a time when most history was read aloud to audiences, not privately digested, the death of Antinous and the noisy grief of the emperor would have made good entertainment; and any out of the ordinary events concerning the imperial family were invariably embroidered, to maximise their dramatic potential.

So what did happen to Antinous, and what role did he play in the emperor's life? Is there anything behind the opaque, slightly demure gaze of a hundred statues, the perfect body, the curls clustering at the nape of the neck? Assessments of his fate can only be circumstantial, but various theories have been examined over the years. At the time of his death there appear to have been just three suppositions concerning Antinous' disappearance. Hadrian's own account, that he quite simply met with an fatal accident, contrasts with the historians' much more sinister suggestions that he either committed suicide or was sacrificed, or induced to sacrifice himself, for the emperor's well-being. But Hadrian's issue of a defensive statement that the death had been an unfortunate accident has echoes of his official disclaimer of involvement in the deaths of the four consuls at the beginning of his reign. Inevitably, Hadrian seemed more, not less, implicated once it had become necessary for him to issue his own version of events.

Antinous drowned some 150 miles south of Heliopolis, close to Hermopolis on the west bank of the Nile. Hadrian's explanation seems not implausible, although evidently the circumstances were problematic. Almost certainly the death went unobserved. By the time the historians whose texts survive brought their pens and their prejudices to examine the deed, both Hadrian and Antinous were long dead. It is not even certain when the corpse was found; details of the retrieval and disposal of the body are noticeably absent. Indeed, the only basis for the assumption that the body was discovered at all is in Hadrian's subsequent behaviour, which was inconceivable in the face of anything other than certainty regarding the death. Nor, despite much conjecture, has it ever been established where Antinous was buried.

An accident is, of course, the most straightforward explanation. The cause of death is not consistently clear in the surviving texts, and not all the sources even give the manner of it, but he is generally said to have drowned. There are no further details of the death itself. It might be assumed that Antinous fell from a boat in the flotilla of royal barges, that he took a smaller craft to explore the river and came to grief, or even that he lost his footing on the bank. Although brought up in a region of lakes and rivers, it is just conceivable that Antinous could not swim; and even if he were a competent swimmer, on a warm night it is possible that a young man might go for a dip and get into difficulties. Summer was over, and cramp is a possibility in water unexpectedly chilly – notoriously so after a heavy meal. It is an old story. Antinous, although always depicted as fit and athletic, would not be the first young man to drown while under the influence of drink, shouts for help or the noise of a struggle being masked behind the activities taking place on deck or on shore. He might have knocked himself out entering the water, or collided with a moving boat in the darkness. Alone and unprotected, the emperor's favourite gave up the struggle.

The seasonal Nile floods had long abated but there were still dangerous currents and drownings were relatively commonplace; at the city of Antinoopolis itself there is a memorial to a young woman who drowned in the river two centuries after Antinous and at Hermopolis a mummy of another victim, a near-contemporary of Antinous, is still preserved. There were indeed local conventions about the treatment of those who died in the waters of the Nile – ones of which Hadrian was quick to take advantage on his favourite's behalf. Long before Hadrian, the god-maker, came to Egypt, extraordinary honours awaited anyone who drowned in the river. A long-established and well-known Egyptian convention was that any victim of the Nile was venerated and deified. If Antinous had drowned then Hadrian might have felt justified by local custom in claiming the young man as a god.

But there are reasons to doubt the simplicity of such an account. If Hadrian's version of events was the most straight-forward, it was also, of course, the only possible one that he could give, whatever the truth. He could stay silent or he could defend himself. But for his enemies, the death left enough loose ends to allow the story to be woven into something much less sympathetic to the emperor. Although stories of sacrifice seem at the other end of a spectrum of plausibility from drowning, at the time this was the prevailing understanding of what had happened. In second-century Rome sacrifice was at the centre of religious observance, and accusations of human sacrifice were occasionally levelled at the members of esoteric religions. It was unlikely, but not impossible, that a man such as Hadrian might have been implicated in the sacrifice of the young man he loved, and recent examinations of the mystery have given credence to this theory.

Several commentators have accepted that the most sensational of the hints in the histories was correct. Willingly or unwillingly, Antinous was sacrificed for the greater good of the emperor and so of the empire. Evidence for this is slight beyond the delightfully sinister statement by Cassius Dio: '*He honoured Antinous, either because of his love for him or because the youth had voluntarily undertaken to die (it being necessary that a life should be surrendered freely for the accomplishment of the ends Hadrian had in view).*'

The imperial party did not arrive in Egypt at a good time. The disastrous failure of the Nile floods, the decline in Hadrian's health and tensions in the east must have weighed heavily on the emperor. Hadrian, it was thought, was also troubled by portents which indicated his continuing decline. Those who could predict the future, whether astrologers or soothsayers, held considerable if precarious power over emperors who were all too eager to clarify an unknown future. Many names are known, among them respected members of court, intellectuals, serious men and women. His own wife's companion, Julia Balbilla, was the granddaughter of Nero's famous astrologer Balbillus, and Balbillus' inclinations may have tended towards areas slightly less benign than astrology; one anecdote finds him suggesting to Nero that a particularly unfortunate prediction might be averted by sacrificing some important person. Echoes of this tale recurred in rumours that Hadrian, a much more able and obsessive reader of signs than Nero, had foretold a crisis in his immediate future and, through Antinous, had decided to take the remedial action recommended by the earlier astrologer.

Even outside such drastic scenarios, attempts to perceive and affect the future did not always end well; stories of tentative fortune-tellers having curiously failed to anticipate the fatal effect of an emperor being told bad news are legion. Emperors who could themselves cast fortunes and acquire the wisdom of the astrologers removed themselves from a dependence on the interpreters of mysteries. For Hadrian, who had taken this course further, who had become so adept at astrology that he was able to calculate the date of his own death, this knowledge became not power but a terrible curse.[5] Consensus – just – seems to support the idea that Hadrian had foreseen some catastrophe bearing down upon him and that Antinous was sacrificed to evade the fates. This was by no means a sign of Antinous' expendability; there is a long tradition that the most effective sacrifice is that of the most precious. Paradoxically, Antinous' loss became the crisis Hadrian sought to deflect.

Modern interpretations which accept this solution believe their case to be supported by coin images of the period; but the iconography of imperial coinage is often ambiguous and the issues used to support the sacrifice scenario certainly are. One shows the emperor standing with his foot on a small crocodile, which might not be a simple depiction of the emperor as ruler of an Egypt symbolised by its most notorious animal inhabitant but rather represent Hadrian as the god Horus. Horus was able to subjugate the forces of evil; he would also dispel individual sickness or curses.[6] The meaning of a statue of the emperor found at Hadrian's villa at Tivoli is even more vigorously debated and much more potentially sinister in its portrayals. The head, which has been identified by comparison to a horde of coins, is of Hadrian in 130 – but of Hadrian restored to youth. A strange inscription on a coin of the same period states that this is Hadrian reborn.[7] Speculation has followed that these few images represent Hadrian, who was known to have been initiated into secret rites of transformation and resurrection, transfigured by the sacrifice of a younger soul – namely, Antinous. The argument is attractively lurid but tenuous.

Over the centuries the rumours gathered gory momentum. By the seventeenth century the story included vivid tableaux in which Hadrian himself, sodden with his lover's blood, ripped out Antinous' entrails, as a priest might in a sacrifice or an augur looking for signs of the future. The most interesting feature of these versions is that they combine aspects from the biographies of two notorious emperors. The other philhellenic emperor, Nero, traditionally condemned of incest and matricide, murdered and dissected his mother, while the youthful but depraved Elagabalus had persuaded doctors to cut new openings in his own body to extend his sexual repertoire. Some commentators have seen in more oblique references associated with Hadrian's love of young men a hint that Antinous had died while being castrated. Again, this must be unlikely; not only did it run counter to Hadrian's own laws, but in practical terms the age that Antinous appears to have been at his death was too late for castration to have prevented the visible signs of sexual maturity.

A scenario in which Hadrian colluded in the bloody destruction of his lover seems to go against what we know both of the emperor's character – his assaults were invariably impulsive bursts of anger, not acts of calculated and cold-blooded destruction – and of the culture he embraced. However, an event which fell somewhere between sacrifice and suicide, the effect of which was that this healthy young body was ceded up in implicit exchange for the emperor's well-being, is not implausible. The relationship had run its course, at least as far as the dignity of both parties was concerned. A final gesture which would at the same time resolve the dilemma of Antinous' situation, ensure his posthumous celebrity and perhaps bring about some restoration of health for Hadrian is not impossible. Nor is it impossible that Antinous drowned himself in a moment of despair. Suicide for the Romans was not the morally nihilistic act that it became under Christianity – in the right circumstances it could be accomplished with dignity – but for a young man who was, in effect, the emperor's possession, to take such autonomous action was not flattering for Hadrian. So any such action might later be elaborated, to enhance the prestige of the emperor, into a more glorious tale of self-sacrifice.

Yet there seem to be three possibilities that did not find their way into contemporary literature: first, that Antinous was removed by rivals or simply those who had had enough of him; second, that he merely disappeared from the imperial entourage, possibly faking his own death; and finally, that he died directly at the hand of Hadrian.

It seems surprising that the first possibility was never considered; in later history favourites were notoriously unpopular and their positions invariably precarious. The balancing act that was still an integral part of imperial power made simmering grievances inevitable. Although a provincial Greek boy was unlikely to have been politically adept – it is not impossible, but we hear nothing at all of any involvement in politics – he had natural enemies in Sabina, Hadrian's childless and at least partly humiliated wife, in the emperor's discarded lovers, and in members of the court who might have objected either to an influence which is now invisible or to the Greek nature of Hadrian's sexuality.

On his accession many years earlier Hadrian had been

neither the popular choice nor, it was believed, that of his predecessor. By 130 there were already young men who found themselves in the same uncertain position that Hadrian had once occupied under Trajan. The possible heirs, Lucius Ceionius Commodus and Pedanius Fuscus, might have seen Antinous as exerting some influence against their cause. There were later rumours that Commodus became Hadrian's lover once Antinous was out of the way – but there were always accusations circulating that young Roman men on the make would encourage a sexual relationship with a politically powerful mentor. It was said that Caligula had a relationship with Tiberius, Domitian with Nero, and so on. It was a very different matter from the idealised homosexuality of Greece. As for Hadrian's great-nephew, Fuscus, well, he was already demonstrating a degree of ambition which would lead to a later and fatal accusation of plotting against the emperor. Either might have acted against a rival to power. If they did, it was of no benefit to either of them; both Commodus and Fuscus were dead within seven years of the trip to Egypt.

Travelling, away from the known territory and the familiar resources of home, produces its own set dramas and accidents. Given the predilection of ancient authors for elaborate set-piece intrigues, the absence of such an accusation from all comment on a death which was evidently not straightforward is remarkable in itself. But in a hot and foreign country, where food poisoning was inevitably endemic, poison would perhaps have been a more likely choice than drowning for a potential murderer, because more certain in its effects. It has been suggested, although it seems far-fetched, that Julia Balbilla, whose grandfather's reputation had been compromised by accusations of poisoning, might have employed some hereditary skills to dispose of this unwanted member of the imperial circle.

It is just possible that Antinous left the imperial entourage of his own accord. Homesick, or unable to cope with the psychological strains of a relationship with a powerful emperor and an irascible man, he might have disappeared into the cosmopolitan community of Egypt despite Hadrian's evident ability to mobilise considerable manpower to pursue him. It is an even more low-key solution than a simple accident, but far more insulting to Hadrian. If he did take himself off, it seems unlikely that he did so with Hadrian's subsequent cognisance; as noted already, the emperor's behaviour was comprehensible only if he was certain that Antinous was dead.

At the centre of all considerations of the event are questions about Hadrian's role in the tragedy. The suspicion that Antinous had been sacrificed quickly raised the likelihood that Hadrian might have been directly involved in his death. At the very least it is feasible that, immersed in the culture of the Egyptian priests, frightened for his own health and possibly believing himself to be under some sort of curse, he might have been persuaded that Antinous' mortality would be for the greater good. Hadrian's preoccupation with death, his involvement with mystery cults, his fondness for astrology and particularly the belief that he used this ability to forecast, and then evade, his own death, implicated him in the demise of Antinous. There is also an oblique suggestion that such dabbling might in itself have brought down disaster on the emperor's head, so that the responsibility for the death, if not the specific intent, was Hadrian's. It was as if behaviour inappropriate for the public figure of the emperor might rebound on the most private area of his life.

What if Hadrian had actually killed his lover, rather than permitting him to be placed at the lethal centre of some ritual process? Such was imperial power that, if Antinous had become inconvenient to the emperor, there is no question that he could have been disposed of or removed, although perhaps not openly. But there is a weight of circumstantial evidence which might suggest that Antinous could have been killed directly by Hadrian, most plausibly during an argument.

Hadrian's outbursts of ill-temper were well known. His capacity for random violence when enraged was the more noticeable because he was on the whole a humane and considered man; but his few surviving letters show an impatient, intolerant side to his personality. The eminent physician Galen recounted how the emperor had blinded a slave by striking him in the eye with a pen, and in his later life there were substantial rumours that Hadrian had killed the brilliant architect Apollodorus, with whom he had had a long-standing professional relationship, merely because the craftsman mocked Hadrian's building designs. At the beginning of his reign the philosopher Euphrates seems to have been forced into suicide, and towards the end of his reign the emperor had an elderly and apparently loyal friend, Servianus, put to death for questioning the wisdom of Hadrian's choice of heir. Hadrian exiled his long-standing friend Favorinus after a trivial squabble. He was a man who bore grudges. But there is also, in the very few descriptions of him with his lover, something else; something altogether more reminiscent of the sadism of Tiberius and the perverse sentimentality of Nero.

And what are we to make of Hadrian's encounter with the magician Pachrates (or Pancrates)? This relationship is overshadowed with menace from the start, and the spectacle raises disturbing questions about Hadrian's personality as much as it demonstrates the frightening range of Pachrates' supernatural abilities. The magician/priest was, after all, a foreigner and a practitioner of strange arts who might be expected to operate outside a Roman system of values; he was a macabre curiosity in the same way that tombs and mummies were. But Hadrian was a Roman emperor in whose hands the welfare of state and citizen rested.

The strange altercation with the philosopher Secundus,

too, goes beyond the normal verbal sparring and conflict of wills that were par for the course in confrontations between emperors and philosophers. Here again, Hadrian, frustrated and enraged, broke the unwritten rules of such engagements, not attempting to outwit his opponent but simply retreating to the power of rank, ordering the man executed if he would not obey an imperial order.

The account of Hadrian as hunter in the fragment of poetry by Pachrates was similar to one given in the late second-century Athenaeus' *Deipnosophistae*, an anthology of dinner-table anecdotes, and was obviously well known at the time. It ostensibly shows a very masculine day of leisure, a lion-hunting expedition, which ended in triumph for the emperor. Not only did he kill his lion, but his intervention when Antinous was in danger saved the young man's life. But Hadrian's behaviour – courageous and skilled, everything that might be expected of an emperor starring in his own poem – can from a slightly different perspective appear taunting and cold-blooded. Whether the point of his action was to display his superior hunting skills or to play out some kind of erotic game, or whether indeed it was reconstructed by the narrator to cover up a situation in which Hadrian inadvertently put Antinous' life in jeopardy, or messed up an attempted kill, Hadrian's instinct does not seem to be loving or protective. The story is one of the very few that exist concerning the behaviour of the two men together and does carry a strong sexual charge, but Antinous emerges from it as some further quarry, hunted rather than protected. Antinous was vulnerable symbolically as well as in reality from the all-powerful man whose possession he was.

It is not impossible that Antinous, too, was dabbling in magic: spells to bind his lover to him, to retard the more obvious advancement of sexual maturity, to confound his enemies. Surrounded by practitioners of magic, astrologers and augurs, possibly having himself seen Pachrates' powerful exposition of the possibility of the supernatural, and with his own future decidedly equivocal, it would be more surprising if he had not. Magic was democratic, available to anyone with the money to pay a magician-priest. If the intellectually sophisticated Hadrian, with earthly power his to command, sought a remedy in Egypt for his own failing health, how much more likely that the powerless Antinous should look to magic to resolve his difficulties? But any hint of magic being practised to influence the actions of an emperor was likely to elicit the strongest response. Invariably it would be seen as a hostile act, an attempt to accrue power to himself by devious means. An act which Antinous might naïvely have regarded as personal would quickly have been perceived as political and treacherous once in the public arena. Had Hadrian argued with his lover, over this or any other matter, he certainly had the strength and emotional capacity to injure him.

Then there is the matter of the dearly bought spell of Pachrates – the eclectic spell that could cause a man to attract, to sicken or to die; that gave dreams to the emperor. If the emperor had attempted to work this magic himself, to bind Antinous to him, to prevent the youth maturing further or to reinvigorate his own sexuality, and it had all gone horribly wrong – as Pachrates' original demonstration suggested it easily could in the hands of a novice – Hadrian must inevitably have panicked.

If, intentionally or unintentionally, Antinous had been killed in a brawl, nothing would have seemed more obvious than to dispose of the body in the Nile. Water, fish and river traffic would soon account for any obvious injuries to the corpse when, if, it was found. Hadrian's excessive reactions to Antinous' death could more easily be understood as a response to the guilt of being complicit in his destruction, whether the emperor struck, or caused to be struck, the blow that killed him. The slave blinded by Hadrian's pen demanded the customary compensation: an eye for an eye. In the years that flowed Antinous' death, was the emperor desperately trying to avert natural retribution?

But perhaps all along Antinous was himself merely a conjuring trick and in the land of magic, of concealment, was summoned up on Hadrian's stage and seen to vanish. The attractive adjunct to the magician's act has always been a integral yet ultimately insubstantial figure of the performance. Perhaps he was just another pretty artefact, a work of art, a Greek game, a joke or even a metaphor. He seems almost over-conveniently to combine so many elements from existing Greco-Roman myth and literature. It is tempting to consider whether the connections with Osiris are just too tidy and whether, given the lack of specific details about the youth's death, an unimportant accident on an unknown date was retrojected on to the existing mystical, and popular, tale of Isis and Osiris, either to make it dramatically attractive or, more calculatedly, as part of a process of creating a new god. A new diversion. A counter to the challenges and special effects of Christianity.

For the powerful aesthete whose interests turned upon beautiful men, Antinous might merely have stood generically as a human representative of the beautiful things which Hadrian could acquire and discard at will.

Looking back over nearly two thousand years, it is the story of Hadrian and Antinous and of Hadrian's grief at his untimely death which has survived through time to prove the most lasting legacy of the reign. It has inspired poetry and novels, polemic and speculation as Antinous became the archetype of classical male beauty cut off in youth, Hadrian of love which transcended rank. Antinous became the erotic and Romantic ideal; his story tapped into existing legends and literature and became a central motif of a pervasive theme. Like so many beautiful boys in Greek and Roman literature – Narcissus, Hylas, Adonis – he had that irresistible combination of youth, allure and premature mortality without the drawback of an intrusive personality.

Hadrian, of course, aesthete and *littérateur*, had it all; he even had a lover who died right, whose behaviour and attributes mirrored the characters of mythology. Like a helpless maiden from Ovid's *Metamorphoses*, Antinous, pursued by a proto-god – Hadrian – slipped into a river and was transformed. His life became incidental; his death in the waters of the Nile and his resurrection as a god, as a star, as (possibly) saviour of Hadrian, as the inspiration of a city, was his whole story. He gazed out implacably over the empire; still gazes, passively, in art collections throughout the Western world, a Galatea turned to stone. The mystery of Antinous will always be more powerful in his absence than it could ever have been in his presence. But if one attempts to examine the story more closely, to move behind the placid beauty, behind the unforgettable image, Antinous starts to slip away.

Until Hadrian's long-lost memoirs are unearthed in some desiccated cache of papyri, the sources for the youth's death are largely second-hand, the nearest chronologically produced text written nearly a century after the disastrous trip to Egypt, the older manuscripts on which they are based having long vanished. The existing sources are inevitably partisan and by modern standards sensational. But the incident in Egypt and its aftermath remains an intriguing tale; and the degree to which the emperor was implicated in Antinous' death might not have been revealed even had more contemporary material survived.

However it occurred, the demise of Antinous was an unheralded event which Hadrian speedily turned into a further episode in the drama of his reign. What was just possibly a genuine tragedy in his life became an opportunity to make an ever closer identification with the most famous Greek of them all, Alexander. Alexander, too, had lost his closest intimate – Hephaestion; Alexander, too, was inconsolable in his grief. Hephaestion had been a friend of nearly two decades, Antinous a companion of probably a very few years at most, but the model was well established. Raising a city to commemorate an event of only personal significance was hardly new; much more trivial episodes than the death of a lover had been the inspiration for such new foundations. Alexander built one on the spot where his favourite horse died; while Hadrian had confined himself to writing a poem for the tomb of his own dead Borysthenes, elsewhere a successful day's hunting had moved him to dedicate a new city.[8] The presentation of the death and its aftermath were all prescripted in the Greek past.

Hadrian was a master of the diversionary tactic; travelling and drama confused and deflected criticism. Antinous' death, though tragic, was a distraction from the internal problems of Egypt. The return to Greece in 131, though demanding, channelled displays of personal grief into massive public benefaction in a country where Hadrian had always been popular. In the same way the subsequent wars in Judea, though burdensome, offered an opportunity to offset Roman criticism of his largely aesthetic agenda in Greece. If censure came from one quarter, Hadrian would remove himself and his entourage to a more congenial context. Throughout his life, ceremonial and munificence disguised the man. It was only later, when he was no longer able to move about his empire, dazzling all who encountered him, to turn away from difficult situations, that the flaws of his reign and his personality became inescapable. As he neared death, guilty and isolated, he was driven to explain and justify his actions in a written account of his life. The confidence with which he strode the empire was at an end, and he no longer trusted the bricks and marble of great cities to ensure his passage into posterity.

Antinous lived on as an Egyptian god, a hunter and a Dionysiac reveller. His fate had become unimportant, but his value was now inestimable. Images of him were uniquely beautiful and their proliferation was to make accurate provenance and even identification complicated in the assessments of history. By the eighteenth century Antinous' statues, copied, reproduced, faked, stolen and smuggled, had found their way into every great collection of classical art in the Western world. His face had become in every sense a monument to desire.

The area of the middle Nile where the cities of Hermopolis and Antinoopolis once stood is currently all but inaccessible. Recent acts of terrorism and notorious local instability mean that all attempts to visit the site are thwarted by officials anxious to contain Islamic extremism. The tourist cruise boats now pass by the ancient sites either side of the Nile from El Minya to Abydos. Today at Hermopolis there are some simple village houses, a dilapidated sugar-processing plant and two great baboon statues which dominate the ruins of the temple of Thoth. All that is left of the city is interred in a few large mounds. On the edge of the desert a short distance away is the city's necropolis.

Just two hundred years ago the French antiquarian Pierre Jomard, surveying the site at Napoleon's behest, was to marvel at the ruins of great Antinoopolis. He recorded the survival of some exceptional architectural features, including a ceremonial gateway, a vast peristyle of columns which gave some idea of the original magnificence of the arcaded main street which once ran parallel to the river. Temples dedicated to Isis and Serapis were recognisable, and Jomard's delicate drawings of columns, palms and causeways are evocative of a city which even in empty dilapidation remained breathtaking in scale and beauty.

None of this is surprising; citizens of the second century who had been persuaded or coerced into populating the new city by financial and legal inducements were dazzled by the opulence of the new construction and the building materials; marbles from around the empire provided the raw material for first-rate masonry and sculpture. Antinoopolis, perhaps in part because of the circumstances of its inception, acquired a reputation for being a place of religion and magic. There were temples, each striving to exceed all others in lavishness, and fine streets. There were, we know, statues of Antinous set up throughout the city, and it is reasonable to imagine that temples dedicated to his cult must have been everywhere in evidence. There is no evidence that Antinous' tomb was ever here, though it remains a tantalising possibility in the absence of any other known burial place. The city was never really excavated; only the third-century Christian tombs in the cliffs at the edge of the desert were ever examined, and they held burials of astonishing lavishness.[9] The rest guards its secrets well.

For today the handsome city of Antinoopolis, set between the mountains and the water, the city which Hadrian intended to be an everlasting memorial to Antinous, is a desolate plain of scree as deserted as when Hadrian, freshly bereaved, designated it for the new Hellenistic foundation. The scattered houses of a tiny modern settlement trickle towards the desert. Neglect, theft, indifference and the rendering down of marble to lime in the nineteenth century have completed the organic process of decay. If the earthly remains of Antinous lie in the city named after him it is unlikely that they will ever now be discovered. On an autumn day, nineteen centuries after Antinous died, the blue sky is hazy, the Nile eddies round a bend in the river, the rushes are as brown as the water and birds hover on the wind which blows up from nowhere over an arid landscape. Nothing beside remains.

Epilogue

Hadrian's successor Antoninus Pius ruled for twenty-three years,

nor did he undertake any expedition other than the visiting of his estates in Campania, averring that the entourage of an emperor, even one over frugal, was a burdensome thing to the provinces.

SCRIPTORES HISTORIAE AUGUSTAE, ANTONINUS PIUS, 7. 4–12.

Notes

Preface

1 K. Hopkins, *Journal of Roman Studies* 3 (1991): 133.

Introduction

1 Cassius Dio, *Roman History*, bk 62, ch. 18.
2 Edward Gibbon, *The Decline and Fall of the Roman Empire*, vol. 1, 3. 78.
3 M. T. Boatwright, *Hadrian and the Cities of the Roman Empire*.

1: The waiting game

1 Cassius Dio, *Roman History*, bk 69, ch. 20.
2 E. L. Bowie, 'Greek Poetry in the Antonine Age'.
3 Julian Bennett, in *Trajan: Optimus Princeps* (p. 203), argues that it was perfectly clear from Trajan's actions, if not his words, that he intended Hadrian to be his successor.
4 Warwick Ball, *Rome in the East: The Transformation of an Empire*, 16.
5 For a fascinating study of distances and travel times, see L. Casson, *Travel in the Ancient World*.

6 *Scriptores Historiae Augustae,* Hadrian, 5. 3.
7 Cassius Dio, *Roman History,* bk 68, ch. 14.
8 Ibid., bk 69, chs 1–4.
9 Pliny the Younger, *Panegyric,* 52.
10 Ronald Syme, *The Roman Revolution,* 50.
11 Suetonius, *The Twelve Caesars,* Domitian, 14.
12 Ibid., 21.
13 John Freely, *The Companion Guide to Turkey,* 361.

2: A travelling court

1 See Martial, *Epigrams,* 3. 63:

Bellus homo est, flexos qui digerit ordine crines,
Balsama qui semper, cinnama semper olet;
Cantica qui Nili, qui Gaditana susurrat.

A man of fashion is one with carefully arranged hair
A man who always smells of balsam and cinnamon
And who can hum every tune from Egypt to Cadiz.

2 The visit to Athens in 116–17 before Hadrian became emperor is contested, though believed by Birley to be likely; see *Hadrian, the Restless Emperor.*
3 C. Julius Antiochus Epiphanes Philopappus, grandson of the last king of Commagene, Antiochus IV.
4 For a general – and stimulating – discussion of religions in the Roman empire, see Keith Hopkins, *A World Full of Gods*; also John Ferguson, *The Religions of the Roman Empire.*
5 Horace, *Epodes,* 2, 1.
6 Petronius, *The Satyricon.*
7 Statistics quoted in Royston Lambert, *Beloved and God,* 24.
8 Pliny the Elder, *Natural History,* 29. 16, 37. 31.
9 Ibid., 15. 9, 8. 89, 7. 130.
10 Alexis de Tocqueville, *De l'ancien régime et la révolution,* 1856.

11 Suetonius, *The Twelve Caesars*, Augustus, 28.

12 Syme, *Revolution*, 50.

13 Boatwright, *Hadrian and the Cities of the Roman Empire*.

14 Lucian, *The Greek Anthology*.

15 In Mary Hill Cole's fascinating study of Elizabeth I, *The Portable Queen*, I came across some interesting correlations in the strategies of two powerful rulers, living 1,400 years apart, attempting to consolidate and control their territories and to strengthen reigns begun in less than auspicious circumstances. It further confirmed my views on Hadrian as a tactical traveller.

16 Cassius Dio, *Roman History*, bk 69, ch. 8.

17 *Scriptores Historiae Augustae*, Hadrian, 11. 4–6.

18 A. Birley, *Hadrian, the Restless Emperor*, 124–5.

19 *Scriptores Historiae Augustae*, 'Antoninus Pius', 7. 4–12.

20 S. Swain, *Hellenism and Empire: Language, Classicism and Power in the Greek World AD 50–250* (75–6 and *passim*) sees Greek culture as manipulated by rather than inspiring the Romans.

21 Cassius Dio, *Roman History*, bk 69, ch. 6.

22 *Secundus the Silent Philosopher*.

23 Galen, *On the Diagnosis and Treatment of the Passions of the Soul*, 17. 1–18.

24 *Secundus the Silent Philosopher*.

3: The shifting sands

1 Virgil, *Georgics*, 4. 287–94; translation from Andrew Dalby, *Empire of Pleasures: Luxury and Indulgence in the Roman World*.

2 Appian, *Roman History*, 2; Lucan, *Pharsalia*.

3 'The Death of Pompey, 48 BC', from Appian, *Roman History*, 2, 84–5.

4 *Scriptores Historiae Augustae*, Hadrian, 19. 2.

5 Athenaeus, *The Deipnosophistae*.

6 Propertius (*The Poems*, 3. 9. 39) refers to the hated (by the

Romans) Cleopatra as 'the whore queen of licentious Canopus' (*incesti meretrix regina Canopi*).

7 Strabo, *Geography* (*c.* 7 BC).

8 H. D. Betz, *The Greek Magical Papyri in Translation*, PGM IV, 2449–71.

9 For further reading on the Nile Mosaic, see P. G. P. Meyboom, *The Nile Mosaic: Early Evidence of Egyptian Religion in Italy*, and the delightfully discursive paper by Susan Walker, 'Carry-on at Canopus: The Nilotic Mosaic from Palestrina and Roman Attitudes to Egypt'.

10 For this fact and other delightful digressions I am indebted to John and Elizabeth Romer's *The Seven Wonders of the World*.

4: Memnon laments

1 Lucian, *Philopseudes*, 33.

2 G. W. Bowersock, 'The Miracle of Memnon', has a good overview of the numerous contemporary commentators, from Strabo to Juvenal, and compelling theories on the eventual restoration of the images.

3 For detailed information on Julia Balbilla, her family and presence in Egypt, and some further details on the statues themselves, I am indebted to Corey Brennan's advice and his accomplished article 'The Poets Julia Balbilla and Damo at the Colossus of Memnon'.

4 A. and E. Bernand, *Les Inscriptions grècques et latines du Colosse de Memnon*.

5 Cassius Dio, *Roman History*, bks 61–70.

6 *Scriptores Historiae Augustae*, Hadrian, 14.

7 Bernand, *Inscriptions*, no. 29. Corey Brennan believes 'pious' is a literary convention for asserting not Julia Balbilla's devotion, but her royal blood.

8 See Bowersock, 'The Miracle of Memnon', 1–4.

5: Cities of gods and ghosts

1   William MacDonald and John Pinto, *Hadrian's Villa and its Legacy.*
2   See Paul Zanker, *The Power of Images in the Age of Augustus* (1990).
3   Cassius Dio, *Roman History*, bk 69, ch. 11; Birley, *Hadrian, the Restless Emperor*, 252.
4   Boatwright, *Hadrian and the Cities of the Roman Empire.*
5   Ibid., 208–9.
6   Pliny the Younger, *Epistles*, 10. 41. 5. Pausanias, travelling only a decade or so after the temple was dedicated, provides a detailed description of the impact of the building (Pausanias, *Guide to Southern Greece*, 1, 6).
7   *Scriptores Historiae Augustae*, Hadrian, 17. 11–12, 19. 2–8.

6: War

1   Josephus, *The Jewish Wars*, bk 5, ch. 12.
2   Ibid.
3   Cassius Dio, *Roman History*, bk 69, ch. 13.
4   Matt. 22: 21.
5   Tacitus, *Annals of Imperial Rome*, 1. 64.
6   Ibid., 1. 12.
7   Josephus, *The Jewish Wars*, bk 5, ch. 12.
8   Cassius Dio, *Roman History*, bk 69, ch. 14.
9   Ibid.
10 *Babylonian Talmud*, Lamentations Rabbah 2. 2; Seder Elijah Rabbah 151.
11 For the figures on Julius Caesar and the Iceni I am indebted to Christopher Kelly (*Times Literary Supplement*, 15 June 2001).
12 Hadrian is mentioned four times in the rabbinical literature: Midrash Tanchuma, Genesis, 7 (mentioned twice); Tanna Debai Eliyahu Rabba, 30; Midrash Rabba, Noah, 1. 'May his bones rot'; Midrash Rabba, Exodus, 51: 5.

7: *The captured world*

1 Martial, *Epigrams*, 94.
2 Colin Wells' *The Roman Empire* is an invaluable, and amusing, source for detailed facts for the period.
3 MacDonald and Pinto, *Hadrian's Villa and its Legacy*.
4 Ibid.
5 Suetonius, *The Twelve Caesars*, Nero, 31.
6 Christopher Tadgell, *Imperial Space: Rome, Constantinople and the Early Church*, 54.
7 *Scriptores Historiae Augustae*, Hadrian, 26.
8 Niels Hannestad and others.
9 J.-C. Grenier and others.
10 *Scriptores Historiae Augustae*, Hadrian, 14.
11 Amanda Claridge, *Rome*.
12 Cassius Dio, *Roman History*, bk 49.
13 Claridge, *Rome*.
14 Papyri Fayum, Pfayum 19=Sm. 123, quoted by Birley, *Hadrian, the Restless Emperor*, 299.
15 For impressively accurate and detailed information on the architectural construction of all the Roman antiquities which are still visible today, see Claridge, *Rome*.
16 Speech, 'La Nuova Roma', given on the Campidoglio by Mussolini on the occasion of the appointment of Rome's first Fascist governor, Filippo Cremonesi, in December 1925.
17 Allied Force HQ, Appendix C-1 to report 20345/0/MFAA 29/12/43, British School at Rome.

9: *Retrospective*

1 Suetonius, *The Twelve Caesars*, Caligula, 57.
2 Cassius Dio, *Roman History*, vol. 8, bk 69; A. G. Pingré, *Cométographie*, vol. 1, 291–2.
3 I am indebted to Michael Hoskin of Churchill College, Cambridge, for this information.

4 Dimitri Meeks and Christine Favard-Meeks, *Daily Life of the Egyptian Gods*.

5 *Scriptores Historiae Augustae*, Aelius, 3: 'Marius Maximus represents Hadrian as so expert in astrology as even to assert that he knew all about his own future and that he wrote down beforehand what he was destined to do on every day down to the hour of his death.' See also ibid., Hadrian, 16.

6 Birley, *Hadrian, the Restless Emperor*, 257–8.

7 Niels Hannestad, *Roman Art and Imperial Policy*, 209, has details of the debate.

8 See Birley, *Hadrian, the Restless Emperor*, 145.

9 A. Gayet, *Fantômes d'Antinoë: Les Sepultres Leukyone et Myrthis et les Sepultres de Thais et Serapion*.

Boardman, J., C
Boatwright, M.
NJ: Princeto
—— Hadrian an
NJ: Princeto
Bowersock, G. W
Clarendon F
—— 'The Mirac
—— Fiction as H
Press, 1994.
Bowie, E. L., 'G
Russell, ed
University P
Bowman, Alan
Museum Pul
Brennan, Corey
Colossus of
Burn, A. H. and
Herbert Pres
Burnett, Andrew,
1987.
Canfora, Luciano
California Pr
Carcopino, Jérôn
Lorimer. Lor
1941.)
Casson, L., Tra
Hopkins Uni
Claridge, Amand
Oxford: Oxfo
Cole, Mary Hill,
Politics of C
Massachusett
Cornell, Tim, and
Oxford: Andr

Bibliography

Primary Sources
This list contains the main classical sources referred to in the text and notes. The page and/or chapter references are given in standard form, so whatever translation is used, the relevant passage will be easy to find. Where available, I have used the Penguin Classics translations, although there are many other reliable editions easily available.

Appian, *Roman History*
Apuleius, *The Golden Ass*
Arrian, *The Campaigns of Alexander*
Athenaeus, *The Deipnosophistae*
Babylonian Talmud
Cassius Dio, *Roman History*
Galen, *On the Diagnosis and Treatment of the Passions of the Soul*
Horace, *Epodes*
Josephus, *The Jewish Wars*
Juvenal, *Satires*
Lucan, *Pharsalia*
Lucian, *How to Write History*

—— *Philopse*

Martial, *Epig*

Ovid, *Metam*

Pausanias, *G*

Petronius, *Th*

Pliny the Eld

Pliny the You

—— *Panegyr*

Procopius, *T*

Propertius, *T*

Scriptores His

Strabo, *Geog*

Suetonius, *T*

Tacitus, *Anni*

—— *Histories*

Virgil, *Georgi*

Secondary *S*

Ball, Warwic
  Empire. I

Bean, George
  (First pu

Beard, Mar
  Duckwor

Bédoyère, Gu

Benario, H.
  Historia

Bennett, Juli
  1997.

Bernand, A.
  de Memn

Betz, H. D.,
  Chicago

Birley, A., *H*
  1997.

Cosgrove, Denis, and Daniels, Stephen, eds, *The Iconography of Landscape* (Cambridge Studies in Historical Geography, 9, ed. Alan R. H. Baker, J. B. Harley and David Ward). Cambridge: Cambridge University Press, 1988.

Dalby, Andrew, *Empire of Pleasures: Luxury and Indulgence in the Roman World*. London: Routledge, 2000.

Dover, Kenneth, *Greek Homosexuality*. London: Duckworth, 1989.

Eck, W., 'The Bar Kokhba Revolt: The Roman Point of View', *Journal of Roman Studies* 89 (1999): 76.

Elsner, Jas, and Masters, Jamie, *Reflections of Nero*. London: Duckworth, 1994.

Evans, Craig, *Jesus and his Contemporaries*. Leiden: Leiden University Press, 1995.

Evans, Penelope, 'The Lost Jewels of the Nile', *Sunday Times Magazine*, 20 August 2000: 16–25.

Ferguson, John, *The Religions of the Roman Empire*. London: Thames & Hudson, 1970.

Freely, John, *The Companion Guide to Turkey*. London: Collins, 1976.

Garzetti, A., *From Tiberius to the Antonines*, trans. J. R. Foster. London, 1974.

Gayet, A. L., *Fantômes d'Antinoë: Les Sepultres Leukyone et Myrthis et les Sepultres de Thais et Serapion*. Paris: Société d'Editions d'Art, 1902.

Gibbon, Edward, *The Decline and Fall of the Roman Empire*. London: Methuen, 1896. (First pub. 1776.)

Gill, C., and Wiseman, T., eds, *Lies and Fiction in the Ancient World*. Exeter: University of Exeter Press, 1993.

Goldhill, Simon, *Being Greek under Rome*. Cambridge: Cambridge University Press, 2001.

Grant, Michael, *The Antonines: A Roman Empire in Translation*. London: Routledge, 1994.

Grenier, J.-C., 'La Décoration statuaire du "Serapeum" du "Canope" de la Villa Adriana', *Mélanges de l'Ecole française de Rome – Antiquité* 101 (1989): 925–1019.

Haag, Michael, *Egypt* (Cadogan Guides). London: Cadogan Books, 1993.

Halfmann, Helmut, *Itinera principum. Geschichte und Typologie der Kaiserreichen im Romischen Reich*. Stuttgart: Franz Steiner Verlag, 1986.

Hall, James, *The World of Sculpture: The Changing Status of Sculpture from the Renaissance to the Present Day*. London: Pimlico, 2000.

Hannestad, Niels, *Roman Art and Imperial Policy*. Aarhus: Aarhus University Press, 1988.

Henderson, B. W., *The Life and Principate of the Emperor Hadrian*. London, 1923.

Hopkins, Keith, *A World Full of Gods*. London: Weidenfeld & Nicolson, 1999.

Hornblower, S., and Spawforth, Anthony, eds. *The Oxford Companion to Classical Civilisation*. Oxford: Oxford University Press, 1998.

Jones, Peter, and Sidwell, Keith, *The World of Rome*. Cambridge: Cambridge University Press, 1997.

Kelly, Christopher, *Times Literary Supplement*, 15 June 2001.

Kleiner, D., *Roman Sculpture*. New Haven: Yale University Press, 1992.

Lambert, Royston, *Beloved and God*. London: Weidenfeld & Nicolson, 1984.

Lefkowitz, M. R. and Fant, M. B., *Women's Life in Greece and Rome: A Source Book in Translation*. London: Duckworth, 1982.

Lucian, *A Selection*, trans. M. D. Macleod (Classical Texts, ed. M. M. Willcock). Warminster: Aris & Phillips, 1991. (Includes a particularly witty translation of *How to Write History*.)

Luttwak, E., *The Grand Strategy of the Roman Empire: From the First Century AD to the Third*. London: Weidenfeld & Nicolson, 1999.

MacDonald, William, and Pinto, John, *Hadrian's Villa and its Legacy*. New Haven: Yale University Press, 1995.

Macmullen, Ramsay, *Romanization in the Time of Augustus*. New Haven: Yale University Press, 2000.

Mathieson, Thomas J., *Apollo's Lyre: Greek Music and Music Theory in Antiquity and the Middle Ages*. University of Nebraska Press, 1999.

Mee, Christopher, and Spawforth, Anthony, *Greece* (Oxford Archaeological Guides). Oxford: Oxford University Press, 2001.

Meeks, Dimitri, and Favard-Meeks, Christine, *Daily Life of the Egyptian Gods*, trans. G. M. Goshgarian. London: Pimlico, 1999. (First pub. in French as *La vie quotidienne des dieux Egyptiennes*, Paris, Hachette, 1993.)

Meyboom, P. G. P., *The Nile Mosaic: Early Evidence of Egyptian Religion in Italy*. Leiden, New York and Cologne: Brill, 1995.

Millar, F., *The Emperor in the Roman World*, 2nd edn. London: Duckworth, 1992.

Ministero per i Beni e le Attiva Culturali, Soprintendenza Archaologica per il Lazio, *Adriano, Archittetura e Progetto*. Rome: Electa, 2000.

Pinch, Geraldine, *Magic in Ancient Egypt*. London: British Museum, 1994.

Pingré, A. G., *Cométographie*. Paris, 1783.

Romer, John and Elizabeth, *The Seven Wonders of the World: A History of the Modern Imagination*. London: Book Club Associates, 1995.

Schafer, Peter, *Judeophobia: Attitudes towards the Jews in the Ancient World*. Cambridge, MA: Harvard University Press, 1998.

Sear, F., *Roman Architecture*. London: Batsford, 1982.

Secundus the Silent Philosopher: The Greek Life of Secundus, trans. B. E. Perry (Philological Monographs). Ithaca, NY: American Philological Association, 1964.

Swain, S., *Hellenism and Empire: Language, Classicism and Power in the Greek World, AD 50–250*. Oxford: Clarendon Press, 1996.

Syme, Ronald, *The Roman Revolution*. Oxford: Oxford University Press, 1992. (First pub. 1939.)

Tadgell, Christopher, *Imperial Space: Rome, Constantinople and the Early Church* (A History of Architecture, 4). London: Ellipsis, 1998.

Vance, Norman, *The Victorians and Ancient Rome*. Oxford and Cambridge, MA: Blackwell, 1997.

Vout, C., 'Objects of Desire: Eroticised political discourse in imperial Rome'. Unpublished doctoral dissertation, University of Cambridge, 2000.

Walker, Susan, 'Carry-on at Canopus: The Nilotic Mosaic from Palestrina and Roman Attitudes to Egypt', paper presented at conference on 'Ancient Perspectives on Ancient Egypt', University College London, 16 December 2000.

Weber, W., *Untersuchungen zur Geschichte des Kaisers Hadrianus*. Leipzig, 1907.

Wellesley, Kenneth, *The Long Year AD 69*. Bristol: Classical Press, 1989.

Wells, Colin, *The Roman Empire*. London: Fontana, 1984.

Yadin, Yigal, *Bar Kokhba: The Rediscovery of the Legendary Hero of the Last Jewish Revolt against Imperial Rome*. London, 1971.

Yourcenar, Marguérite, *Memoirs of Hadrian*. London: Penguin, 1978. (First pub. as *Les Mémoires d'Hadrian*, Paris, 1951; this edn first pub. 1959.)

Zanker, Paul, *The Power of Images in the Age of Augustus*. Ann Arbor: University of Michigan Press, 1990.

Index

EMMA DARWIN

EDNA HEALEY

When Charles Darwin published *The Origin of Species* in 1859 his place in history was assured, but of his wife Emma little was known. Charles and Emma – both grandchildren of Josiah Wedgwood – married in 1839, three years after Charles's return from the voyage round the world in the *Beagle*.

As young women Emma and her sisters made the Grand Tour and kept lively diaries, to which Edna Healey has had privileged access, as well as to many unpublished family letters. But most of Emma Darwin's life was overshadowed by tragedy: the early death of her sister, Fanny, the loss of two of her ten babies, the death of her 10-year-old daughter, Annie.

Emma Darwin's portrayal by Edna Healey is a perfect example of beautifully researched and elegantly written ninteenth-century history which will fascinate everyone interested in the notion of a 'wife of fame'.

NON-FICTION / BIOGRAPHY 0 7472 6248 9

THE CELEBRATED CAPTAIN BARCLAY

PETER RADFORD

'Fantastic fun . . . gives a fascinating insight into
enduring aspects of the sporting impulse' *Sunday Times*

In the summer of 1809 Captain Robert Barclay
Allardice set out on one of the greatest sporting
challenges ever undertaken. His attempt to walk for 'a
thousand miles in a thousand hours for a thousand
guineas' drew huge crowds to Newmarket to witness
this extraordinary event. Six gruelling weeks later,
Barclay achieved the seemingly impossible, winning
himself a fortune and gaining a reputation as one of
the leading athletes of his time.

This unusual and beautifully written biography tells
the story of a unique and complex man whose life was
reckless, extravagant and thrilling and gives a
fascinating glimpse into the little-known Georgian
world of pugilism, horse racing and pedestrianism,
a world mad on sport and entranced by the
excitement of gambling.

NON-FICTION / BIOGRAPHY 0 7472 6490 2

Now you can buy any of these other bestselling non-fiction titles from your bookshop or *direct from the publisher*.

FREE P&P AND UK DELIVERY
(Overseas and Ireland £3.50 per book)

Geisha   *Lesley Downer*   £7.99
A brilliant exploration into the *real* secret history of Japan's geisha from an award-winning writer.

The Floating Brothel   *Siân Rees*   £7.99
An enthralling voyage aboard *The Lady Julian*, which carried female convicts destined for Australia to provide sexual services and a much-needed breeding bank.

The World for a Shilling *Michael Leapman*   £7.99
The intriguing story of London's Great Exhibition of 1851, which attracted a quarter of Britain's population to witness the latest wonders of the emerging machine age.

Eight Bells and Top Masts *Christopher Lee*   £6.99
The compelling tale of life on a tramp ship in the 1950s and of a young boy growing up as he travelled the world.

Old London Bridge   *Patricia Pierce*   £7.99
The story of this magnificent bridge, its inhabitants and its extraordinary evolution – for over 600 years the pulsating heart of London.

TO ORDER SIMPLY CALL THIS NUMBER

01235 400 414

or visit our website: www.madaboutbooks.com

Prices and availability subject to change without notice.